Latinos and the U.S. Political System

TWO-TIERED PLURALISM

Latinos and the U.S. Political System

TWO-TIERED PLURALISM

Rodney E. Hero

TEMPLE
UNIVERSITY
PRESS

Philadelphia

Temple University Press, Philadelphia 19122
Copyright © 1992 by Temple University. All rights reserved
Published 1992
Printed in the United States of America

Library of Congress Cataloging-in-Publication Data

Hero, Rodney E., 1953–
    Latinos and the U.S. political system: two-tiered pluralism / Rodney E. Hero.
    p.   cm.
    Includes bibliographical references and index.
    ISBN 0-87722-909-0. —ISBN 0-87722-910-4 (pbk.)
    1. Hispanic Americans—Politics and government.   2. Hispanic
Americans—Colorado—Denver—Politics and government.   3. Denver
(Colo.)—Politics and government.   I. Title.
E184.S75H48   1992
323.1′168078883—dc20   91-20104
                                                              CIP
                                                              REV.

To my family

Contents

Tables and Figures

Preface

Latino politics has not been studied extensively. This book brings together the political science research that has been undertaken in an effort to understand Latino politics within the larger U.S. political context and U.S. politics from the vantage point of the Latino political condition. The book is generally structured along the lines of a conventional textbook in government because that format seemed most useful for the book's purposes. After presenting background issues in the first several chapters, the focus turns to major political activities and institutions of the U.S. political system, with specific reference to Latinos. In addition to presenting and summarizing basic issues and research findings, the book addresses normative and theoretical issues throughout. The work culminates in a chapter that synthesizes the discussion and offers an interpretation I call *two-tiered pluralism.*

Chapter 1 introduces a number of background points and broad issues, underscoring the significance, and the difficulty, of studying Latino politics; these points and issues guide much of the subsequent discussion. Chapter 2 provides an overview of major theoretical perspectives that have been used in seeking to understand U.S. politics generally and Latinos and the rest of U.S. society more specifically. The perspectives include pluralism, coalitional bias, and internal colonialism. The chapter examines the different views in terms of their assumptions and arguments, differences and similarities, strengths and weaknesses, discussing specific aspects of the U.S. political system that are particularly significant for Latinos and other minorities from the standpoint of their relevance to the theoretical perspectives and their general impact. This chapter introduces the idea of two-tiered pluralism.

Chapter 3 provides historical overviews of the three major Latino groups—Mexican Americans, Puerto Ricans, and Cubans—comparing and contrasting each group's experiences. Another section of the chapter delineates variables hypothesized to be related to minority-group status and assesses the three groups with respect to those variables. This chapter also presents specific data regarding the socioeconomic statuses of the several Latino groups and discusses their implications for political activity.

Chapter 4 considers the political attitudes of Latinos regarding general predispositions toward politics, levels of political activity, ideology, and partisan leanings. This chapter also examines the orientations of interest groups that advocate for Hispanic concerns, seeking to delineate dimensions of group activities and provide a scheme for summarizing, and thus better understanding, those groups and their roles in Latino politics.

Chapter 5 examines Latinos and national institutions—the presidency and the executive branch, Congress, and the Supreme Court—and how Latinos have sought to influence and have been influenced by these decision-making bodies. The chapter draws on the limited research that has addressed these concerns and presents additional research and issues.

Chapter 6 considers Latinos and state politics in the United States. Although Latinos are concentrated in a handful of states, little research has examined politics in these states with specific reference to Latinos. Therefore, the chapter draws on the available literature on state politics and examines the political and policy characteristics of states with substantial Latino populations, suggesting—and examining to the extent possible—the implications of this evidence for Latinos and state politics.

Chapters 7 and 8 discuss Latinos and urban politics. Chapter 7 focuses specifically on the elections of Federico Peña as mayor of Denver. The detailed attention to these elections is useful, given the importance of elections from theoretical standpoints and for several other reasons. Chapter 8 turns to several unique qualities of urban politics, presenting and discussing theoretical arguments regarding several policy arenas of urban politics and the "natural" bias toward certain policies. Discussed, too, is other evidence regarding the historical or formative stages of American cities in terms of their implications for Latinos. The chapter also examines the different structural forms of urban government and their impacts. Finally, the chapter considers the political status of Latinos in a number of cities.

Chapter 9 examines several policy areas. Education, one of the most important issues to the Latino community, is the first concern. Despite the high salience of educational policy among Latinos, Latino educational levels remain very low. The chapter examines research that has attempted to discover why this is so. A second policy area the chapter considers is public employment, followed by language policy, particularly as manifested in Official English or English Only initiatives in the mid to late 1980s.

Chapter 10 is devoted to a critique of the way that Latino politics is, or is not, studied in the United States. A variety of assumptions and related problems have affected the extent, foci, and findings—interpretations of Latino politics. In many respects, these problems both reflect and contribute to an understanding, or *misunderstanding*, of Latino politics.

Chapter 11 presents an overall interpretation of Latino politics in the United States, that of two-tiered pluralism. The interpretation links, modifies, and extends other views into a distinct perspective on Latinos in the U.S. political system.

Although the materials are organized as indicated here, it is important, if obvious, to recognize that some issues intertwine and, to some degree, overlap. For instance, in considering participation in such formal political processes as voting, several chapters focus on participation at different levels of government. Group history is another example, as it is shaped by, and shapes, particular interest-group actions.

In short, the book seeks to provide a careful and critical overview and to offer a distinct interpretation of Latinos and politics in the United States.

Acknowledgments

Many friends and colleagues have been very supportive of me and my work on this project and to them I am most grateful. Among those who most directly encouraged me in my research on Latino politics are Rodolfo de la Garza, Joe Stewart, Jr., and F. Chris Garcia. A number of my colleagues at the University of Colorado at Boulder read parts of the manuscript and shared their thoughts with me on the analysis and ideas presented. These include Dennis Eckart, Larry Dodd, Susan Clarke, Frank Beer, Anne Costain, Walt Stone, John McIver, Cal Jillson, and Estevan Flores. David Caputo has also been a central and very supportive influence.

Also important in the writing of this book was the financial support provided by a Summer 1990 grant given through the University of Colorado's Implementation of Multicultural Perspectives and Approaches to Research and Teaching (IMPART) program and its director, Al Ramirez, and a Rockefeller Foundation grant for Minority Group Scholars (1987–1988). Any shortcomings in the book are, of course, mine alone and not attributable to any of the aforementioned.

Finally, my wonderful family has always been most generous and caring. I express appreciation to my mother, sister, and father, as well as to my grandparents, Caridad and José Valdes and Lena Hero, and to Kathy and Lindsay, Chris and Jennifer.

Latinos and the U.S. Political System

TWO-TIERED PLURALISM

1

Introduction

Latinos—U.S. residents of Mexican American, Puerto Rican, Cuban, or a variety of other "Hispanic" backgrounds—are the nation's second-largest minority group, after African Americans, comprising about 8 percent of the population. They are also one of the nation's fastest-growing groups and may well be the largest minority by early in the twenty-first century. Latinos already constitute 25 percent or more of the population in California and Texas. Latino students in elementary and secondary schools represent disproportionately large shares of the school-age population and probably actual school attenders; in the future, this disproportion will probably increase. Yet, despite their numbers, Latinos in the United States have not received much attention in political science research, and there has been little effort to bring together or systematically discuss the implications of the analyses that do exist (Avalos 1989; Wilson 1985; Barber 1990). The dearth of research on Latino politics is itself notable and suggestive. (We speculate on this in Chapter 10.)

Latino politics has particular characteristics that should be recognized and understood in and of themselves; at the same time, it must also be viewed in relation to the larger U.S. political system (see M. García 1989, 302). For example, because of population concentration, urban politics is the arena in which we would expect Latino political activity to be greatest; we therefore need to look at recent theoretical and "empirical" work regarding the broader urban political system.

1

Similarly, education, a major policy concern in U.S. society in general, is especially salient for Latinos, given their low socioeconomic status, because of its significance for economic and social mobility.

Understanding Latino politics in the United States has proved challenging and elusive, for a number of interrelated reasons. First, there is a question whether something that can be defined as Latino or Hispanic politics really exists. The question arises partly from the diversity of the Hispanic population. Indeed, several identifiable Latino groups can be identified by nationality. Mexican Americans make up about 62 percent of the total Latino population, Puerto Ricans about 15 percent, and Cubans 5 percent; the remaining 18 to 20 percent are "other Hispanics." Moreover, substantial differences exist, for instance, within just one of the Latino groups, Mexican Americans, in terms of socioeconomic status, historical experience in the various southwestern states, and so on (Connor 1985; Garcia and de la Garza 1977). Consequently it is not readily apparent that there is *a* Latino politics. Latinos may be a group in name—a nominal group—but not necessarily a politically identifiable group. Some observers see this lack of political and related social-psychological identification, within as well as between groups, as a major explanation for the lack of Latino political influence. "Latino politics" assumes certain similarities within and between groups of Americans of Hispanic descent that have not always been borne out in political action or in research.

Nevertheless, as Joan Moore and Harry Pachon (1985) point out, viewing "Hispanics" (their word) as a distinctive group may be appropriate. First, the life situations of all Hispanic minorities in the United States seem to be converging; this is occurring despite their distinctive histories and separate identities. "Second, the Hispanic populations are increasingly being treated as a group with common characteristics and common problems. In some respects, they are beginning to think of themselves as sharing many problems" (Moore and Pachon 1985, 2). Moreover, there has been a very large increase in the total number of Hispanics.

A related issue is identification, that is, the appropriate name or label to attach to a group. In this book I use the term "Latino," although it should be noted that "Hispanic" has become widely and popularly accepted. Considerable, and often heated, debate has taken place over the more correct or appropriate name. Despite precedents for its use, several scholars have criticized "Hispanic" as a label largely imposed by government agencies, particularly the U.S. Census Bureau, for the sake of convenience and simplicity. The methods and definitions used by government entities to describe Latino groups in the United States is itself an important example of the social and political "structuring of ethnicity" (see Muñoz 1989; Acuña 1988; Gimenez 1989).

Some have also criticized "Hispanic" as masking the diversity within and between Latino groups. As such, it acts as a form of stereotyping (Melville 1988). The term emphasizes, or overemphasizes, the Spanish or European aspects of the Latino political experience, while it deemphasizes experiences in the Americas, particularly the experience of conquest by the United States.

"Latino" is preferred by some because it strongly recognizes the New World, that is, the non-European aspects of historical experience, and, perhaps, because similar terms were used relatively early by prominent groups. One of the first and major Mexican American groups, the League of United Latin American Citizens (LULAC), formed in the 1920s in Texas, may be the best example of this. Also, beginning in the late nineteenth century, Cubans and Spaniards (and Italians as well) in Tampa, Florida, were generally referred to collectively as "Latins" (Mormino and Pozzetta 1987), and the term's Spanish equivalent, "Latino," was frequently used by the Spanish and Cuban populations in that area.

Group identification is complex and perhaps should be viewed as a process involving social, political, and individual dimensions. Individuals may perceive themselves to be members of a particular ethnic–racial group, but self-definitions emerge at least partly, or primarily or even solely, in response to social and political structures and policies. And they are reinforced by them. Ethnic–racial identification cannot be simply taken for granted or as a given. It is a "dependent variable," something to be understood and explained. This need results from the importance of individual designation for political and policy purposes.

The U.S. Constitution (Article I, section 1, later modified by the Fourteenth Amendment) specified that representation in Congress was to be determined by numbers, "which shall be determined by adding to the whole Number of free Persons, *including those bound to Service for a Term of Years*, and excluding *Indians* not taxed, *three fifths of all other persons*." Well before the rise of the major Latino interest groups, the U.S. Census Bureau began grappling with ways of defining groups for census purposes. Such practices underscore the political and social structuring of ethnic politics. In short, demography plays a large part in social and political definition—and in the way and degree to which government, politics, and related processes are factors not adequately explored in U.S. political research as it pertains to minority groups.

Definition is or can be both enabling and delimiting —and perhaps both simultaneously. On the one hand, individual and group identifications may serve purposes of pride and self-esteem; self-identification may also serve "strategic" purposes, leading to greater access to government programs and benefits. On the other hand, certain labels may serve as cues to the broader society that a group is a subordinate one, that it contributes little positively to society and has, perhaps, little to contribute. In any event, group labels suggest the political nature of issues and the difficulty in even specifying the group(s) of interest.

Another issue is ethnicity in relation to other variables, particularly socioeconomic ones. Political observers generally have viewed race–ethnicity as an "independent variable," that is, as a variable that explains some other phenomenon, such as voting. And, many times, race and ethnicity are treated as simple, and static, phenomena. It is not unusual, for instance, to find social science research that codes data in the following way: black = 1; white = 2. This seems to occur both at the levels of political analysis, theorizing, and research and in practical or day-to-day politics. Whether it is appropriate (see Barrera 1979) to consider ethnic–racial background as just another variable along with, or in contrast or opposition to, traditional socioeconomic measures such as education and income, in terms of inquiry has been a matter of substantial debate.

Some observers have claimed that at the practical political level, race–ethnicity has been made a focus of attention in order to deflect attention from other, perhaps more fundamental social divisions (e.g., social or economic class) and from fundamental policy questions (e.g., the distribution of wealth in society [Wolfinger 1974, 61–73]). Other analysts have been more inclined to see linkages between social class and substantive policy, on the one hand, and ethnic politics on the other. In this view, ethnic consciousness is a shorthand way of referring to social class that avoids Americans' distaste for the idea of class distinctions. In any event, the interplay of class and race has sometimes led to conceptual ambiguity from the standpoint of analysis.

Recently it has been said that "arguments about whether the real problem is race [ethnicity–culture] or class, and arguments whether recent U.S. racial progress is real or a sham, are miscast. We can understand the conditions of [ethnic–racial minorities in the United

States] only by specifying the complex and changing *connections* among race and class, progress and regress, not by posing one against the other" (Hochschild 1988, 188; emphasis added). These questions of ethnicity–race and class, from the standpoint of both the study and the practice of politics, are important. Yet they have often complicated our understanding of the matter. They are addressed a number of times in later chapters.

Another issue to think about is that of specifying and developing appropriate theoretical frameworks—ways to study or understand Latino politics. Political science research has not been especially helpful in this regard (again, see Avalos 1989). This, according to some observers, is because the emphasis in political science theory and research has been overwhelmingly on the experiences of European groups in the northeastern and midwestern United States. This Atlantic immigration, immigrant analogy, or Eurocentric focus does not seem especially useful for understanding Latinos or blacks (Blauner 1969; Omi and Winant 1986; Barrera 1979; Garcia and de la Garza 1977). Relatedly, common notions or assumptions about interest groups, and interest-group theory, may not necessarily apply to Latinos (as developed in Chapter 4).

What is suggested, then, is that understanding Latino politics is challenging because of its theoretical placement. According to Pachon (1985), for example, the Mexican American experience differs from the European immigrant experience in several ways. First, Mexican Americans were discriminated against on a racial basis, while Europeans were not. Second, Mexican Americans were "associated with a traditionally subordinate and conquered population," the American Indians. Third, Europeans came to cities in the eastern United States at a time when urban political machines could be used to pursue their interests. Machine politics was much less common in the Southwest, where Mexican Americans were concentrated; where political machines did exist, Chicanos scored political gains. In contrast, color or race barriers have been less extreme for Mexican Americans than for blacks.

Similarly, as Falcón (1988) points out, important differences between Puerto Ricans and blacks in New York City, to take one example, emanate in large part from different historical experiences. "The effects of the black experience with slavery in the United States compared to the Latino colonial experience are critical to any understanding of many of the current values and perceptions of each group"; and "while American blacks have developed a distinctive heritage after close to four hundred years in the United States, Latinos come from culturally and/or politically foreign countries. Compared to the *black rootedness in the U.S. experience*, albeit in a subordinate relationship, *Latinos* have a *more tenuous* relationship" (Falcón 1988, 184, 176; emphasis added). The "distinct" and "tenuous" nature of Latino status in the United States has made it difficult to develop explanatory frameworks appropriate to their unique status.

Furthermore, unique structural features have been noted in discussions of Mexican Americans relative to other ethnic groups in the United States (Glazer 1985). These structural features also are relevant, to greater or lesser degrees, to Puerto Ricans and Cubans in the United States. One feature is the common border, Mexico's proximity to the United States, which would also seem important for Puerto Rico and Cuba. Puerto Rico is a U.S. commonwealth, its citizens are U.S. citizens; Cuba is only ninety miles from the coast of Florida. A second feature is conquered territories: "that the American Southwest was once a part of Mexico is a reality in the listing of structural features even if it has no present consequence," according to Glazer (1985). But some interpretations would contend that the long-term consequences of conquest have been more important for Mexican Americans than Glazer suggests. Puerto Rico was obtained subsequent to the Spanish-American War and was administered as a colony for a number of years; Cuba was administered by the U.S. government for a brief period after the same war and was subsequently closely linked to the U.S. government.

Donald Horowitz (1985) has asserted that "the history of Mexicans in the United States has two sides, and both are important." On the one hand, a "fairly small but significant Mexican population was encapsulated" in the United States as a result of the war with Mexico, which ended in 1848; its treatment "was consistent with the treatment of a conquered population." On the other hand, there is another, later, arguably more important side, "voluntary immigration," which began most clearly coincident with the Mexican Revolution, in about 1910. In some respects, then, "the history of Mexican-American immigration parallels that of the great voluntary migrations of Europeans, which took place for the most part somewhat earlier. Both push and pull, both political and economic incentives played a part. The experience of Mexican Americans reflects their dual origins in the United States" (Horowitz 1985, 70).

Some scholars have placed primary emphasis on the first side, the initial contact or the conquest aspect; others have emphasized the "voluntary immigration" aspect of Mexican American presence in the United States. Still others argue that both sides are significantly interrelated. It has been said for instance, that the initial contact of Mexican Americans as U.S. citizens was important in "setting the stage" for later developments. Mexican Americans, and Native Americans, may have been seen as obstacles to America's "manifest destiny" in a way that other groups, such as Orientals and blacks, were not. These different emphases implicitly seem to affect how the Mexican American, and the broader Latino, situation has been viewed (these issues are revisited later).

A third important feature of the Mexican American situation is economic differences. Glazer (1985) contends that the contemporary Mexican economic situation in relation to the United States is unique in that "no other highly developed country shares a long land frontier, or indeed any land frontier at all, with a developing country." Puerto Rico, while also a developing country, is a U.S. entity. The significance of this feature regarding the Cuban population is less clear.

Another aspect that has implications for politics seemingly important for Latinos, yet is difficult to pin down, is their categorization. There are parallels between the Latino—particularly Mexican American and Puerto Rican—and black situations. But Latinos have generally been considered to be white by Census Bureau definitions, and often in terms of self-definition. Yet the Latino historical experience in the United States has diverged from that of most Anglo and other ethnic groups (and the word "Anglo," as used in the Southwest, means non-Hispanic white), including those eastern and southern Europeans who settled in the Northeast and Midwest in the late nineteenth and early twentieth centuries. Some areas make a tripartite distinction between white, nonwhite (i.e., Mexican or Mexican American), and black. Thus neither ethnicity nor race seems entirely appropriate in discussing Latino politics, although "racism" has often been used to describe Anglo attitudes and behaviors toward various Latino groups.

Perhaps a distinctive quality of Latino politics is that of cultural politics, although a central component of culture, language, has lessened in use over time among Hispanics. A central component of the "Chicano" Movement in the mid 1960s to mid 70s was cultural pride, or cultural nationalism. This broad cultural notion seems to be sufficiently strong to maintain the notion of a Latino politics. But that notion has not been sufficiently powerful to provide a clear-cut, action-oriented political program. That is, culture has been a source of pride, something precious to be defended against implicit and explicit denigration; what it has actually meant beyond this in the context of U.S. politics has not been made clear (Muñoz 1989). Culture does, however, seem to have an important impact in terms of political participation and policy outcomes (see Chapters 4 and 8).

Related to cultural politics and its somewhat diffuse, even ambiguous, focus are several questions. What are the goals of Latino politics? Does Latino politics mean specific attention to government policies and programs focused on the Latino population, or does it mean attention to general policies that are particularly salient for Latinos because of their socioeconomic status? Or does it mean both? Does it mean a greater emphasis on symbolic politics? Do Latinos merely have interests like any other interest group, or do they, like other minority groups, raise different issues and, at least implicitly, more fundamental value questions? One suspects that they are more likely to have to do both.

Part of what is implied in our discussion, then, is that Latinos are "different" politically (Browning, Marshall, and Tabb 1990; Meier and Stewart 1991). In many ways, a theoretically intriguing aspect of understanding Latino politics may lie in its uniqueness or its "betweenness" relative to dominant (Anglo or white) or other ethnic immigrant groups (e.g., the Irish and the Italians), on the one hand, and other minority groups (e.g., African Americans or Native Americans) on the other. That uniqueness has made the study of Latino politics particularly difficult and elusive. For better or worse, the discussions and analyses presented in this book reflect the intellectual elusiveness of Latinos' unique status.

An understanding of Latino politics seems to require a reliance on concepts and perspectives, and perhaps methodological approaches, that lie somewhere between several concepts and theoretical models. Similarly, an understanding of Latino politics seems to lie between race and ethnicity, or race–ethnicity and class. It reflects concerns for equality and community, the relation and tension between interests and values, and between symbols and substance. The uniqueness, and challenge, of Latino politics can be illustrated by the position of Latinos relative to the other large minority group in the United States: blacks. By several, though not all, measures of socioeconomic status, Latinos fare better than blacks; this would be expected because Latinos did not endure slavery and the formal discrimination blacks experienced. But Latinos have had substantially less political success than blacks to this point (Welch 1990), at least in the ways that such success is typically defined, by levels of political participation, electoral successes, and the like.

One focus of this book is its attention to the uniqueness and "between-nesses," and the resulting paradoxes and tensions that are evident in Latino politics. Apparent are the dilemmas faced by Latinos in terms of the group itself (or groups themselves), and important contextual or politicosocial structural factors that have not been sufficiently emphasized in examinations of Latino politics. As part of this, I link micro and macro perspectives.

Any study of Latino politics requires that we focus at several levels. We need some understanding of the internal dimensions of the group—the basic differences within a particular group and the degree of social, economic, geographical division within the group (e.g., the Mexican American group). A second issue requiring attention is the essential similarity, the "core qualities" of a particular group. A third focus is the bases for coalition among several groups, for example, Mexican Americans, Puerto Ricans, and Cubans, in the Latino category.

At the broad level, the study of Latino politics is valuable for a variety of reasons. A focus on what is often referred to as minority politics implies an alternative perspective on majority politics—the political operations and activities of the U.S. "mainstream." A political system needs to be viewed and understood in terms of its contradictions and weaknesses, as well as its strengths. Latino and minority politics brings attention not only to numerically smaller groups but, more important, to "marginalized" groups and to the problem of how these groups practice a politics that both draws on and challenges American values. It is a politics that to a considerable degree seeks to be part of the mainstream but has not succeeded in its efforts and therefore often functions at the margins of U.S. society and politics. Thus the study of Latino politics leads us to examine several assumptions and theoretical questions in U.S. political science.

How does our democratic theory account for the disadvantaged status of Latinos? Do such groups and their circumstances imply a need to question or redefine our understanding of democracy and power? If so, how; if not, why not? Considerable political and social theorizing has focused on blacks as an exception to the broader embrace of our "democratic creed." Latinos—and perhaps Native Americans and others—may be additional exceptions.

Other issues arise. Do ostensibly universal principles, such as procedural fairness and government neutrality, hold up when applied to all groups, or do they result in differential outcomes and impacts? What happens when the activities of government, which are supposed to be neutral at worst and ameliorative at best, seem to maintain, reinforce, and perhaps worsen social inequality? Are the concepts, methods, measures of the study of politics able accurately, adequately, and appropriately to address questions of Latino politics?

In this book there is a perception that much of the existing scholarly work on Latino politics has been lacking in several respects. Moreover, there has not been sufficient effort to synthesize or critically assess the existing research. A goal of this work is understanding and comprehension, a goal that differs from the narrower and more common goals of explanation and prediction evident in much political science research. This book is trying to explain something, but what is more important, it hopes to provide insights into Latino politics in the United States and, indeed, minority politics in general.

2

Theoretical Perspectives and Latino Politics

Latinos are in a disadvantaged position politically, socially, and economically in the United States. They fare considerably less well than Anglos, and less well in some instances than blacks, on a variety of measures of political representation and socioeconomic status (see Chapter 3). Although political science research has not addressed these issues extensively, some theories or interpretations of power and authority have been put forth that are relevant to the political and social status of Latinos and other disadvantaged minority groups.

This chapter summarizes several major theories and comments on their assumptions and arguments. The theories provide different ways of looking at the U.S. political system and the condition of Latinos within it, each theory organizing information and structuring evidence about Latinos and the political system somewhat differently. For example, depending on the theory, the same "factual" information is in some way factored in or factored out, is perceived as more important or less so, and is consequently interpreted differently. From a discussion of the strengths and weaknesses of these theories, a picture emerges of how different theoretical perspectives define and shape the perceived relationship between the political system and Latinos.

An early effort to examine the Chicano political experience focused on three perspectives of politics in an attempt to understand the status of ethnic and racial minority groups in U.S. society: pluralism, elitism, and internal colonialism (Garcia and de la Garza 1977). The discussion that follows to some extent takes up that earlier examination, but also departs from it and expands on it in order to account for various developments that have occurred in the years since it was published.

—————PLURALISM

Since at least the mid 1950s, pluralism has been the dominant perspective in political science research on U.S. politics (Manley 1983; Hero 1989). Minority politics, by extension, has also been largely examined and understood in pluralist terms. What exactly is meant by pluralism, however, may vary based on the time period or the particular scholar one consults. The concept of pluralism, somewhat complex to begin with, has become more so through the theoretical modifications made in the concept by scholars (e.g., Dahl 1982; Lindblom 1980). The discussion that follows makes certain distinctions between early and later pluralism (see Manley regarding pluralism I and pluralism II, or pluralism and neopluralism). Along with other clarifications, these distinctions are necessary to update the theoretical perspectives identified in early political science discussions that addressed Latinos or Chicanos.

Garcia and de la Garza (1977) identified several "essential qualities" of pluralist interpretations. Pluralism—what some would call early pluralism or pluralism I—assumed that there were multiple centers of power, not a single center, in society and in politics. Power was considered to be widely dispersed among a variety of groups and institutions in society. These groups, according to Garcia and de la Garza, had some degree of essential political resources (if not equal resources), including group size, financial resources, social status (including prestige), cohesiveness, intensity, and geographical dispersion. A related, and important, assertion was that these resources were "noncumulative." Thus groups advantaged in one resource (perhaps wealth) would probably be weak in another resource (say, group size). A poor but numerically large group might thus stress elections as a major form of political influence. One group might have more of a particular resource than another, but overall these differences could at least partially be compensated for or balanced out. Resource equality was maintained through the noncumulative pattern of group resources.

Later pluralist writings, however, suggest that many (not necessarily all) groups or interests frequently (not always), in some manner or another, depend on the availability of a variety of resources, "the skill and intensity with which the resources are employed, and the legitimacy of the group . . . organizing and defending themselves" (Dahl 1982, 207–209). Still later pluralist writing qualifies or modifies assertions about the nature of group resources and the ability of groups to have an impact in the political arena. Yet those who criticize this later pluralism say that it has not made clear how much inequality of resources can exist before the label pluralism is no longer a legitimate description.

Early pluralism implies that if a minority group is too small in number or otherwise lacks power, it can make its voice heard by forming coalitions with other groups. If a group is discriminated against, this happens at least partly because it has not used its resources effectively. In any event, certain legal protections, or minority rights, presumably assure that all groups, including ethnic and racial groups, have the rights of free association, free speech, and so on. Those rights are essential to the enjoyment of full civil liberties and to liberal democracy—and they limit the existence and extent of legal and political discrimination. But later pluralism, and critics of early pluralism, argue that such protections are necessary but are not sufficient guarantees. In fact, they may be empty rhetoric in the face of substantial social inequality and its implications.

Pluralism also talks of separate spheres of influence. Some groups are influential on policies of particular importance to them, while other groups have extensive influence in different areas. For example, teachers would probably be influential regarding education, or some specific aspects of education, while doctors would be especially important in health policies. Critics, and later pluralist writers, are more skeptical of this argument, seeing the scope and impact of certain interests and interest groups as broader and more "privileged" than others (Lindblom 1980). In any case, early pluralist writing would imply, for instance, that if one could identify an issue or issues particularly important to Latinos, then one would expect Latinos to be somewhat influential regarding that issue, and probably more influential on that issue than other groups.

Pluralism also contends that individuals and groups possess *slack resources*. Even if a group appears weak or inactive at one point in time, elected officials are aware that the group can become active. Officials therefore act in anticipation of that potential and are therefore held accountable.

Another assumption of pluralism is that there are *multiple access points* in the political system. A group that has been denied or frustrated in its efforts to influence politics at one point or place in the system can pursue its political goals in other places or arenas. For example, if a group has been unable to influence the executive branch, it may seek judicial redress; or, if local government does not prove responsive to group needs, the group may seek to influence the state or federal government.

Pluralism also views the political process as *incremental.* Because power is dispersed, policy change requires extensive bargaining and compromise between groups, which, in turn, generally leads to only small or marginal political and policy change. This incrementalism may appear to leave the status quo basically unchanged, but pluralist writings suggest that the cumulative impact can be, and in some instances has been, substantial. In the long run, at least, most groups can have some opportunity to influence policies important to them, or so pluralism suggests.

More often than not, early pluralism tended to assume, or to take as givens, many issues that, while relevant to politics, are not themselves political questions or issues unless groups are somehow able to force them onto the political agenda. Much research indicates, for example, that socioeconomic status affects the likelihood of political participation and influence, but early pluralism in general tended not to view the distribution of wealth in society as a political question. Early pluralism was less inclined than other perspectives to ask what, if any, political factors influenced or caused existing social and economic relationships to come about in the first place. There was not a theoretical predisposition to inquire into the historical origins or dimensions of these circumstances. Early pluralism tended not to place much emphasis on the broad social and political structure.

Overall, then, pluralism assumes that most groups—and we would assume, by extension, minority groups as well—have some resources to draw on to make their political influence felt. They may lack money, but can at least partly compensate for the lack with other resources. At least in the long term, all "legitimate" interests get a fair chance to influence the political process because the political rules of the game are basically fair and apply equally to all groups. If a group's goals are not achieved, pluralism implies that (1) the group's goals are not sufficiently widely shared—that is, there is not enough political support or consensus for the group's policy preferences to be enacted—;(2) the group has not used its resources effectively; or (3) both. Later pluralism, however, has become more negative about the entities at the heart of its model, interest groups or independent associations.

The leading pluralist scholar, Robert Dahl, has recently raised the claim that interest groups often can and do promote harmful defects in a political system. In protecting and furthering their own interests, entrenched groups can "stabilize injustices and inequalities." Because they are well-entrenched and powerful groups, they can minimize or nullify changes that, by some standards, are deemed necessary to lessen political inequality. Interest groups can also "deform civic consciousness" in that they encourage people to think only, or primarily, in terms of narrow self-interest and in the short term. They also "distort the public agenda" because they may keep certain issues off that agenda or define issues in ways advantageous only to themselves. They may also "wrongfully appropriate public functions"; they take major roles not only in defining but in implementing public activities and policies, and they do so in a narrowly self-interested manner (Dahl 1982).

Pluralism itself, and research that implicitly holds pluralist assumptions (see Chapter 10), seems to imply that ethnic–minority groups are but one more interest group in the society. The minority–group situation is not seen as all that different in relation to the larger political system from that of nonethnic–racial groups competing to make their voices heard. Similarly, pluralism seems to make little distinction between the situation of earlier immigrant ethnic groups, such as the Irish and Italians, and that of Latinos and blacks (Omi and Winant 1986). In these respects, pluralism is similar to other perspectives that might address minority politics, such as elitist and class analysis.

COALITIONAL BIAS

Coalitional bias, a second perspective on American politics, is a modification of *elite theory*. Elite theory argues that there are essentially two major groups in society, a small group of powerful elites and the powerless masses. In elite theory, minority groups are simply part of the powerless mass and do not have a unique status within it. The elite group is well organized and controls, directly or indirectly, the major economic, social, and political institutions in society. While the masses influence government through elections and related processes, their influence is seen as marginal and not as a serious challenge to elite dominance, which is imbedded in socioeconomic institutions and reinforced by beliefs and attitudes.

Coalitional bias brings to bear sociological arguments regarding the nature and importance of social stratification to understand group power relationships better (Stone 1986; cf. Stone 1980). Socioeconomic equality or the lack of it puts groups in more or less advantageous positions to influence politics; these different positions have clear and major implications for the distribution of power in the political and social system. Public or government officials depend heavily on upper-class groups or interests because such groups possess many of the resources necessary to advance governmental activity and policies. Indeed, many would contend that some upper-class groups, including large businesses and corporations, hold what is essentially public power. Not only do upper-strata interests have a greater quantity of resources, they also have a greater range of resources, more durable and more indispensable resources than others do (Stone, Whelan, and Murin 1986, 203; cf. Dahl 1982; Lindblom 1980).

Essentially, coalitional bias suggests that the resources of the upper strata are so wide ranging, ever present, and significant that this group holds substantial advantages in terms of both actual and slack resources, often overwhelming other interests and groups. Upper-strata interests are a factor in all that public officials do; the interests of lower-strata groups are not. This means that "groups are not uniformly valued as partners in governance; not all have an equal opportunity to become and remain" part of governing coalitions (Stone 1986, 203).

The importance of coalitional bias for understanding minority politics is the theory's attempt to link issues of class with those of racial–minority politics. A group's social-class position serves as a clear indication of its attractiveness as a coalition partner because of the strong association in people's minds between social class and racial–minority status. Minority status is a metaphor or cue for a group that is undesirable, perhaps undeserving, and that probably has little to offer politically. Minority groups thus make less desirable coalition partners. Coalitional bias contends, then, that some groups—the dominant or advantaged groups—"prevail consistently, though not totally. Over time, those that prevail do so in part because they enjoy a systemic advantage in the governmental process. Other groups lose consistently, though not totally. Over time, those that lose do so in part because they suffer a systemic disadvantage and are outsiders in the governmental process" (Stone 1986, 203). That is, a relationship between class and race exists, and minority political opportunities and influence are especially damaged by that relationship. In some ways, coalitional bias is compatible with another view, internal colonialism.

_____INTERNAL COLONIALISM

Internal colonialism, a third perspective, is an expansion and "modification of classic colonialism adopted to the situation of American minorities." The internal colonial model is complex (Barrera 1979). According to Garcia and de la Garza (1977), an essential feature of internal colonialism is a "situation where one group of people dominate and exploit another, and, generally the relations occur between culturally different groups." A major difference between classic colonialism, which is the domination of one nation or society by another within the dominated group's own territory, and internal colonialism is that with internal colonialism the colonized minority population has the same formal legal status as the dominant group, or "colonizers" (Barrera 1979, 189–204). Members of the minority group have the same political and legal rights as majority-group members.

Moreover, the internal colonial interpretation suggests that the colonized or minority group entered the dominant society involuntarily, through a forced process. The minority group is, therefore, not an immigrant group as are other ethnic groups, like the Irish and Italians, for example. Internal colonialism sees this as a crucial historical difference. Several related aspects of internal colonialism are *cultural genocide*, policies that denigrate native values and culture, often including language; *racism*, both at an individual and institutional level; and *external administration*, the system where political–administrative and economic control rests with persons and institutions outside the group, despite nominal indications that the "colonized" group is in control and holds official positions and power.

The internal colonial model is in some ways similar to and a variant of the elitist model. Garcia and de la Garza (1977) suggest, however (also see Barrera 1979), that internal colonialism emphasizes unique historical circumstances and factors, contending that there are important differences between racial–minority groups and other groups, including ethnic groups, in society. The internal colonial interpretation claims that the present disadvantaged position of Latino groups is in large part the result of past oppression, an oppression that was severe.

The oppression continues, although it is no longer overt and may no longer be directly supported by formal government policies. It may well occur institutionally, through "normal practices." Despite the formal openness of the political system, political access is significantly foreclosed because of the magnitude and nature of the inequality of social and economic resources, along with discrimination, prejudice, and the like. (As discussed by some scholars, particularly some political sociologists, the internal colonial model has a Marxist or class-analysis flavor; indeed, some have sought to synthesize it with Marxist analysis, as I later suggest.)

─────ASSESSING THE PERSPECTIVES

The perspectives may be further evaluated now that they have been summarized. Pluralism has been challenged on several grounds. The early pluralist claim that groups are essentially equal in resources or that group resources are noncumulative has been most strongly questioned. The inequality, critics argue, is simply too great to hold to that contention. Groups lacking in one resource tend to be lacking in others; groups with abundant resources in one arena tend to have them in others as well. Also, access and influence are not necessarily one and the same, and access may be only a prerequisite to influence. The argument that there are multiple access points is likewise challenged; critics contend that, with few exceptions, groups that lack political influence at one level of politics tend to lack influence at others. It can be noted at this point that this may be especially so for Latinos, given that they are concentrated geographically and given the significance of federalism, and state and local governments, in the U.S. political system (these are discussed in later chapters). Relatedly, pluralism is criticized for not being sufficiently attentive to the larger socioeconomic system and for treating such matters as the distribution of wealth in society as natural and largely outside the realm of politics. To the extent that pluralism does address such issues it views them as one among a number of independent variables. Later pluralist theoretical writing is less culpable in this regard, but it does not appear that this writing has had much impact on most of the mainstream empirical research that has addressed Latino politics (this is discussed further in Chapter 10).

Pluralism also has been criticized for treating the situation of blacks, Latinos, and other such groups as essentially the same as that of groups that voluntarily migrated to the northeastern and midwestern United States around the turn of the century. Pluralism has applied the immigrant analogy and has assumed that the Atlantic (European) experience can explain the sociopolitical situation of minority groups. Pluralism seems to want to make the groups fit the theory, rather than have the theory fit the groups. This, critics argue, is simply wrong, empirically, theoretically, and ideologically.

Coalitional bias seems a more cogent interpretation than its theoretical predecessor, elitism, and is more attentive to certain issues than is its ostensible theoretical antagonist, pluralism (Isaac 1988; Dahl 1982). As coalitional bias recognizes, sociopolitical relations are more complex than "simple" elitism suggested. Coalitional bias also is more attentive to the larger social structure, rather than activities in a narrowly defined political arena. Coalitional bias suggests that group resources cannot be understood outside the socioeconomic context; resources are more or less crucial in relation to particular circumstances. With this contextual emphasis, coalitional bias provides an important macroperspective as a counterpoint to pluralism's frequent microperspective. Nevertheless, pluralists typically respond, locating power in social structures, institutions, and the like is in some respects too easy and in others too difficult. It is too easy, pluralists say, in that it is a ready-made argument that fits all situations. The difficulty that interpretations such as coalitional bias may encounter is in pinpointing the exercise of power in particular situations. Pluralism has stressed that the exercise of power must be demonstrated, made evident and measurable; it cannot merely be assumed.

Coalitional bias arguments respond that understanding how power is imbedded in institutions and is "systemic" in nature, and how power operates in the long run, is crucial to understanding politics, but that pluralism tends not to focus on such issues. Indeed, coalitional bias and internal colonial arguments imply that pluralism too often and easily explains away, rather than explains, the power or lack thereof of all groups.

Although coalitional bias is more attentive to unique historical circumstances than is pluralism, it is not so historically attentive as internal colonialism. Nor is coalitional bias especially clear about how and why the complex relationships between class and race have come about. Like other theories that have a political economy emphasis, coalitional bias often implies that racial–minority politics derives from economic relationships; ethnic politics is seen as effect, rather than cause. Whether this implication is accurate is open to debate; the point is that race and minority status often do not seem to be the central focus of coalitional bias.

An interesting aspect of the internal colonial interpretation, compared to the other two perspectives, is its attentiveness to historical uniqueness and different group experiences, and, in turn, its stress on lingering individual and institutional impacts of cultural denigration. These concerns are not so evident in the other theories. Internal colonialism has come under criticism, however, on several grounds.

Over time, there have been theoretical and ideological debates about the validity of the internal colonial model. Recently, several scholars of Chicano history and politics have argued that internal colonialism probably has overstated its case, perhaps substantially so. Major criticisms, which can be noted only briefly here, argue, for one thing, that internal colonial interpretations give insufficient attention to both the significance of internal class stratification within the Mexican population before and after the U.S.–Mexican war and the class nature of racial conflict after U.S. annexation. Second, these interpretations may fail to appreciate the degree to which the claim that Chicanos are victims of colonization on their own land is a dubious contention at best. Third, the claim that Chicanos were victims of colonial systems based on racial domination is also seriously open to question, given the racial status accorded Mexicans after U.S. annexation and the modest advantage they held over other minority groups. Fourth, when viewed comparatively, the experience of Chicanos in nineteenth-century California (and, for that matter, in the entire Southwest) diverged from that of other racial minorities and raises questions about the commonality of the colonized minority experience. Finally, works that suggest a continuity between the nineteenth- and early twentieth-century Chicano "colonial" experience fail to appreciate the enormous differences that actually existed between these two historical periods (Almaguer 1987, 11; cf. Morris 1975, 22–23; Gómez-Quiñones 1990, 19). These criticisms of internal colonialism cannot be taken lightly.

At the same time, a number of scholars have not agreed with the criticisms (Acuña 1988; Barrera 1979). The model may raise certain points and provide certain insights that other theories do not; internal colonialism may have been overstated, but its insights are not irrelevant. Moreover, the unique structural features indicated by Glazer (see Chapter 1), among others, as well as much evidence of very low Latino socioeconomic status (detailed in the next chapter), suggest that plu-

TABLE 1
A Comparison of Three Theoretical Perspectives on Issues Relevant to Latino Politics

Issue	Pluralism	Coalitional Bias	Internal Colonialism
Importance of history	Not very important	Somewhat important (implied)	Very important
How groups in society are seen	Essentially similar	Quantitatively and perhaps qualitatively different	Qualitatively different
How ethnic–racial groups are seen	Not very different	Somewhat different	Very different
Significance of prejudice	Not insurmountable	A major issue	Deep-seated, enduring
How power is seen	Dispersed	Somewhat skewed	Highly skewed
How group problem is seen	Within group; bias against group	Political–economic; social structural; historical	Historical; political–economic; social structural
Implicit group reference	Europeans; immigrant analogy; Atlantic migration	Sees groups as different	Conquered people; non-Europeans; Third World

ralist and coalitional bias arguments alone are probably not sufficient explanations of Latino politics.

Clearly, none of the theories is without problems. To some degree, however, the problems of one theory are compensated for by the insights of the others. The interplay of micro factors, socioeconomic institutions and structures, and historical attentiveness are all important to understanding Latino politics. The relative contributions of these theories generally, along with how well they have been applied to Latino politics, are significant. Notably, there has been substantial theoretical convergence; the theories have incorporated elements previously excluded or downplayed. For instance, later pluralist writing has paid increasing attention to issues of social structure that early pluralist writings did not emphasize. Coalitional bias has modified various assertions of (earlier) elitist theory. In fact, coalitional bias and later pluralism look somewhat similar. But pluralism stresses that individuals and groups, not social and economic structures, act; coalitional bias and similar views stress that action takes place within social structures.

Notwithstanding the shortcomings of internal colonialism, its implication that history has been overlooked and that unique histories have been overlooked is a point that itself should not be overlooked. This neglect has been particularly strong in political science, and neither early or later pluralism nor coalitional bias have entirely avoided this problem.

Table 1 summarizes some of the major points of the several theories discussed in this chapter and the ways in which they differ on certain questions.

————RELATED SOCIOLOGICAL PERSPECTIVES

Sociological discussions of social inequality complement the theoretical perspectives on Latino–minority politics. The sociological theories also parallel and inform, or misinform, political and political scientific discussion. Although some of these popular sociological views have often been discredited by social science research, they nonetheless seem to underlie certain assumptions of political analysis and popular debate.

Barrera (1979, esp. chap. 7) identified and discussed several theories of racial inequality. These theories are important because of the assumption that racial inequality in the broader social arena spills over into the political arena. The implication or corollary for politics is also suggested in the discussion of the theories.

————DEFICIENCY THEORIES

The first sociological theories of inequality are deficiency theories. These theories explain the low status of certain groups, particularly minority groups, by arguing that the problem lies within the groups. Specifically, group members are said to have certain deficiencies that prohibit or at least impede their ability to function and succeed in the U.S. social, economic, and political system. These deficiencies may take several forms, and sometimes the several forms are interrelated. Three varieties of deficiency theory are linked to biological, social structural, and cultural factors.

Biological deficiency theories attribute racial inequality to the genetic and thus hereditary inferiority of certain groups. Most frequently, lower-status groups are said to have lower levels of intelligence, which leads to less social and economic success. *Theories of social structural deficiency* contend that shortcomings in various relationships within a group, such as links to the immediate or extended family and inadequate or insufficient social organization, explain the status of minority groups. For instance, an overly strong loyalty to family is sometimes perceived as a deficiency in the Latino family structure; a weak family structure has been claimed to be a major problem for blacks.

The ostensible political implications of the alleged social structural deficiencies of Latinos can be noted. Very strong ties to family lead to a heavy focus on family interaction, which in turn lowers social and economic mobility; these are important factors in developing an interest and participating in politics. More directly, family ties may consume time that could otherwise be spent on political activities.

Group attitudes and values are the focus of *cultural deficiency theories.* According to this perspective, Latinos and other minority groups do not have the "right" attitudes and values, those necessary to succeed socioeconomically and, by extension, politically, in the United States. For example, cultural deficiency theories argue that minority groups do not place sufficient value on education and financial success; also, individual members of the groups have a present, rather than a future, orientation. This inability to plan for the future leads to limited opportunities. Regarding politics, there may not be the "right" attitudes about civic responsibility and political participation; or, to the extent that the "right" attitudes are held, they may not be acted on.

Biological deficiency theories have been largely discredited (Barrera 1979). For example, a group's performance on IQ tests, which is the major evidence for those who put forth biological deficiency arguments, has been found to be socially biased. A number of problems with the social structural and cultural deficiency theories have been indicated by Barrera. Assuming that clear and significant differences between advantaged and disadvantaged groups in social structures and attitudes can be established—and it is by no means certain that this can be done—it must then be ascertained whether those differences are a cause or an effect of a minority-group's disadvantaged status. That is, if members of minority groups indeed hold different attitudes from majority groups, is that what has caused their lower socio-economic or political status? Or are the group's allegedly different attitudes a result of, an adaptation to, their unequal status? It must also be demonstrated that the values held by the group are necessarily negative. For instance, it is quite possible, and indeed a common perception, that strong family ties are an important and redeeming value. It would also have to be shown that there are no other positive cultural values to compensate for the supposedly negative ones. Similar "proofs" would also have to be extended specifically to politics (Barrera 1979).

Within-group structure and cultural deficiency theories have been criticized as being at best superfluous and at worst legitimizing myths. They are criticized as superfluous in that they assume that "equal opportunity exists and has existed for minority races in American society, and that [the minority groups] have failed to seize the opportunity because of their own deficiencies" (Barrera 1979, 181). Yet substantial evidence exists that such opportunity often has not been present for Latinos and other minority groups and that, when economic opportunities have existed, Latinos have pursued them. Contentions regarding social structural and cultural deficiencies thus are challenged as merely ways of justifying, rather than explaining, Latino or other minority-group inequality.

—————BIAS THEORIES

A second set of theories of inequality are bias theories. These theories "focus on prejudice and discrimination as the sources of minority inequality, and thus tend to put the responsibility on the Anglo majority rather than on the minorities" (Barrera 1979, 182). These theories contend that dominant groups, that is, whites or Anglos, have negative or unfavorable attitudes toward, and discriminate against, minorities. The biases and discrimination lead to a set of self-reinforcing inequalities, such as poor education, unemployment or underemployment, and powerlessness among minorities; in turn, these inequalities may lead to a self-reinforcing set of social pathologies, such as crime, drug, and mental problems within disadvantaged groups. Ultimately, these inequalities and social problems justify, reinforce, and exacerbate prejudice and discrimination against minority groups.

_____STRUCTURAL DISCRIMINATION THEORIES

Structural discrimination theories, a third kind of theory of racial inequality, point to the social structure of the society as a whole as the source of minority disadvantage. Structure refers to the regular patterns of human interaction in society and can be either formal or informal. Formal structures have some publicly legitimated or recognized status, such as schools or government. Informal structures would include the class system. Structural theories differ from deficiency and bias theories in emphasizing that discrimination need not be overt and visible, that it can occur institutionally, in what is taken to be the "natural course of things." Sociological theories tend to place greater importance on the implications, or spillover affects, that informal structures have for a variety of political phenomena than does political science.

Internal colonialism is one structural discrimination theory developed by sociologists. "The central dynamic of this model is provided by the concept of interests; the interests referred to are those which originally gave rise to European colonialism, of which internal colonialism is an extension, as well as the contemporary interests of privileged groups" (Barrera 1979, 196). Dominant groups and individuals in the society benefit from and therefore have strong interests in creating and maintaining those socioeconomic structural relationships that bring about benefits. The internal colonial model does not dismiss the importance of racial prejudice, which bias theories emphasize, or the role that perceived or claimed minority-group deficiencies might have, but it views these factors in a different light than do the bias and deficiency theories, as being a product of racial ideologies developed to justify structural discrimination.

Some scholars contend that internal colonialism is an incomplete interpretation in that it does not link racial oppression and conflict to dominant economic relations, more specifically, capitalism. Because of this, some have sought to synthesize internal colonial theory with Marxist or class segmentation theory. One argument is that there are two major intraclass divisions in capitalist political economy, with each division having subdivisions. The structural class segment consists of divisions based on the structure of occupations. The second, ascriptive class segments, are based on ascribed characteristics, such as race–ethnicity or gender. "Chicanos have been incorporated into the United States' political economy as subordinate ascriptive class segments, and they have historically been found occupying such a structural position at all class levels" (Barrera 1979, 212).

─────RELATING POLITICAL AND SOCIOLOGICAL PERSPECTIVES

A fuller theoretical understanding may be provided by pointing out the parallels and relationships between the political and sociological views. Pluralism focuses on within-group abilities and resources; deficiency theories also have within-group focus. To a substantial extent, pluralism attributes political inequality, or an absence or deficit in political influence, to factors such as inadequate group cohesion or mobilization, poor leadership, and unpersuasive policy arguments. These organizational shortcomings may be tied, if only implicitly, to within-group problems, as deficiency theories would suggest. Pluralism may also acknowledge certain biases, as in bias theory, but implies that such biases can probably be overcome with adequate mobilization, coalition building, and the like.

Despite major differences between bias theories and pluralism, on the one hand, and structural theories on the other, there are also similarities. Structural theories, bias theories, and pluralism all recognize the significance of prejudice and discrimination. Bias theories, however, see prejudice and discrimination as a cause of inequality; pluralism sees bias as a problem for minority political groups, but implies that bias can be surmounted with adequate mobilization (Browning, Marshall, and Tabb 1984). Structural theories see prejudice and discrimination as growing out of a need to justify the structural inequality.

There are also clear parallels between sociological and political structural theories. The political and sociological internal colonial models are essentially similar. The coalitional bias theory and Barrera's synthesis of class segmentation with internal colonialism are also similar. Both imply that economic interests are central divisions in society, and both indicate that ethnic–racial equality is a related, yet distinct, component of social and political inequality. Internal colonial perspectives make this argument more forcefully. Coalitional bias theory recognizes the importance of economic relations in society but, unlike internal colonialism, does not necessarily see them from the standpoint of Marxism or radical political economy (Barrera 1979).

How are these theories to be evaluated, and what do they mean for Latinos in society and politics? Pluralism, the dominant perspective on

American politics, does not seem to explain the Latino political situation well, or may explain it away or explain it too easily. Pluralism seems more suited to understanding the experience of immigrant ethnic groups; its usefulness for understanding groups whose initial entrance into American society was involuntary or in other ways divergent from the Atlantic migration model, seems limited. Other of pluralism's assumptions, such as those concerning group resources and the noncumulative nature of resources, also seem questionable. In short, pluralism may be accurate to some extent, and perhaps Latino groups will "fit" this model increasingly in the coming years; conceivably, the political process might evolve toward the conditions and outcomes suggested by pluralism. Generally, however, until now pluralism does not seem to be a fully adequate or appropriate interpretation of the political situation of Chicanos (Mexican Americans) and Puerto Ricans. Therefore, the structural theories deserve further attention. Pluralism may be more accurate regarding Cubans.

While scholars have questioned internal colonialism, it nonetheless highlights issues that pluralism overlooks or deemphasizes. Central in this respect are contentions that racial–ethnic groups, especially Latinos, Native Americans, and blacks, have had different experiences in the United States. Coalitional bias does not emphasize history per se, but it is well aware of enduring characteristics of the political system and related political economy that shape the political situation of minorities.

Overall, much of mainstream political science would claim that political–sociological views, particularly in their more radical forms, exaggerate the role of economic structures and fail to give sufficient attention to the role of politics, political rights, and political equality and for understating the importance of free and open elections, civil liberties, and the like. Political scientists, particularly those holding pluralist views, might point to the civil rights movement and the civil rights and voting rights legislation of the 1960s and subsequently as evidence of pluralism working, and working well. Others would argue, however, that such evidence overlooks the continuing, and in some ways increasing, inequalities experienced by minorities. They would say that the impact of political "success," such as the election and appointment of minorities to important official positions, has left the situation of the masses largely unaffected.

Table 2 summarizes the relationships and comparisons between the political science and sociological perspectives.

TABLE 2
Political Science and Sociological Perspectives on Minorities:
Comparison and Contrast

Political Science Perspective	Sociological Perspective

Problem lies within minority group	
Pluralism (poor use of resources)	Deficiency theories; biological, social structural, cultural
Problem lies within dominant group (prejudice/discrimination)	
Pluralism sees bias as possible additional impediment to some groups	Bias theories
Problem lies with social structural system	
Elitist; coalitional bias; internal colonialism	Political economy (class segmentation); internal colonialism

---

———OTHER CHARACTERISTICS OF THE U.S. POLITICAL SYSTEM

Other major characteristics of the U.S. political system are significant for minority politics. One is the belief that there should be, and to some degree is, formal or legal equality—equality before the law and equality of opportunity to compete in society. Equal opportunity has been called the keystone of American liberal democracy. The concept of equal opportunity is crucial in that it bridges "the gap between the promise of political and social equality and the fact of economic inequality" (Hochschild 1988, 168). Nevertheless, the concept of equal opportunity may be a double-edged sword, for several reasons.

First, equal opportunity for members of one social group is often perceived as coming only at the expense of opportunity for even more disadvantaged members of a different group. It may lead to competition between minority groups. Another double-edged condition can occur when opportunity for members of one group occur at the expense of even more disadvantaged members of the *same* group. A third reason is that "if the promise of equal opportunity is not fulfilled in practice, it can backfire" on the political system that promises it (Hochschild 1988).

Federalism, another important part of U.S. politics has been both hailed and criticized in terms of its implications for minority politics. Political observers, particularly pluralists (Dahl 1976), in asserting that there are multiple access points, argue that the the existence of many local and state governments offers various groups many opportunities to participate in, learn about, and influence the political process. In contrast, others claim that federalism permitted and facilitated the massive denial of basic rights embodied in the institution of slavery and later mechanisms that have diminished political and social equality. Federalism's impact on minority politics continues to be the subject of much theoretical and practical political debate. (These issues arise in Chapters 6–8, addressing state and local politics.)

Another aspect, majority rule in the electoral process, is notable in the light of evidence of considerable ethnic–racial bloc voting in the United States. Especially at the local government level, data indicate that nonminorities vote for nonminority candidates and that minorities vote for minority candidates. Thus the practice, as distinct from the ideal, of majority rule and minority rights, in the context of substantial socioeconomic inequality, figures in the chapters that follow.

_____TOWARD A NEW PERSPECTIVE

The political and social theories delineated in this chapter should serve as a backdrop in organizing and making better sense of the materials that follow. In several instances, we draw on additional theoretical insights to complement and modify those presented here. At the same time, the important shaping effects of the American political system are emphasized to provide a context for the analysis of Latinos in the political system. At this point, however, it may be useful to suggest another interpretation of Latino politics, one that is extensively developed in Chapter 11.

Latino politics, as well as that of other minority groups, is best understood through a perspective of *two-tiered pluralism*. That is, because of historical, socioeconomic, and other factors, minority individuals and groups have largely been relegated to a lower social and political tier or arena. Despite the equal legal and political status of Latinos formally, distinct factors and processes have led to systematically lower political and social status. Only occasionally have minorities had political influence comparable to nonminority segments of society. Individually, Latinos sometimes have gained political successes; on the whole, however, Latinos and Latino politics have been relegated to a lesser place in the U.S. political system. That place is not well explained by conventional pluralism, nor do the other interpretations fully capture what that place is and how it came about and continues to exist. The evidence leading up to this interpretation is suggested in the chapters that follow.

Important structural features of the Latino situation were suggested in Chapter 1. The importance of those features, along with historical and socioeconomic factors, require extensive attention. It is to these that we now turn.

3

The History and Socioeconomic Status of Latino Groups

_____As suggested in the previous chapter, a historical and social background is necessary if we are to place the Latino political situation, as well as that of the several Latino subgroups, in perspective. There are important differences in the historical and contemporary situation of the Latino groups; there are also similarities.

According to Moore and Pachon (1985), U.S. views of, and hostility toward, Hispanics have been influenced by "roots that go as far back as England's conflict with Spain in the sixteenth century" (pp. 4–5). Not only had Spain been a competitor with England for New World dominance, but its Roman Catholicism and the perception of the Spanish "black plague," based on the treatment of native populations in what is today Latin America, also served as a justification for criticism and the subordination of Hispanics. Also, Hispanics early became a problem for U.S. expansionist activities. Their presence in Florida, Texas, and the Southwest, and the continued Spanish control of such Caribbean areas as Puerto Rico and Cuba, were obstacles to emerging U.S. ideas regarding territorial expansion and hemispheric influence symbolized by the Monroe Doctrine and the theory of "manifest destiny." Moreover, the mixture of races characteristic of Hispanics, plus their levels of poverty, seemed to support U.S. notions of Latino racial inferiority (Moore and Pachon 1985; Hietala 1985). These perceptions were in turn reinforced by Spanish and Mexican upper-class ideas about race, which also supported social stratification and inequality.

31

These and related ideas helped create an ideology—if not a pronounced indifference—among Anglos that their actions toward or against Latino groups were actually beneficial to or "liberating" of Hispanic populations and lands under Hispanic control (Acuña 1988). The ideology of liberation was evident, for instance, in the support for the "just war" that led to the annexation of Texas and the Southwest (Moore and Pachon 1985). (Similarly, some observers have noted that the U.S. military intervention in Panama in 1989 was called Operation *Just Cause*.) This ideology and its supporting stereotypes were powerful enough to permit Anglo Americans "to stifle any guilt feelings about the rapid conquest of Mexican and other Hispanic territories" (Moore and Pachon 1985, 6). Thus, partly because Spain had been a colonial power, and probably more so because as well-developed ideology emerged over the years along with American expansionism, the United States had few doubts or second thoughts about its actions toward Hispanics.

The treatment of blacks and Native Americans may have been viewed as "original sins" and the sources of ideological inconsistency, or a moral dilemma, as Gunnar Myrdal (1944) called it, in U.S. society and politics. The historical treatment of these groups has been subsequently criticized, if not rectified. The status of Hispanics has been less a source of agonizing, perhaps because of its somewhat different nature; but it may also have been that because the supporting ideology was unchallenged, intellectual, theoretical, or emotional concern was deemed neither necessary nor appropriate.

Another commonality among Latinos is the similarity of their cultures, especially their attachment to the Spanish language. Cultural attachment, including language, may vary considerably, affected by such factors as length of time in the United States, generation, and regional concentration. But a common cultural attachment appears to be important (Caplan 1987). And it may be that such attachment is growing, as high levels of opposition to Official English measures among *all* Latino groups, including Cubans, would attest; attachment may be a defense of one's culture against perceived attacks. Cultural attachment does not mean political commitment to the "homeland" nation, however (de la Garza 1985).

There are also major differences between Latino groups. These historical differences are central to understanding the social and political standing of Latinos.

————MEXICAN AMERICANS

This section presents various ways of characterizing and summarizing the history of Mexican Americans, or Chicanos, in the United States in order to suggest the broad outlines of that history and to indicate how scholars have perceived and conceptualized it. There are significant similarities in the descriptions and characterizations, although different authors use different language in their accounts.

Villareal (1988) summarizes Chicano political history in terms of five major periods: the politics of resistance (1850–1925), accommodation (1915–1945), social change (1945–1965), protest (1965–1975), and moderation and recognition (1974-present). Garcia and de la Garza (1977, 19–33) specify four periods: the stage of forced acquiescence (1848–1920s), the politics of adaptation (1920s–1940s), the politicization period (post–World War II to mid 1960s); the Chicano Movement (mid 1960s–mid 1970s).

Barrera (1985; also see Chapter 4) discusses Chicano history in terms of several broad goals of Chicano groups during four different eras: (1) "communitarian" (mid nineteenth century until around 1920), in which the mid nineteenth century is described as a "period of decline" and the late nineteenth century to the 1920s as the "mutualista period"; (2) "egalitarian" (1920s through 1950s); (3) the revival of community and a (unique) linking of communitarian and egalitarian goals in the cultural nationalism of the Chicano Movement (mid 1960s to about 1973); and (4) "post–Chicano Movement," a time of "fragmentation, radicalization, re-traditionalization" (mid 1970s to present).

Some differences are implied in these scholars' views of the earliest period, the 1850s to early 1900s. They, and others, tend to stress Mexican American resistance to Anglo domination, and Anglo force to subdue that resistance (also see Acuña 1988). Mexican Americans resisted domination resulting from the U.S. "conquest," the acquisition or annexation after the war with Mexico of what now comprises much of the U.S. Southwest. Some scholars believe this war was precipitated by the United States because the country perceived a quick and easy victory with tremendous gains to be achieved in land and other resources (Acuña 1988; Estrada et al. 1988; Hietala 1985). Concluded by the Treaty of Guadalupe Hidalgo in 1848, the war is seen by these scholars as a conquest of the Mexican American population in the Southwest at the time.

The Treaty of Guadalupe Hidalgo guaranteed such basic rights as freedom of religion, the right to own property, and political liberty, but for many Mexican Americans, the U.S. federal and state governments failed to adhere to the guarantees. "The consistent lack of enforcement of this treaty set the stage for the disenfranchisement and significant political fragmentation of Americans of Mexican descent" (Villareal 1988, 2). Land grants are a major example of this treaty violation.

In the war's aftermath, certain policies had the effect of displacing and dispossessing Mexican Americans. First, Mexican Americans, who were generally small-scale subsistence farmers, lost land because they were "unprepared and generally unable to raise the capital to meet . . . newly imposed tax liabilities" resulting from different tax policies under U.S. and Spanish-Mexican practice (Estrada et al. 1988) Second, the Anglo judges sitting on courts established to resolve land claims "had very limited knowledge and understanding of Mexican and Spanish landowning laws, traditions, and customs. Their judgments, based on Anglo legal practices, greatly contributed to the dispossessions" (Estrada et al. 1988, 33).[1]

Domination and an underclass status were not always passively accepted. Alienation and withdrawal may have been the most common response, but other responses occurred at various times and places during this era (Garcia and de la Garza, 1977). One response has variously been referred to as limited insurrection, direct action, guerrilla warfare, and social banditry. For instance, one Chicano group, Las Gorras Blancas (White Caps), opposed the systematic loss of land by resorting "to direct action . . . by cutting down fences and burning the property" of Anglo ranchers who had "acquired" the land (Barrera 1985). Direct action seems to have had broad support among the Mexican American population. Still, many members of the numerically small Chicano–Hispano elite allied with the Anglo community, emphasized electoral politics, and built a political base; in this way they sought to hold on to some of their declining social and political status. The Chicano elite was "more interested in defending its own interests than in defining a broader 'community' interest with a traditionally subservient class," the nonelite Chicanos (Barrera 1985, 2–3).

The *mutualistas* (mutual aid societies), another response to Anglo domination, were probably most important from the late 1800s to the early 1930s. Their activities were spurred by the enormously increased Mexican migration that resulted from political upheaval in Mexico, including the Mexican Revolution of 1910. These societies offered life insurance coverage and a wide range of social activities, and "a few provided other services, such as employment agencies, adult education, health clinics, and libraries" (Barrera 1985).

Efforts at accommodation and adaptation to mainstream American society became common around 1915 to 1920. Systematic resistance was less evident as Mexican Americans made a greater effort to deal with U.S. society on its own terms. The emergence, goals, and styles of several Latino groups during this period demonstrate this tendency. One of the most visible and significant Latino groups (historically and at present) was the League of United Latin American Citizens (LULAC), formed in 1929 (see M. García 1989; Barrera 1985; Marquez 1988; also see the discussion in Chapter 4). The emergence of this group and its pursuit of formal equality—for example, equal access to and equal treatment from public institutions—through civic and political activities distinguished it from earlier groups. LULAC claimed to speak for the Latino population, although its ideology was grounded strongly in mainstream American ideas, including individualism and patriotism. The group "rejected political action that was based exclusively on race or ethnicity" (Barrera 1985).

Notably, LULAC and its immediate predecessor organizations were indicative of a "diverging identity" between the more established Mexican American middle-class residents and newly arrived Mexicanos. While many of the goals LULAC sought might benefit all Latin Americans, to a substantial degree the group accepted existing social and political processes and maintained some distance from the larger immigrant population. "It was tacitly assumed that poverty and unemployment would continue to exist, the only difference being that the distribution of these economic hardships would not be allocated according to race or ethnicity" (Marquez 1988, 23). That assumption must have been difficult to maintain in view of the repatriation of many "Mexicans," including the extensive and illegal deportation during the Great Depression of Mexican Americans who were U.S. citizens.

Other organizations during the 1930s and 1940s also exhibited ambivalence in their attitudes toward ethnic pride and identity, on the one hand, and full acceptance of and by U.S. society on the other. Symptomatic of this ambivalence was a reluctance to enter into, or define, group activities in an explicitly political fashion.

Scholars differ considerably on the extent of, and reasons for, the approaches and perspectives of Mexican American groups during this accommodation or adaptation period. Some writers contend that the groups were composed mostly of middle-class members concerned about maintaining the status in the eyes of U.S. society. Because they felt that the large influx of Mexican immigrants might undermine that status, they chose a moderate, "accommodationist" stance (Barrera 1985; Marquez 1988). Others argue that such moderation must be understood in terms of the levels of ethnic–racial hostility at the time. These organizations set out to accomplish what they thought was possible in the circumstances. According to this view, the middle-class organizations were stronger advocates for the Latino masses than a pejorative "accommodationist" interpretation recognizes (M. García 1989, 16–18; Muñoz 1989).

The 1940s and 1950s saw a period of change and increasing politicization among the Mexican American population. The post–World War II era witnessed the formation of several organizations that, along with a service orientation, were involved in activities that questioned discriminatory government policies. They also engaged in such political activities as voting and campaigning to a greater extent than had been common previously. Some examples are the G.I. Forum and the Community Service Organization (CSO), both formed in 1948.

The G.I. Forum initially focused on problems regarding government benefits to Latino war veterans and was involved in various social concerns, among them school segregation. Although formally nonpartisan, the Forum participated in political campaigns, especially for Democratic candidates, relatively early in its existence. The CSO, organized in Los Angeles and locally oriented, came into existence in response to social concerns and participated in local elections as part of those concerns.

The late 1950s are important in Chicano political history because it was at this time that the first groups openly to refer to themselves as political came into existence. The Mexican American Political Association (MAPA) was formed in California in 1959, and the Political Association of Spanish-Speaking Organizations (PASSO) was organized in Texas in 1960. Both organizations "concentrated on voter registration, political education, lobbying," and the like (Barrera 1985).

Throughout this period, the major focus of the most active elements of the Chicano population was on pursuing the American dream of equal opportunity and political participation in the civic arena. Much effort was spent on exposing the gap between the ideal and the reality of U.S. society and politics. Nevertheless, the ideal was accepted almost without question; only minor modifications in existing social and political processes were called for. Whether this was so because the groups felt that circumstances would not permit anything more, because of a true faith in the American system, including the "melting pot" notion, because of a belief that the social–political situation was not all that bad, or some combination of all these reasons remains open to debate.

During the early 1960s, a number of social and political activities could be seen as immediate precursors of the Chicano Movement. One was the "Viva Kennedy" effort in the 1960 presidential campaign. Others were more localized and specific, but nonetheless they had broad significance because of their focus and approach. One was a movement to reclaim the land in northern New Mexico that had been lost to the Chicano population following U.S. acquisition. This movement, or alliance, led by Reies Tijerina, sometimes relied on direct-action tactics. Another was the farmworkers' movement, especially the United Farm Workers (UFW), led by Cesar Chavez, which gained visibility in the early 1960s. Although the UFW was (and remains) primarily a labor organization, "its aura of a moral crusade, and the self-conscious use of Mexican symbolism" brought attention to the plight of Mexican Americans. Coincident with the emerging civil rights movement, the UFW used marches, strikes, and boycotts as ways of pursuing its goals (Muñoz 1989).

The Chicano Movement was, in some ways, the Chicano equivalent of the black civil rights movement of the period. According to one assessment, by the mid 1960s it had become

> clear to Mexican Americans that a conventional approach to social and political change produced little of benefit to them. On the other hand, it seemed that the civil rights movement and black militancy were achieving a great deal. To many aware and concerned Mexican Americans, therefore, it made sense to emulate the black example. Thus was born the Chicano Movement. (Garcia and de la Garza 1977, 31).

This movement encompassed several groups and a variety of ideas. The groups ranged from paramilitary organizations focused on the barrios to student groups actively involved on campuses and in campus communities to a political party, La Raza Unida, (United Race, or United People/Culture party). Despite the various concerns, there was a consensus among the groups that the social and political system had both ignored and discriminated against the Mexican American population, which had not been treated with proper respect. There was at the same time a perception in the movement that conventional approaches to social change, such as voting, were inadequate to address the breadth and depth of Latino problems. New ideas and new approaches were needed.

The Chicano Movement emphasized ethnic unity and pride, explicitly rejecting the myth of Anglo superiority. It also emphasized Aztec and North American Indian ancestry, downplaying Spanish and western European ancestry. It sought to focus attention on the distinct experience of these groups in the New World, including the period since the conquest by the United States. The movement called for self-determination and community control. Latinos felt that control of political, social, and economic institutions in the community was necessary if they were to receive equitable and respectful treatment. Some elements of the Chicano Movement went even further, challenging the capitalist economic system.

Despite a consensus on broad concerns, the Chicano Movement declined in the early 1970s. Authors put forth several reasons for that decline. First was the general decline in the civil–minority rights movement. Government harassment of the movement was also cited. Another reason involved ideological divisions along with ideological uncertainty and ambiguity within the movement. Although there was agreement regarding the inferior status of Chicanos in U.S. society, Chicano Movement members disagreed about what should be done about it and how they should best address these conditions. Yet the Chicano Movement had a lasting impact. From it emerged a group of activists that, while moderate in its ideas and approaches, maintained an interest in political and policy concerns that was different and more assertive than that of previous generations of Latinos (Muñoz 1989).

With the decline of *Chicanismo* and related organizations, many movement members became involved in, or returned to, liberal reformist politics. Liberal reformism, which has predominated since the mid 1970s, has stressed moderate political activities, such as voter registration, voter turnout, legal challenges to electoral obstacles, and the support of particular policies through lobbying. To a considerable degree, some of the older organizations, such as LULAC, have become more active and assertive than they once were, although some claim LULAC has recently become somewhat more conservative than it was in the early 1980s (Muñoz 1989). The reemergence of older groups has been referred to as "re-traditionalization" (Barrera 1985). Also, social service-oriented groups have become common at the local level. Examples are the Citizens Organized for Public Services (COPS) in San Antonio and United Neighborhood Organizations (UNO) in Los Angeles. There has also been first a rise and then a decline of small radical groups espousing Marxist–Leninist ideas. The major impact of these groups, according to Barrera (1985), has been in influencing Latinos to rethink their social, economic, and political status in the United States.

_____PUERTO RICANS

The island of Puerto Rico became U.S. territory in 1898, following the Spanish-American War. It was a U.S. colony from 1898 until 1952, when it became a commonwealth. Immediately following the U.S. acquisition, Puerto Ricans were in a political "limbo; neither citizens of the United States nor citizens of an independent nation" (Moore and Pachon 1985, 31). With the passage of the Jones Act in 1917, Puerto Ricans became U.S. citizens. According to one scholar, the Jones Act "imposed U.S. citizenship on the people of Puerto Rico over the objections of the island's legislature" (Falcón 1984, 21). Today, residents of Puerto Rico are U.S. citizens "subject to military draft, but they do not pay U.S. income taxes and do not fully participate in federal government social service programs" (Moore and Pachon 1985, 31). As U.S. citizens, Puerto Ricans are also free to travel to, and move within, the United States.

There were steady, if moderate, levels of Puerto Rican emigration to the U.S. mainland in the 1920s and 1930s, but after World War II it grew substantially. Scholars often have attributed Puerto Rican migration to the economic policies of the United States and the island's government, which have encouraged industrialization and capitalist investment. These policies have affected the Puerto Rican subsistence economy and have had the effect of making Puerto Ricans a source of cheap labor. In the words of one writer:

> Puerto Ricans leaving their country were encouraged by the particular economic relationship between the mainland and the colony. . . . Part of the government's strategy in Puerto Rico was to establish a "safety valve" for the economic costs of industrializing Puerto Rico. The Puerto Rican migration can be perceived as "involuntary" in that it was organized between the governments of the United States and Puerto Rico. For no other migrant group, except perhaps for the Mexicans under the Bracero program, has the

United States government systematically and over a period of decades arranged entry into this nation. (Jennings 1988, 66–67)

Writers have disagreed about the level of Puerto Rican political participation in the United States, particularly in New York City, where
the population is most concentrated, during the first several decades of
the twentieth century. By the 1930s, however, the Puerto Rican population in some parts of the city had become too large for politicians to
ignore. The first Puerto Rican official from New York City was elected
to the New York State Assembly in 1937. Yet, throughout the 1940s
and 1950s, there was a "virtual absence of Puerto Ricans from New
York City politics" (Falcón, 1984). Several theories have been offered
for the ostensibly low levels of political activity.

One explanation is that machine politics and the patronage it offered earlier ethnic minorities in return for electoral support had declined by the time of major Puerto Rican population growth in New
York City. Also, the Democratic party had become increasingly conservative, and there was a perception that Puerto Ricans were nonwhite
and hence a threat to the city's white population. Puerto Ricans were
also considered to be a "troublesome" group because they had strongly
supported leftist congressional candidates in New York City, and Puerto Rican nationalists had attacked President Harry S. Truman and
congressmen in the U.S. House of Representatives. Finally, the Puerto
Rican government sought to assure that Puerto Ricans in New York
City would remain in the city and not return, that New York might act
as a "safety valve." Toward that end, the Puerto Rican government set
up a Migration Division in the city "that took on the functions that
ethnic politicians had served for earlier immigrant groups. As a consequence, the presence of the Division slowed the growth of a Puerto
Rican leadership cadre in New York City" (Baver 1984, 44–45). Related to these reasons is another, broader one: Because Puerto Ricans
often do *not* see themselves as permanent residents on the U.S. mainland—that is, they feel that they will someday return to the island—
they do not develop deep political attachments on the mainland.

Puerto Rican political activism increased in the 1960s, in part as a
result of the funding directed to minority communities through the
War on Poverty programs that were part of President Lyndon Johnson's Great Society. Poverty agencies provided social and political resources to the community that the local Democratic organization had
been reluctant to offer. But "poverty-crats could never play the same

political role of developing ethnic power" as had been true for groups in the early 1900s (Jennings 1988, 71). The bureaucratic rules, regulations, and procedures that constrained these programs meant that they could not address the concerns of particular ethnic–racial groups.

Militancy also arose in the Puerto Rican community in the 1960s. Probably the clearest manifestation of it was a group known as the Young Lords. Characterizing themselves as "socialists and revolutionary nationalists," they used a strategy that was a mixture of confrontation and community service. Another characteristic of New York's Puerto Rican militants was "their linking of the Puerto Rican struggle for social justice in New York with the struggle for independence of the island. In the political analysis of many militants, Puerto Ricans on the island live in a U.S. colony, while Puerto Ricans in mainland ghettos live under conditions of internal colonialism. Both situations are seen as resulting from the needs of American capitalism" (Baver 1984, 47). (A similar, but occasionally even broader, "internationalist" perspective has been voiced by radical segments of the Chicano community.)

Along with the antipoverty and militant groups, the major political activity of the 1960s occurred in the electoral arena. Several Puerto Rican politicians emerged from the reform wing of the city's Democratic party. Perhaps most important was Herman Badillo, "a moderate . . . working in relatively mainstream context" who later became a U.S. congressman (Baver 1984).

From the mid 1970s to the present, Puerto Rican politics has emphasized expanded participation and a practical orientation. A significant development has been that the local Democratic party has been more receptive to Puerto Ricans, to the extent that most Puerto Rican politicians now have some link with the party. In another development, efforts have been made to assure the fair drawing of council districts in the city so that Puerto Ricans can gain a more meaningful political voice.

CUBANS

Cuban tobacco workers migrated to the United States in the late 1800s, settling mostly in Key West and, later, Tampa, Florida. The immigrants to Tampa "eventually formed the backbone of the Cuban movement for independence against Spain" and in the early 1900s "organized the most radical wing of the American Federation of Labor" (Torres 1988, 82). This Cuban–Hispanic population has been referred to in some historical accounts as a "colony" within the larger community (Mormino and Pozzetta 1987).

Like Puerto Rico, Cuba was acquired by the United States as a consequence of the Spanish-American War in 1898. Unlike Puerto Rico, "Cuba was ruled by an American army of occupation for only three years. The Republic of Cuba appeared, in 1902, [as] a close, independent, but dominated neighbor of the United States" (Moore and Pachon 1985, 36). The Cuban constitution included provisions, in the Platte Amendment, that "allowed the U.S. to intervene in the island's internal affairs" (Vigil 1987, 24).

The first half of the twentieth century saw both political dictatorships and instability in Cuba. The largest and most visible influx of Cubans to the United States came following the overthrow of Fulgencio Batista by Fidel Castro's forces in 1959. Castro established a communist state that nationalized business, expropriated foreign properties, and took over the economy (Vigil 1987, 24). The initial postrevolutionary immigrants from Cuba were those most adversely affected by the programs of the revolution. They tended to be politically conservative—some would say reactionary (Torres 1988); they also were generally well educated and affluent, and most did not intend to stay in the United States.

As the prospects for returning to Cuba diminished after the unsuccessful Bay of Pigs invasion in 1961, the idea of permanent residence in the United States presented itself, and Cuban naturalization rates increased. In the mid 1960s, large numbers of Cubans were airlifted to the United States. The entry and settlement of this wave of Cubans was greatly facilitated by the U.S. government, which set up special resettlement programs that included food, clothing, medical care, and cash benefits. This facilitation largely grew out of the U.S. government's desire to discredit Cuba's communist revolution (Torres 1988, 82–83). The most recent large Cuban immigration to the United States, the *Marielitos*, took place in 1980. This migration, numbering about one hundred twenty thousand, was made up of people of lower socioeconomic status, the darker skinned, and of some criminal elements.

The politics of Cuban immigrants in the 1960s was strongly influenced by their exile status and their desire to overthrow the Castro regime and return to Cuba. This intense "foreign policy" focus caused an initial inattentiveness to U.S. domestic politics. During the 1970s, however, some "pluralization" took place in the Cuban community, with political attention broadening to focus on such issues as better and more social services for needy sectors of the population. Also, actions to establish a dialogue with the Castro regime took place, particularly during the Carter administration. New and expanded political activities in the Cuban community emerged around such issues as bilingual education. They are most evident in elections for state and local offices.

The 1980s saw an expansion of Cuban American political participation in lobbying and partisan electoral activities. There was also a reassertion of Cuban American conservatism, spurred on by the Reagan administration. For instance, the Cuban-American National Foundation, formed in 1980, lobbied for several projects and programs closely linked to Reagan administration goals. These included the creation of Radio José Marti, the administration's radio station beamed at Cuba, and aid to the Nicaraguan *contras* (Torres 1988, 90–92). Since 1980, a cohesive Hispanic voting bloc has played a major role in electing Republican candidates in Dade County (the Miami area) to the Florida state legislature.

Given the form that Cuban immigration to the United States generally has taken, many scholars have been inclined to use pluralist–immigrant interpretations of the Cuban situation, rather than perspectives that seem appropriate to the Mexican and Puerto Rican situations. According to some writers, however, "tension has been a constant element in nearly two centuries" of relations between Cuba and the United States, much of it resulting from the proximity of Cuba to the United States. Proximity has also shaped expectations, "and in the United States the expectation took hold early that destiny had manifestly meant for Cuba to be part of the [United States]. It was simply inadmissible if not inconceivable that Cuba, so near, so strategically situated, could somehow remain outside the sphere of U.S. control (Perez 1990, 364–365). What some observers have suggested, then, is that historical factors shaped by geographic proximity have made the Cuban social and political situation in the United States unique and more complicated than it initially appears to be.

OTHER HISPANICS

A sizable population exists of Hispanics who do not come from one of the three population groups discussed. A few are from Spain, but most are of Central or South American origin—Salvadorans, Nicaraguans, and so on. It is difficult to ascertain their political leanings, but one would anticipate that the more the individual or group experience parallels that of another group—for example, Nicaraguans as similar to Cubans—the more political similarities there may be.

_____The history of major Latino groups suggests that important events, what might be called formative events, occurred in each instance. The Mexican American historical experience is the longest and most complex. The Mexican American presence in the United States is attributable to conquest as well as to what some would call simple immigration. There was also "arranged" immigration through the Bracero program. Some scholars also contend that Mexico's proximity to the United States, as well as the treatment of Mexican immigrants as merely a source of cheap labor, were other significant factors. Both conquest and immigration occurred somewhat differently in different regions of the Southwest. Some claim that economic reasons were primary in immigration. Yet the formative event, conquest, and subsequent and contemporary circumstances growing out of U.S.–Mexican economic and political relations make it difficult to define post-1900 Mexican immigration as "simply" economic (Pedraza-Bailey 1985).

For Puerto Ricans, the fact that they are U.S. citizens and are free to return to their "homeland," which in many respects is viewed as an independent nation by Puerto Ricans, is important. At the same time, economic need was the main reason for their northward migration, a movement encouraged or arranged by the U.S. and Puerto Rican governments, and this is important in understanding both their history and their present status. The initial contact with the United States as a colony also should be noted.

The Cuban situation is one in which voluntary immigration certainly occurred. Yet it is possible that the island's brief colonial status and its functional closeness, what some have called domination, by the United States after Cuba's formal independence in the early 1900s can at least partly be interpreted as a relationship that was not fully voluntary.

_____ASSIMILATION, SOCIOECONOMIC STATUS, AND RELATED ISSUES

A number of variables that can help explain the extent and speed of a social group's assimilation have been identified by sociologists. Assimilation is a complex phenomena; Yinger (1985) has emphasized that assimilation refers to a *process* and that the process is *multidimensional*. An ethnic group that has assimilated is a "group of persons with similar foreign [or ethnic] origins, knowledge of which in no way gives a better prediction or estimation of their relevant social characteristics than does knowledge of the behavior of the total population of the community or nation involved" (Yinger 1985, 30–31). In other words, a group may be definable as a group, but as it becomes more assimilated it becomes less noticeably different—socially, politically, economically—from the rest of society. Regarding one subprocess of assimilation, integration, *political* integration means "similar rates of registration and voting and similar ratios and levels of officeholding" (addressed in Chapter 4). In economic matters, "full integration would mean that occupational and income distributions of an ethnic group matched those of the whole society." This would also seem to apply to levels of employment (or unemployment), levels of education, and so on (Yinger 1985, 32).

Many, perhaps most, Latino groups seek some degree of assimilation or integration. There may well be differing attitudes as to the desirability of other subprocesses of assimilation, however. It is not clear that complete amalgamation or identification, for instance, is desired by most Latino individuals and groups. In fact, some Latinos have been critical of these degrees of assimilation.

_____VARIABLES ASSOCIATED WITH ASSIMILATION

Table 3 lists the variables associated with assimilation, along with their predicted impact and an assessment of the several Latino groups in these terms. In looking at the table, two points should be noted: (1) Yinger (1985) provided the assessment of the Mexican American situation for most of the variables; (2) assessments of the Puerto Rican and Cuban situation on the variables are mine, based on evidence from the historical discussion and from other scholars.

The degree of assimilation would be expected to have a substantial bearing on a group's political status and influence (see Chapter 2). In general, the variables, and the hypotheses associated with them, seem consistent with actual conditions.

GROUP SIZE. Mexican Americans are a large and growing group, which works against assimilation or could be said to have "dissimilative" influence. Puerto Ricans are a somewhat smaller portion of

TABLE 3
Variables That Affect the Speed and Extent of Assimilation and Their Application to Latino Groups

Variables	Mexican Americans	Puerto Ricans	Cubans
1. Size of group relative to total population (small = +, large = −)	−	−	+
2. Regional concentration (no = +, mixed = m, yes = −)	m	m	−
3. Residential segregation (low = +, moderate = m, high = −)	m	−	+
4. Long-time residency, i.e., low proportion of newcomers (high = −, medium = m, low = +)	m	m	m
5. Return to homeland difficult (yes = +, no = −)	−	−	+
6. Speaks majority language (moderately well = m)	m	−	m
7. Adheres to a majority religion (yes = +, no = −)	+	+	+
8. Belongs to majority race (yes = +, mixed = m, yes = −)	m	−	+
9. Voluntary U.S. entry (yes = +, mixed = m, no = −)	+	m	+
10. Homeland culturally similar (yes = +, mixed = m, no = −)	m	m	+
11. Interest in homeland politics (yes = −, no = +)	+	−	−
12. Diverse in class and occupation (yes = +, mixed = m, no = −)	+	m	+
13. High average level of education (yes = +, moderate = m, no = −)	m	−	+
14. Little discrimination experienced (yes = −, mixed = m, no = +)	m	−	+
15. Resides in open-class society (yes = +, mixed = m, no = −)	+	m	+

Source: Variables and assessment of Mexican Americans drawn from Yinger 1985.

the overall population and the Hispanic population, but they are experiencing above-average population growth rates. Cuban Americans are the smallest of the three major Latino groups and have the lowest growth rate. Overall, the Latino population is increasing, having grown from about 6.5 to almost 8 percent of the total U.S. population between 1980 and 1990.

REGIONAL CONCENTRATION. Each of the major Latino groups is concentrated regionally. About 85 percent of Mexican Americans reside in the five southwestern states of California, Texas, New Mexico, Arizona, and Colorado. California and Texas alone accounted for almost 75 percent of all Mexican Americans in 1980. Puerto Ricans are concentrated in the Northeast, with about 49 percent in New York and 12 percent in New Jersey. Almost 60 percent of all Cuban Americans live in Florida, with another 10 percent residing in New York and New Jersey. Not only are the groups regionally concentrated but they also tend to concentrate *within* regions and states.

Mexican Americans, although still regionally concentrated, increasingly are dispersing; the same is true of Puerto Ricans. In fact, Latinos in general are now increasingly dispersed.

RESIDENTIAL SEGREGATION. Mexican Americans, although somewhat residentially segregated in urban areas, are less so than blacks. Some recent evidence indicates, however, that Mexican American residential segregation may be increasing (Bullock and MacManus 1990). Puerto Ricans are more residentially segregated than Mexican Americans, with Cubans the least residentially segregated of the three major groups. Thus Cuban Americans would appear to be the most assimilated by this indicator.

LONG-TIME RESIDENCY. Mexican Americans' "immigration is extensive, but the proportions of second- and third-generation group members are increasing." Yinger (1985) suggests that as this pattern increases, assimilation too will increase. Mexican Americans are also long-time residents, even if the initial residence was not voluntary. Puerto Ricans' and Cuban Americans' residence has been shorter, which presumably is not conducive to present assimilation; but the proportion of newcomers is not especially high, which is conducive to assimilation. Overall, the impact of this measure for Latinos is mixed.

RETURN TO THE HOMELAND.   For many Mexican Americans, return to Mexico is "easy and frequent"; this is also true for Puerto Ricans. Given the diplomatic relations or nonrelations, between the United States and Cuba since the 1960s, return visits to that nation have been difficult. These patterns of homeland visits indicate dissimilative impacts for Mexican Americans and Puerto Ricans, and an assimilative one for Cuban Americans.

LANGUAGE.   The variable of language has a mixed or neutral influence for Mexican Americans because "the use of the Spanish language continues, but English is the main language by the third generation" (Yinger 1985). A general pattern of adoption of the English language seems similar for Cuban Americans and Puerto Ricans, if somewhat stronger for the Cubans (but cf. Meier and Stewart 1991, 40).

RELIGION.   Most Mexican Americans are Roman Catholic, and church segregation is on the decrease. This has a mainly assimilative impact on Mexican Americans. Patterns for the other two groups seem similar. Although there has been no elaboration on this theme, some political scientists have suggested that Latinos' Catholicism is a significant factor that makes them different from blacks (Browning, Marshall, and Tabb 1990).

RACE.   Many Mexican Americans "belong to a minority race, but the racial line is increasingly blurred and of decreasing importance" (Yinger 1985). This factor is the reason for citing a mixed influence of the race variable for Chicanos. Puerto Ricans are the most likely and Cubans the least likely to be dark-skinned. Thus Puerto Ricans are disadvantaged, while Cubans benefit with respect to this assimilation variable (Horowitz 1985).

VOLUNTARY ENTRY.   As we saw in Chapter 2, this variable is central to any analysis of Latino politics. Yinger (1985) indicates an overall assimilative impact regarding this variable, saying that "most [Mexican Americans] entered voluntarily; but early entrants were forced by annexation." Some observers perceive that involuntary and voluntary aspects of Mexican American inclusion in the United States are of probably equal significance (Horowitz 1985, 68–69). Yet others, particularly those who take an internal colonial interpretation of Chicano politics, contend that the involuntary aspect outweighs the voluntary. Some go further, contending that the voluntary aspect is not as "voluntary" as it might appear, that the voluntary nature is more apparent than real. The formative experience of Mexican Americans has had a more dissimilative impact than Yinger's assessment recognizes, as implied earlier in this chapter (see also Chapters 1 and 2).

The Puerto Rican situation is also complex. Puerto Rico became a U.S. colony or territory following the Spanish-American War. Puerto Ricans gained U.S. citizenship (some would say it was imposed on them) about twenty years after the island's acquisition. Extensive migration eventually occurred. Some view this migration as essentially voluntary; others claim that it "can be perceived as 'involuntary'" (Jennings 1988, 66). Overall, then, the rating of Puerto Ricans on this variable is, at best, mixed or neutral; more likely, it is dissimilative.

The Cuban entry was the most voluntary of the three major groups. But, as noted earlier, this may be more involved than the Yinger framework recognizes. Perhaps further distinctions regarding this dimension need to be made.

CULTURE. This variable is seen as having a mixed or neutral influence concerning Mexican Americans because Mexico is becoming increasingly similar to U.S. society. While this assessment may be accurate for recent Mexican immigrants to the United States, it is less clear how valid the assessment is for those who arrived at earlier periods, and whether the two cultures are as monolithic as implied by the criterion. For instance, with respect to Cubans, both the middle-class immigrants of the mid 1960s and the 1980 *Marielitos* were from the same society. But their ability to fit into the United States has been quite different because of their prior socioeconomic status in Cuba. This variable may be linked to another variable, class and occupation.

The social cultures of Puerto Rico and Cuba are similar to that of the United States in some respects. Both societies have been heavily influenced historically by American corporate, economic, and social interests.

CLASS AND OCCUPATION. This variable of diversity in class and occupation is a plus in the process of Mexican American assimilation because the group is becoming increasingly diverse (although data presented later suggest that this may be an overly positive assessment). It does, however, seem an accurate evaluation for Cubans; the situation for Puerto Ricans is mixed (see Table 3).

INTEREST IN POLITICS AND ECONOMICS OF HOMELAND. According to several observers (Yinger 1985; cf. de la Garza and Weaver 1985), there is no strong pull or interest toward political and economic developments in Mexico among Mexican Americans; this is said to have an assimilative impact. In contrast, Cubans and Puerto Ricans are quite interested in "homeland" political and economic issues and concerns.

LEVEL OF EDUCATION. While considerable data suggest that Mexican American educational levels are well below those of others, Yinger (1985) and several other scholars (e.g., Horowitz 1985) stress the importance of accounting for change and rates of change, generation, and similar factors in assessing educational levels. When such factors are accounted for, the evidence is more positive, Yinger and others claim. Thus, level of education is rated as having a mixed influence; the "educational gap is significantly reduced by the third generation." Cuban education levels are close to that of the total population; Puerto Rican levels, perhaps surprisingly, are higher than those of Mexican Americans. Thus, extending from Yinger's assessment, one would rate Cubans as assimilative and Puerto Ricans as close to that. Recent research on Latinos and education policy is discussed in Chapter 9.

DISCRIMINATION. The assessment for Mexican Americans on this dimension is mixed; "discrimination persists but is declining" (Yinger 1985). For Cubans, the situation seems to be more positive; for Puerto Ricans, it is probably more negative.

CLASS. Many Mexican Americans "experience fairly extensive mobility in the United States" (Yinger 1985); this suggests an assimilative impact. One would assume a similar or lower assessment for Puerto Ricans and, for Cubans, one at least equal to, and probably greater than, that for Mexican Americans.

OTHER FACTORS. To the variables considered by Yinger one can add others that have been discussed or implied in previous

considerations of minority-group social status and politics. One significant factor seems to be the age makeup of the group. Younger groups
seem to be disadvantaged, while those that have an older profile seem
to benefit. This probably reflects individual maturity, adaptability, likelihood of socially deviant behavior, social threat, and the like. On the
age variable, Cubans are advantaged (assimilative), while Mexican
Americans and Puerto Ricans are disadvantaged because of their overall youthfulness (Meier and Stewart 1991, 40).

Other factors are related to economic conditions and structures.
Northern and western Europeans who immigrated around the turn of
the century benefited from an emerging American industrialization
and the opportunities that industrialization presented; they were also
aided by the labor movement. Chicanos, in contrast, were for many
years concentrated in some of the least dynamic economic sectors and
regions of the United States, agriculture in the Southwest. And these
regions were among the least likely to have strong labor movements.
Also, as relative latecomers to New York City, Puerto Ricans were not
well positioned to benefit from the city's earlier economic opportunities and dynamism. Cubans, because of their socioeconomic background and population concentration in Miami, have created an economic and social ethnic enclave.

Other variables revolve around political ideas and government
structures. Political ideas seem important in terms of how a group's
immigration is defined. For instance, Cuban immigration was supported ideologically and materially by the U.S. government because it
helped discredit a competing world ideology, communism. Given different times and different circumstances, the ideology concerning Mexican Americans and Puerto Ricans was a negative one.

Finally, regional and local politics and governments proved to be an
important variable. The Southwest had state and local political structures and processes, "reformed" structures, that generally did not lead
to Mexican Americans being seen as necessary or desirable political
allies. There were some exceptions to this, particularly in south Texas,
where political machines were active and seem to have led to greater
levels of political activity among Chicanos in the long term. South
Florida also had (and has) predominantly "reformed" structures, yet
various conditions made it possible for Cubans to have substantial political impact. Despite New York's unreformed political structure, Puerto Ricans have achieved only moderate levels of political integration.
These factors are considered further in later chapters.

_____INCOME AND STATUS

The data in Table 4 speak directly to the socioeconomic status of the Latino groups—more specifically, to their income, education, and occupation. Two important qualifications should be noted about this table. First, the data do *not* control for nativity or generation. Research indicates that having been born in America and having lived in the United States for longer periods of time are associated with greater socioeconomic equality. Second, most of the data are presented in terms of family, not per capita, measures. This is important because Latinos, particularly Mexican Americans and Puerto Ricans, have larger families than do non-Latinos. In this respect, the data probably understate the level of income of individual Latinos relative to individual members of other ethnic–racial groups; that is, Latino socioeconomic status is probably lower than the data suggest. Indeed, when per capita, rather than family, is the unit of analysis, Latino socioeconomic status on several indicators is lower than that of blacks (Hispanic Policy Development Project 1990).

The items in the table are the numbers for Latinos–Hispanics divided by the numbers for non-Hispanics; the closer to 1.00, the more the Latino situation approaches that of non-Latinos.

Latino median family income in the late 1980s was about two-thirds (.66) that of the non-Hispanic population; notably, the 1989 and 1987 data indicate a decline from 1982. There are major differences between groups. Cubans, who are closest to the non-Hispanics pattern, fluctuated somewhat during the 1980s. Mexican American median family income relative to non-Hispanics dropped from .75 in 1982 to .63 in 1989. Puerto Ricans have median family incomes that are only about half that of non-Hispanics.

Hispanics have poverty rates dramatically higher than the non-Hispanic population (Moore and Pachon 1985, 79). The Puerto Rican poverty rate is about four times as high as that for non-Hispanics. Even for the relatively affluent Cuban population, poverty rates exceed those of non-Hispanics by a considerable amount (Meier and Stewart 1991, 40).

Latino males were, in 1989, less than half as likely (.44) than other males to hold managerial and professional jobs. Mexican Americans are only a third as likely to have such occupations. And the parity score for the Latino subgroup that does best on this measure, Cubans, lags somewhat behind that of non-Hispanics.

In 1987, the level of education, calculated from the median number of school years completed, for Hispanics overall was about 94 percent

TABLE 4
The Socioeconomic Status of Latinos (Hispanics) Relative to Non-Hispanics (Parity Ratios)

	All Hispanics	Mexican Americans	Puerto Ricans	Cubans	Other
Median family income ($)					
1989	.66	.63	.57	.81	.72
1987	.66	.64	.48	.89	.77
1982	.72	.75	.51	.80	.79
Families below poverty level (%)					
1989	.40	.38	.31	.56	.51
1987	.40	.40	.26	.74	.52
1982	.45	.47	.25	.77	.61
Managerial and professional occupations, males					
1989	.44	.32	.38	.90	.65
1987	.41	.33	.48	.72	.53
Education					
[1989]	.65	.54	69	.80	.82
1987	.94	.85	.95	.98	.97
1982	.86	.77	.84	.93	.98

Note: The brackets around the 1989 data entry for Education indicate the data are different from the 1987 and 1982 data. The 1989 education data are based on those twenty-five years or older who have four or more years of high school education; the 1987 and 1982 data are based on the median number of school years completed.

Sources: U.S. Bureau of the Census, "The Hispanic Population in the United States: March 1989; Current Population Reports"; and "The Hispanic Population in the United States: March 1986 and 1987 (Advanced Report)," August 1987. The entries are, essentially, parity ratios; the closer to 1.00, the more similar or equal Hispanics are to non-Hispanics, the farther from 1.00, the more "disadvantaged" Hispanics are.

of non-Hispanics. The ratio was somewhat lower for the Mexican-origin population. And evidence suggests that these levels increased rapidly in the short time from 1982 to 1987. This improvement is notable, but it must be remembered that there is a ceiling on the level of formal education; sixteen to twenty years of schooling is about the limit for most people. Thus the improvement for Latinos is affected by the fact that the top end of the education scale is constrained. Such constraints are less a factor with respect to other indicators of socioeconomic well-being, such as income.

Overall, the socioeconomic data indicate a clearly lower status of Latinos relative to the non-Hispanic population. This is much less so in regard to education than to the other indicators. What is interesting, however, is that the increases in educational levels seem not to be strongly related to increases in relative levels of income or decreases in poverty. There are, also, substantial differences between the Latino groups. Cubans and "other Hispanics" generally rank highest on the measures, although there are exceptions to that overall pattern.

Additional data underscore the relatively low socioeconomic position of Latinos in American society. Data from 1988 on wealth—including not only yearly income but money in bank accounts, home-ownership, automobiles, stocks and bonds, and so forth—indicate that the wealth of Hispanic households is only about one-eighth that of white households, $5,520 versus $43,280 (*Denver Post,* January 11, 1991). The wealth gap between the households is much wider than the income gap. Nevertheless, Latino household wealth is slightly above that of blacks. Moreover, data from fourteen metropolitan statistical areas (including Los Angeles, Miami, New York, and San Antonio) indicate that Latino socioeconomic status on a number of measures declined between 1979 and 1989; and when per capita, rather than family, measures are used, Latinos are often more disadvantaged than African Americans.

_____SUMMARY AND CONCLUSION

The historical background presented in this chapter noted similarities among several Latino groups. Here, as in Chapter 1, it appears that there are unique historical and structural features common to the major Latino groups. Among the most important factors is the geographical proximity of the Latino "homeland" to the United States. At the same time, there are important differences between the groups and *within* groups. Both historical similarities and differences seem central to explaining the Latino situation in the United States and that of particular groups, as the extensive consideration of the variables and factors associated with group assimilation indicates. Furthermore, and consistent with the unique, and disadvantageous, historical situation, the socioeconomic status of Latinos is substantially below that of non-Latinos. Again, however, there are differences between Latino groups. This background is important to keep in mind as the extent and impact of Latino political participation and behavior in the U.S. political system are considered.

4

Political Participation

—————Dominant interpretations of U.S. politics hold that if citizens exercise the right to vote and participate in politics in other ways, the system can be responsive to their concerns and preferences. This chapter examines various dimensions of Latino political participation, addressing both mass and group politics. Among the issues to be considered are Latino political behavior, group identity, political ideology, attitudes regarding and actual levels of political participation, and several specific policies. This chapter also discusses Latino interest groups and activities plus Latino attachment to political parties. As with a number of issues concerning Latino politics, these areas have not been extensively studied. And the relatively few existing studies have produced inconsistent findings.[1] Once again, the evidence seems to indicate that Latino politics is unique. In turn, this implies the inadequacy of conventional pluralist interpretations of Latino politics and the need for alternative theoretical frameworks.

That Latinos are at least somewhat different politically has been assumed and has subsequently been borne out in research (Nelson 1979; Browning, Marshall, and Tabb 1990, 220; Jackson 1988; Meier and Stewart 1991). The data substantiate the view that there is such a thing as Latino politics, but understanding the various aspects of that politics, including Latino participation, has proven elusive.

_____PERCEPTIONS OF DISCRIMINATION

One factor would appear to be related to group identity and cohesion, if only in the negative sense of a group's feeling a need to protect itself, and that is the perception of being discriminated against. Nevertheless, a sense of discrimination is less strong among Latinos than might be expected, given "objective" evidence pointing to their low social and economic status (see Chapter 3). An early study published in 1976 found that 49 percent of Mexican Americans, versus 76 percent of blacks, thought they were treated unfairly compared to Anglos in regard to housing; on the question of jobs, 51 percent of Mexican Americans felt they were treated unfairly relative to Anglos (compared to 80 percent among blacks). When it came to schooling, only 35 percent of Mexican Americans, versus 74 percent of blacks, complained of unfair treatment. Yet this study also found that Mexican Americans ranked consistently, and in most cases substantially, lower than blacks (and, of course, Anglos) in Denver at this time in terms of family income, education, and occupational standing (Lovrich and Marenin 1976).

This lesser perception of discrimination at the time is difficult to explain. It is possible that Mexican Americans had lower socioeconomic status yet were not overtly treated unfairly or discriminated against in housing, schools, and jobs. Or the discrimination might have been so subtle that Mexican Americans did not perceive it as much as blacks did. Perhaps Mexican Americans were not yet an "awakened" minority (Lovrich and Marenin 1976). Perhaps the questions asked did not, or could not, tap less visible, or "institutional," discrimination. Later research (Meier and Stewart 1991; James et al. 1984) provides substantial evidence of low socioeconomic status (again, see Chapter 3) and institutional discrimination in the field of education against Hispanics (see Chapter 9).

A 1989 Colorado survey suggested that "racial prejudice and discrimination" was a substantial, but not overwhelming, concern of the "Spanish-surnamed" (LARASA 1989). When people were asked if they were "very concerned" (scored as 3), "concerned" (scored as 2), or "not concerned" (scored as 1) about "discrimination and prejudice," the average response was 2.46, which would suggest that they were concerned to very concerned. Taken as percentages, 55 percent said "very concerned," 36.3 percent said "concerned," and 8 percent said "not concerned." These and other data indicate that Latinos are increasingly aware of discrimination toward them.

————**GROUP IDENTITY**

As suggested in Chapter 1, a major issue in examining Latino politics is group self-identification. A number of studies have examined individual self-reference—the ethnic–racial names or labels people use to identify themselves—which is thought to be important for several reasons. First, self-identification has implications for group cohesion; persons who do not identify as a group are less likely to act as one. Second, self-identification is important because of what it means for group assimilation or acculturation in relation to the larger society. The extent and kind of self-identification situates a group relative to other groups in society. Finally, how one identifies oneself is thought to be relevant regarding political participation and ideology.

Early research found a rather high degree of division among Mexican Americans in terms of self-identification. A Denver study in the mid 1970s found that 21 percent of the Mexican Americans interviewed preferred the term Mexican, while 10 to 15 percent preferred one of several other terms, such as Mexican American, Spanish American, Spanish, Hispano, or Chicano (Lovrich and Marenin 1976). Blacks, in comparison, were in much greater agreement regarding self-identification, with 52 percent preferring to be called black and 29 percent choosing Negro. This has been interpreted as suggesting less social and, by implication, less political cohesion among Mexican Americans than among blacks. This lack of cohesion is especially notable because Mexican Americans in Denver at the time were worse off than blacks in terms of several "objective" measures of socioeconomic status.

A survey of 5,404 Latinos in five southwestern states (Arizona, California, Colorado, New Mexico, and Texas) also found considerable diversity in terms of ethnic self-identification (Garcia 1981). Mexican American was the most preferred term (50.7 percent), but the sociodemographic characteristics of those who chose this label were highly diverse, the most diverse of all the self-defined groups. Mexican and Other Spanish were each preferred by about 20 percent, and Mexicano and Chicano were each selected by fewer than 5 percent. A study in Houston, Texas, found that 81 percent of Spanish-surnamed registered voters preferred Mexican American, American, or Mexican (MacManus and Cassel 1988). Only 3.5 percent chose the Chicano label. Again, there is evidence of considerable diversity in terms of ethnic self-identification among the Hispanic population.

In the Colorado survey of the Spanish surnamed, Spanish American was the most preferred term (26.6 percent), with Mexican American second (24.8 percent), Hispanic third (22 percent), and Mexican fourth (10.7 percent). Chicano was the preference of 5.8 percent, while Latino was preferred by only 1.8 percent (LARASA 1989).

Although research indicates continuing diversity in terms of self-identification, recent data from Colorado found that those relatively few Spanish-surnamed who called themselves Chicano or Latino were twice as likely to be "involved in any Hispanic organization" than those who preferred Hispanic or Mexican, and were about three times more likely to be so involved than Mexican Americans or Spanish Americans. Two points should be added. Overall, only 10.7 percent of the entire sample were "involved in any Hispanic organization"; those who called themselves Chicano or Latino were also the most educated and had the highest incomes. It is possible that sociodemographic characteristics alone or in association with ethnic identity are related to organizational involvement. Those calling themselves Chicano were also the most likely to be concerned about prejudice and discrimination. Thus, self-identification does seem related to perception and attitude.

Other commentary regarding ethnic self-identification can be noted. Some have pointed out that a considerable portion of what might be defined as the Mexican American population often does not label itself in a fashion that indicates *any* Mexican heritage. This finding has been taken as indicating little attachment to a Mexican "homeland" and little perception of being a member of a minority group, particularly with relevance to politics (Connor 1985). Whatever the accuracy of this assertion, some changes that may be occurring in Latino self-perception and definition need to be recognized. That is, "Mexican-ness" may have been modified, supplemented, or transcended by broader definitions.

The U.S. Census Bureau may have encouraged a broader self-identity with its use of the term Hispanic. And in Chicago, various groups, such as Mexican Americans and Puerto Ricans, have invoked the broader Latino label for strategic political purposes (Padilla 1985).

Other research suggests that in 1984 more Hispanics thought of themselves "as Hispanics first and Americans second" than had been the case in 1981. This finding further supports the idea of a Latino or Hispanic politics. Additional findings, reported between 1981 and 1984, are these: (1) There was a significant increase in the desire to perpetuate Hispanic traditions through succeeding generations; (2) a growing emphasis on tradition was also evident in Hispanics' desire to see their culture appreciated by others; and (3) the Spanish language was increasingly seen as the most important mechanism for preserving Hispanic culture and identity. In addition, there has been a distinct blurring of differences between Hispanics of various nationalities and how they feel about one another (Caplan 1987, 165–166).

Thus, the choice of a particular name or label, or the diversity of labels that persons with ethnic–racial affinity might use, may be important. At the same time, the emergence of new labels probably suggests social and political developments among groups. There is a "politics of ethnicity" tied into self-identification and government identification of individuals and groups (Muñoz 1989). The use of the terms Hispanic and Latino is increasing, but considerable diversity in self-identification remains.

POLITICAL PARTICIPATION ORIENTATIONS

A strong case has been made that an identifiable "ethnic political culture" shapes the attitudes of group members toward political participation (Nelson 1979). A study of ethnic–racial groups in New York City suggests that ethnic–racial political culture is independent of, and often more significant than, socioeconomic status in explaining political participation. A Los Angeles study also found that ethnic background was more strongly related to political participation patterns than was socioeconomic status (Jackson 1988).

The New York City study (Nelson 1979) found that several Latino groups—Puerto Ricans, Cubans, and Dominicans—have "weak participant political cultures," while blacks and other groups (e.g., Irish and Jews) have distinctively stronger orientation to political participation. A study of registered voters in Houston, Texas, found that "Mexican-Americans are less interested in politics than Anglos or blacks." That study also claimed that Spanish, rather than English, language orientation explains some of the lower politicization of Mexican Americans than blacks (MacManus and Cassel 1988). It thus appears that "ethnic political culture," including that of Latinos, is distinctive and that Latinos are not disposed to political participation.

But other evidence counters the findings of the New York City study and similar claims of a "weak participant culture" among Latinos. To take one Latino group, the 80 to 90 percent voter participation rates of Puerto Ricans *in Puerto Rico* are substantially higher than voting percentages among *all* citizens in the United States, regardless of ethnic–

racial background (see Jennings 1988, 72). This suggests the importance of context and perhaps other factors, such as sense of "attachment" and language, in understanding Latino political participation.

Also, there is evidence of positive and strong attitudes toward politics among Chicanos (Garcia and Arce 1988, 136–137). Chicano "civic orientations"—defined as attitudes focusing on political activities that an active member of the political system pursues, such as voting as an individual expression, getting people of Mexican descent to vote, and supporting demonstrations to change unfair laws—were found to be high. Attitudes reflecting a sense of ethnic identification, or a "collectivist orientation," were also positive and strong among Chicanos. "With this pattern of political orientations, one might expect active levels of political participation. Yet the political participation rates [of Chicanos] are rather low" (Garcia and Arce 1988).

This study also found Mexican-born Chicanos to have higher levels of civic orientation than did American-born Chicanos. "This could represent some degree of internalization of civic duty norms and an immigrant perspective." Moreover, those of lower occupational prestige and with lower educational attainment had higher levels of civic orientation. Also, the level of collectivist orientation, a sense of ethnic community, was higher among those who were older, Mexican-born, closer generationally to Mexico, of lower occupational prestige, and of lower educational attainment. Higher levels of socioeconomic status are usually associated with greater participation orientations, but the evidence in this study belies the predicted pattern. Garcia and Arce (1988) speculate that a distinction between "immigrant" and "minority" group perspectives might help explain this unusual pattern.

Recent findings from Colorado (LARASA 1989) are not entirely in agreement with those of the Garcia and Arce study. The Colorado study found that among Spanish-surnamed Coloradans, the native-born were more likely to be "involved in a Hispanic organization" than were the Mexican-born, as were the better educated and those with higher incomes. Another study, in Houston, found that Mexican American participation is lower than that of Anglos and blacks even when socioeconomic status is controlled. This study also found that only 9 percent of survey respondents report belonging to a Mexican American community organization (MacManus and Cassel 1988, 204).

Cubans in Miami have rates of voter registration and turnout comparable to other groups in the city (after controlling for citizenship) and rates that are higher than for the Hispanic population nationwide (Portes and Mozo 1988). Puerto Ricans, in contrast, have low levels of political participation. Evidence from New York City indicates that in 1982 and 1984 Puerto Rican voter registration was about 4 percent below that of blacks and about 10 percent lower than that of whites. Latino turnout rates in those two years were only slightly less than that of blacks and about 8 percent less than that for whites. Additionally, Latinos were more likely to enter the voting booth, but *not* to vote on some ballot issues (Falcón 1988, 182).

One of the most extensive studies of Hispanic political participation contends that "Hispanics are less likely to participate in politics than are other Americans" (Calvo and Rosenstone 1989, 2). Data on various forms of participation indicate that the Hispanic to non-Hispanic participation ratio was closest with respect to having "attend[ed] a public meeting" (.95), "turned out to vote" and "trying to influence how others vote" (both .78), and "belong[ing] to a political club" (.75). For none of the other forms of electoral participation (e.g., attending political rallies, working for parties or candidates, contributing money) or nonelectoral participation (e.g., writing to a congressman, signing a petition, doing committee service for a local club, or belonging to a political club or group) did the Hispanic to non-Hispanic ratio reach .70. Thus, "as the cost of participation rises, Hispanic participation trails farther and farther behind that of other Americans" (Calvo and Rosenstone 1989).

Even after controlling for socioeconomic status, Hispanics were less likely to register and turn out to vote than were non-Hispanics (Calvo and Rosenstone 1989). To a considerable degree, however, Cubans departed from this pattern, often being *more* likely to vote than non-Hispanics, controlling for socioeconomic status. But, outside the Miami area, Cubans and other Hispanics in Florida seem not to be especially politically active or influential (MacManus 1990, 461). Overall, socioeconomic status has less significance in differentiating Latino registration and turnout within and between the several Latino groups than is true within the non-Hispanic population. Some part of the gap in overall Latino participation (excepting Cubans in Miami) is attributable to socioeconomic disadvantage, such as low levels of income and education, but that does not account for the entire difference.

Two other factors thought to account for the differences are language and attachment. Difficulty with the English language may depress political participation (Calvo and Rosenstone 1989; MacManus and Cassel 1988; but see Meier and Stewart 1991). Others point to evidence that Latinos have difficulty in *understanding* U.S. politics and the political system (Vigil 1987, 43). Several scholars have suggested that noncitizenship, because of a lower sense of attachment to and permanence within the United States, is a leading cause of Latino non-participation. As much as a third of the Mexican-origin population may be noncitizens, and Puerto Ricans have a unique dual-citizenship status that apparently diminishes participation in the mainland setting.

Organizations such as political parties and interest groups are often claimed to be important in mobilizing political participation. Cubans living in Miami were 22 percent more likely to vote than Cubans living outside the city, which Calvo and Rosenstone (1989) attribute to political interest-group activity in Miami.

Another set of factors that affects voter participation is probably especially significant for Latinos. "The current maze of laws and administrative procedures that govern voter registration suppress [overall] voter turnout in the United States by about 9 percentage points and have their greatest suppressive effect on the turnout rates of the young, the poor, and those with few years of formal education" (Calvo and Rosenstone 1989, 24). As we have seen, Latinos are disproportionately younger, poorer, and less educated than the general population; the suppressive effect of registration procedures is probably greater among Latinos than the 9 percent for the overall population.

Other variables have been claimed to affect Latino political participation. Prominent among them is gerrymandering, the drawing of legislative districts to diminish or dilute the impact of particular groups on electoral outcomes (see, e.g., Regalado 1988). The impact of gerrymandering is most directly felt in local and state legislative elections, although the difficulty a group faces in having certain (legislative) candidates elected might well be expected to have implications regarding how group members perceive the efficacy of voting.

Levels of Hispanic registration and voting continue to be lower than those for non-Hispanics, as indicated by U.S. Census Bureau data. In the 1988 presidential election, 56.6 percent of eligible Hispanics were registered to vote, compared to 71.1 percent of non-Hispanics; Hispanic registration was about 80 percent that for non-Hispanics. In the same election, 45.9 percent of Hispanics actually voted, while 61.4 percent of non-Hispanics did; Hispanic voting was 75 percent of that for non-Hispanics. Of the eligible electorate, then, about 26 percent of Latinos actually registered and voted, while about 44 percent of non-

Hispanics did so. General patterns of lower Hispanic registration and voting in this election hold regardless of education and income levels, with some exceptions. Among those with four years or more of college, Hispanic registration and voting reach 95 percent of that for non-Hispanics; among those with annual family incomes of $50,000 or more, Hispanic registration and voting are 96 percent of that for non-Hispanics. While the socioeconomic "resource bias" of political participation has been recognized for some time, the Latino political situation goes beyond that.

Some additional points regarding Latino voting should be noted briefly. First, there is evidence that Latinos do not automatically vote for Hispanic (Spanish-surnamed) candidates. Mexican Americans are a "responsible electorate"; they have voted for Anglo, rather than Spanish-surnamed, candidates when the position on issues of the former were more compatible than those of the latter (de la Garza, 1974). Another finding is that Latinos are *less* likely to turn out to vote in initiative–referenda versus candidate elections. Apparently, issue-based elections present somewhat more confusing and abstract matters than do candidate-based elections. This is consistent with the evidence that a significant reason that Latinos do not participate is because they have difficulty understanding politics. In any event, the data show that elections in the United States have not produced many Hispanic elected officials. Latinos constitute only about 1 percent of all elected officials in the United States.

POLITICAL IDEOLOGY

How do Mexican Americans and other Latinos identify themselves in terms of political ideology, that is, as liberals, conservatives, and so on? This is difficult to answer, for once again the findings are not clear. The 1976 Denver study found that Latinos were more likely to characterize themselves politically as conservative (31 percent) or right-wing (1 percent), than as liberal (25 percent) or left-wing (1 percent). The authors of this study were especially struck by the finding that 41 percent of Mexican Americans refused to apply *any* of the ideological self-identification terms, including "moderate." In that same study, blacks were considerably more likely to call themselves liberal (42 percent), and much less likely to refuse to label or characterize themselves using one of the various ideological categories (Lovrich and Marenin 1976). The authors interpreted this as suggesting that Latinos were not a very "awakened" minority.

Recent state-level surveys (SWVRI 1988) indicate that Latinos in the

Southwest tend to view themselves as "moderate." About half the Hispanic voters in New Mexico, Texas, and California identify themselves as "in-between" liberal and conservative ideologically, presumably meaning they are moderate. In all three states, the percentage identifying as liberal is greater than the percentage identifying as conservative, but the difference is less than 5 percent. Other research indicates that the most frequent self-identification of Hispanics (in California, Texas, and New York State in 1984) is as moderates (35, 44, and 33 percent, respectively); in California and Texas, Latinos were more likely to call themselves conservatives (34 and 28 percent, respectively) than liberals (25 and 24 percent, respectively). In New York City, Latino identification as liberal or conservative is about equally split (31 to 30 percent).

Other findings regarding Hispanics in Texas should be noted. One study found that, overall, 28 percent of Hispanics identified themselves as liberals, 34 percent as moderates, and 37 percent as conservatives. There were interesting patterns according to levels of education and levels of income. For the most educated (college graduates) and the least educated (less than high school), the most common ideological self-identification was as conservatives (Dyer and Vedlitz 1986, 29). Generally, the liberal identification of Latinos was close to that of blacks and about 9 percentage points above Anglos (Dyer and Vedlitz 1986). The level of moderate and conservative identification among Hispanics was 7 percent less and 2 percent less than comparable numbers among Anglos. Latinos' self-identification as moderates was 7 percent less, and as conservatives was 9 percent more, than the similar percentages for blacks. Overall, the study suggests that "Hispanics are nearly as liberal as blacks and nearly as conservative as Anglos. This is possible because of fewer 'moderates' among the Hispanics who are willing to place themselves on the scale. As a group, Hispanics are more split ideologically than either blacks or Anglos" (Dyer and Vedlitz 1986, 11).

Other data on Texas, from 1980 to 1985, further suggest that Hispanics view themselves as decidedly more conservative (45 to 60+ percent) than liberal (20 to 38 percent) or moderate (3 to 12 percent). At the same time, this polling indicates that Texas Hispanics vote heavily for Democratic party candidates (Tarrance 1987, 64–66). Cubans in south Florida would probably also heavily self-identify as conservatives.

Finally, some national-level data have compared "Latin Americans" with Americans of various backgrounds: blacks, Asians, American Indians, lower- or working-class whites, northern/western Europeans, and southern/eastern Europeans. After blacks (39.6 percent) and Asians (35 percent), the Latin Americans (33.3 percent) were the most likely to call themselves liberals. Latin Americans' self-identification as moderates (42.7 percent) was close to that for American Indians (45.1 percent), lower- or working-class whites (44.6 percent), and southern or eastern Europeans (42.2 percent); ideological identity as a moderate was somewhat higher than that among northern or western Europeans (38.8 percent), blacks (37.2 percent), and Asians (32 percent). Latinos (23.9 percent), along with all lower- or working-class whites (20.4 percent) and blacks (23.2 percent), are among the least likely group to call themselves conservatives. The gap between Latinos and the group most often identifying as conservatives (northern or western Europeans, 36.5 percent) is substantial but not dramatic (Harrigan 1989, 146).

Although the data on political ideology are difficult to disentangle, one point seems relatively clear. Latinos do not heavily or overwhelmingly identify themselves as liberals. Nor do they depart dramatically from the mainstream in terms of ideological self-identification. And Cubans in Miami are probably more conservative than the mainstream. Latinos are also ideologically diverse. These patterns seem contrary to popular perception.

Finally, other research further addresses, albeit indirectly, the issue of Latino ideology and other political attitudes, and compares it with that of other groups. An analysis of a number of ballot propositions in San Francisco found that Hispanics tend to vote "broadly progressive," while blacks vote "narrowly liberal," by local political standards. For instance, on such "radical proposals" as "local corporation taxes and municipalization of utilities, Hispanic voters are *alone among racial minorities* in their strong support" for those measures (De Leon 1988, 21; emphasis added). Hispanic and black similarities are confined to policy areas of shared *material* concerns, such as jobs, housing, and education, that are congruent with Democratic party politics.

A better understanding of Latino political ideology requires more reliable and consistent findings. Also important to ascertain or verify is whether the terms liberal, conservative, and so on necessarily have the same meaning for Latinos as they do for other groups, and whether those meanings necessarily apply to specific issues or dimensions. Finally, more comparing and contrasting of the various Latino subgroups, as well as examining Latinos in relation to blacks, Asians, Anglos, and the rest, is necessary.

_____POLICY CONCERNS

As often as not, research has found that Latinos have somewhat different concerns than others do. For instance, Latinos (and blacks) in Denver were substantially more concerned than Anglos about social services in the city, such as crime and law enforcement, community relations, health and welfare services, and inadequate police services. Anglos evidenced greater concern about environmental protection and quality-of-life issues, such as public transportation, pollution, and government efficiency. Moreover, these differences in policy preferences and concerns remained after controlling for socioeconomic status (Lovrich 1974).

Recent survey data from Colorado indicate differences between Hispanics and non-Hispanics in terms of policy concerns. Asked in an open-ended question about the most important problem facing the state in 1989, the greatest policy concern of Latinos (39 percent) was "the economy, and jobs" (LARASA 1989). The state's population as a whole more frequently mentioned the economy as its first issue of concern (46 percent). Latinos were much more likely to mention education as a major problem facing the state (14 percent) than were Anglos (2 percent), and to see crime and substance abuse as a major problem than were Anglos (8 percent versus 2 percent).

The Colorado Hispanic population responded somewhat differently when asked to indicate their level of concern (scored 3 = "very concerned" to 1 = "not concerned") about problems in Colorado. When asked in this way, in closed-ended questions, the major concerns, listed in terms of the average response, were crime (2.64), education (2.57), alcohol–drug abuse (2.55), the homeless (2.50), discrimination and prejudice (2.46), taxes (2.44), unemployment–jobs (2.43), government mismanagement (2.41), environment–pollution (2.22), housing and neighborhoods (2.21), transportation–highways (1.93), and urban growth (1.75).

An analysis of Texas Latino voters in 1988 that asked about the "most important problem facing people . . . in your neighborhood" found that 55 percent answered "crime and drugs," 24 percent said "jobs and poverty," and 10 percent cited "municipal services." Four years earlier, 20 percent had mentioned crime–drugs, 39 percent jobs–poverty, and 17 percent municipal services (Flores and Brischetto 1989).

A San Antonio study found that although Anglos and Mexican Americans differ on a few important issues, overall they do not constitute distinct electorates. They differ primarily in their views of government spending on minority-related issues; somewhat with regard to spending on education, environment, space, and welfare; and not at all in their evaluation of spending on crime, drug addiction, defense, foreign aid, and urban problems (de la Garza and Weaver 1985).

In late 1988, the Southwest Voter Research Institute (SWVRI) examined the views of Latinos, Anglos, and blacks in three southwestern states (California, Texas, and New Mexico) on fourteen issues. Latinos differed from Anglos by 10 percent or more on five issues: military aid to the *contras* (12 percent less supportive of aid than Anglos); increased spending on bilingual education (42 percent stronger support); English as the only official language of the United States (44 percent stronger opposition); for national health insurance (16 percent greater support); and more support than Anglos for federal funding of day care (14 percent). Latinos differed by 10 percent or more from blacks on four issues: cutting defense spending to reduce the federal deficit (11 percent less approving than blacks); increasing spending on bilingual education (25 percent more favoring); making English the only official language (30 percent more opposing); and exacting the death penalty for murderers (13 percent greater support). The issues on which Latinos differed by 10 percent or *less* from both Anglos and blacks were increased defense spending, temporary amnesty for Central American refugees, increased taxes to reduce the federal deficit, making abortion illegal except in cases of rape and incest, providing tax credit for children in private schools, and banning handguns for citizens.

Thus, the similarities between Latinos and Anglos are substantial. And some of the differences are readily explainable. For example, the difference between Latinos and Anglos (as well as blacks) regarding bilingual education and Official English measures are not surprising, given the salience of the language issue for Latinos. Latino–Anglo differences regarding national health insurance and federal spending for day care probably reflect socioeconomic status and social need (these are not accounted for in some of the research concerning policy preferences). The Latino–Anglo difference regarding aid to the *contras* probably has to do with Latino concern about U.S. interventionism in Latin and South America. Notably, the level of Latino and black opposition to military aid to the *contras* is similar, 66 and 67 percent.

Another study found several policy priorities—schools, immigration, and employment—that "make Mexican Americans distinctive in local [Houston] politics," although there may be "no single overwhelming political issue which mobilizes the Mexican-American community such as the civil rights issue mobilizes blacks" (MacManus and Cassel 1988, 208).

LATINOS AND POLITICAL PARTIES

Discussions of political parties in the United States typically distinguish three aspects of the parties: the party in the electorate, the party in government, and the party organization. Stated otherwise, there are (1) those who just affiliate with the party, the rank and file; (2) elected officials, whether Democrats or Republicans; and (3) those who hold positions within formal organizations of political parties.

Considering parties in the electorate, Latinos overall are strongly linked to the Democratic party in terms of both registration and voting patterns. But Latino Democratic strength does not equal that of blacks in the Democratic party. And Cubans in the Miami area depart from the pattern. Various estimates indicate that, overall, the Latino vote for Democratic presidential candidates has been substantially higher than that of the general populace. In 1988, for instance, Democratic presidential candidate Michael Dukakis received an estimated 65–69 percent of the Latino vote.

MEXICAN AMERICANS

The party affiliation of Mexican Americans is heavily Democratic. In Arizona, 77 percent of Mexican Americans are registered Democrats; only about 15 percent are Republicans, versus 45 percent Republicans and 43 percent Democrats of all registered voters. In California, Texas, and New Mexico, Mexican American affiliation with the Democratic party is 75–80 percent. These high levels are reflected, and sometimes magnified, in voting totals for Democratic candidates for national, state, and local offices.

Republican George Bush carried California in the 1988 presidential election, but the state's Latino population gave the Democratic candidate 65–75 percent of its vote (Guerra 1989). Data from Arizona also indicated very high levels of Hispanic support for Michael Dukakis, although in the state as whole, Bush received over 58 percent of the vote. Such high levels of Mexican American support for Democratic candidates for president are equaled and, in some cases, surpassed in congressional elections and elections for state offices. Through the 1960s and well into the 1970s, Chicano support for Democratic congressional candidates was 85 percent or greater (Garcia and de la

Garza 1977, 104). In 1988, California Latinos strongly supported (60–69 percent) the Democratic candidate for the U.S. Senate, who was defeated. Mexican American support for Democrats in House races generally runs even stronger.

_____PUERTO RICANS

In New York City about 80 percent of Puerto Ricans were registered as Democrats in 1982 and 1984, a pattern that probably still holds. This level of Democratic party affiliation is about the same as that of blacks and is somewhat higher than that of whites (about 65 percent) in the New York City area. Puerto Rican support for Democratic candidates in 1984 was 61.3 percent, which was about 12 percent lower than for blacks and about 13 percent higher than for whites. Election patterns in 1982 were similar. In the 1988 presidential election, the Democratic candidate received 79.6 percent of New York City's Latino vote, while the black and white vote were 87.5 and 58.7 percent, respectively (Falcón 1988, 12).

_____CUBANS

Little if any of what has been said about Latinos and party activities pertains to Cubans. Party registration of Hispanics in Dade County, Florida, which includes Miami, is heavily Republican, 68 percent; only 24 percent are registered Democrats. This represents a change from the 1979 pattern, when 49 percent of Dade County Hispanics were registered Democrats and 39 percent were Republicans. This strong Republican leaning is clear in Cuban voting patterns. The 1988 Democratic presidential candidate received only 15 percent of the vote in Dade County's heavily Hispanic precincts, while he received 45 percent in the county as a whole. Similarly, the Democratic candidate in the 1986 U.S. Senate race received 24 percent of the vote in Hispanic precincts, but 56 percent of the total county vote.

Observers have claimed that Republican–conservative Cuban political leanings are *not* the result of their relatively high socioeconomic status compared to other Latino groups: "Although the data cannot support a definite conclusion, they point . . . in the direction of the unique history of this minority and the attitudes rooted in its home country experience" (Portes and Mozo 1988, 164) as the source of Cuban conservatism and Republican leanings.

Also important is the extent to which the political parties have sought to recruit and involve Latinos in the political process. The presence of strong political party organizations seems to have had a substantial impact on Latino voter registration and turnout (Calvo and

Rosenstone 1989). (On state politics, this is examined further in Chapter 6; local politics are discussed in Chapter 8.)

As for Latinos and the party in government, the vast majority of Latinos holding elective positions at the national level, specifically Congress, or as state legislators are Democrats (Martinez 1990). Throughout the 1980s, nine of the ten Hispanics in the U.S. Congress were Democrats. All but two of the eighty-eight Latino state legislators (including state senators and representatives) in the five southwestern states were Democrats (in 1990). In contrast, only one of the eleven Hispanics in the Florida state legislature is a Democrat, and the only Latino governor in the late 1980s was Republican Robert Martinez of Florida.

As for Latinos and the party organization, Latinos are much more numerous in Democratic than Republican organizations. Data on Chicanos in the Southwest suggest that there are eight Chicanos on the Executive Committee of the Democratic National Committee and that fifteen of the more than three hundred members of the Democratic National Committee are Hispanics. In 1990, seven of the one hundred and fifty members of the Republican National Committee were Chicanos (Martinez 1990).

Table 5 presents data on *state* party central committees. They imply a stronger presence of Hispanics in state *Democratic* party executive committees and central committees, but it is difficult to measure without specific data on the proportion of Latinos among a state's party identifiers relative to the percentage of Latinos among party organization officials.

_____INTEREST GROUPS

Many scholars see interest groups as the linchpin of U.S. politics and U.S. pluralism. Whether or not one accepts that interpretation, a focus on interest groups that advocate in behalf of Latinos is essential. But before turning to a discussion of Latino interest groups, we should make several points. Scholars of Latino politics have argued that the conventional approaches to and understandings of interest groups in the United States do not directly apply to Latino (Mexican American) groups. Latino groups, as often as not, have not been inherently political. That is, the group's existence may have resulted from perceived political and social discrimination and needs, but the group's activities may not be political in the usual sense. In fact, it has been suggested that Mexican American organizations often have been reluc-

TABLE 5
Chicanos as Party Officials

State and Party	Executive Committee Members	Central Committee Members
Arizona		
Dems	0 of 32	35 of 400 + voting members
Reps	0 of 8	1 of 120 positions
California		
Dems	21 of about 300	
Reps	2 of 18	112 of 1,000 + voting members
Colorado		
Dems	0 of 13	28 of 338 voting members
Reps	0 of 5	8 of 369 voting members
New Mexico		
Dems	17 of 47	103 of 242 voting members
Reps	8 of 38	62 of 360 voting members
Texas		
Dems	13 of 85	19 of 254 voting members
Reps	5 of 70	8 of 424 voting members

Source: From data in Arthur D. Martinez, *Who's Who: Chicano Officeholders, 1990–91*, 8th ed. (Silver City, N. Mex.).

tant to use the term political in their names or statements of purpose, "perhaps because of a fear of sanctions from the dominant society, or perhaps potential members would shun affiliation with a 'political' organization" (Vigil 1987, 100). Some also contend that Latino organizations are commonly multifunctional. Group activities may be "not strictly political, not strictly economic, not strictly social, but respond to all kinds of problems." Thus, it is difficult to know the most useful approach for discussing the various Latino interest groups (Vigil 1987).

Before we turn to the typology developed here and a discussion of specific groups, several points should be noted. To my knowledge, there has been no systematic effort to assess a substantial number of Latino interest groups in terms of their political influence. Nevertheless, based on the evidence from previous chapters, Latino interest groups are probably not resource rich or influential; indeed, the evidence points to low levels of resources. Some research that has addressed this issue contends that Latino "organizations which are active in attempting to influence the policy process, e.g., LULAC, NALEO, NCLR, have either one or two person operations in Washington, or are able to allocate only portions of their resources to the time-consuming task of legislative and executive lobbying. In contrast, other ethnic organizations such as the Urban League, the NAACP, the American Jewish Committee, with their million dollar budgets, their large staffs, and their decades of history, indicate the relative disparity of organizational development and political influence of the Hispanic community vis-à-vis other ethnic groups" (Pachon 1985, 307).

According to Barrera (1985), Mexican American organizations have had somewhat different goals in different historical periods (see Chapter 3). Building on Barrera's work, we can form a typology that emphasizes group goals and related ideology. Communitarian goals were most prevalent among Chicano groups from the mid nineteenth century until around 1920; communitarian goals focused on "maintaining the physical and cultural integrity of the Mexican communities, which were under heavy pressure from the expansion of the American political economy into the Southwest." Beginning with the 1920s and continuing through the 1950s, "there was a shift in emphasis to an 'egalitarian' ideal, which aimed at securing for Chicanos the statuses and privileges of the dominant, Anglo group" (Barrera 1985). "The 1960s saw the birth of the Chicano Movement, which for the first time linked communitarian and egalitarian goals in a distinctive ideological phase known popularly as 'Chicanismo,' or cultural nationalism" (Barrera 1985).

Communitarian and egalitarian concepts are useful in order to categorize and thus help understand the goals, ideologies, and approaches of Mexican American–Chicano organizations historically and in the present. An extension of these concepts is also useful. Both egalitarian and communitarian goals may be expressed more or less assertively or defensively, actively or passively. For example, an instance of a defensive (protective community) goal would be the mutual aid societies, or *mutualistas*, which sought to protect the Mexican population during the late 1880s and early 1900s. Such organizations played important roles in early periods (and sometimes well beyond them) for other Latino communities (see Mormino and Pozzetta 1987). At the assertive end of the communitarian continuum is the Chicano Movement with its strong accent on distinct, desirable, community values that are put forth as alternatives to dominant Anglo values.

Egalitarian goals also can be thought of in assertive and defensive terms. But a more useful distinction here is between the goals of formal or procedural equality and "full" political or substantive equality, that is, equality of condition. Formal–procedural goals are associated with notions of equal opportunity, equality before the law, due process, and so on, and are common to traditional American politics. Goals of substantive equality are concerned with equality of outcome and strong support for specific affirmative policies that go beyond "mere" equality of opportunity.

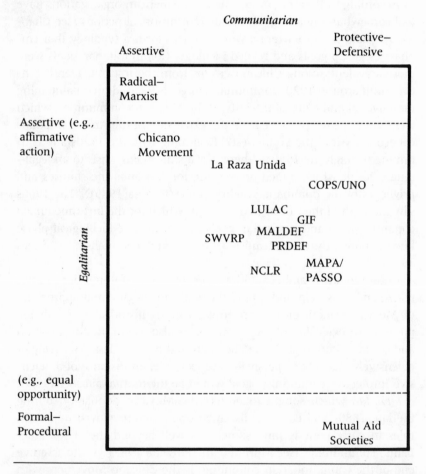

FIGURE 1
Toward a Typology of Latino (Mexican American) Interest Groups

Figure 1 provides two interrelated continua with respect to these dimensions and a placement and implicit assessment of Latino (Mexican American) groups. The figure does not rule out evolution or change. In fact, it implies an evolution from the bottom right to top left of the figure (cf. Barrera 1985), an implication that is important for several reasons.

First, evolution in a general direction is implied, from bottom left to top right of the figure, that is consistent with what has been referred to as liberal reformism. And the evolution suggests continuity or linkage, as well as change. More generally, groups may vary over time in terms of their position with respect to egalitarian and communitarian concerns. For example, internal changes, such as the partial or full achievement of goals, membership change, and turnover can cause variations in concern. Change may also occur through external forces, such as general shifts in public opinion and public policy enactments. Nevertheless, original goals should, to some degree, "anchor" a group within a political space in the political arena.

A brief discussion of several groups can help in understanding the groups and their placement. Some of the most visible mainstream Latino groups are national groups, such as the League of United Latin American Citizens (LULAC), Mexican American Legal Defense and Education Fund (MALDEF), and National Council of La Raza (NCLR). Some local groups, such as Citizens Organized for Public Services (COPS) in San Antonio and United Neighborhood Organizations (UNO) in Los Angeles, have also gained recognition beyond their locales. The particular placement of the various groups may be questioned, but the heuristic benefits of the diagram are not entirely lost thereby. For instance, that LULAC, NCLR, MALDEF, and the Southwest Voter Research Project (SWVRP) are located near the center of the figure implies that they are moderate mainstream organizations. In any event, the figure serves only as a starting point; it is meant to aid in understanding the groups, and to encourage further analysis.

Before the 1920s, the major goals of Latino organizations were communitarian and only implicitly political. When resistance to Anglo domination and efforts at electoral politics emerged, the communitarian tendency was manifested in the *mutualistas* (mutual aid societies). "The central concern of the mutualistas during their 'golden age' appears to have been the social cohesion of the Chicano community. Membership of a mutual aid society provided a kind of social 'safety net' . . . that helped preserve the integrity and the peace of mind of the working class Chicano family. At the same time, the social activities that were very important to most mutualistas afforded a focus for community interaction that was provided by no other mechanism" (Barrera 1985, 7; also see Mormino and Pozzetta 1987). The *mutualistas* generally eschewed the explicitly political arena.

LULAC, created in the late 1920s, has emphasized "equal access to and equal treatment from public institutions." LULAC has focused extensively on issues of socioeconomic and political equality in the United States and has shown "very little concern with issues of community cohesion as such" (Barrera 1985, 13). Among the specific issues in which LULAC has been involved are school integration, public accommodations, and discriminatory voting practices (Meier and Stewart 1991). Interestingly, while LULAC has been involved in a number of antidiscrimination activities for many years, and although it has used formal, legal, and political processes such as litigation as a tool, the group has often downplayed its "political" nature. LULAC has been, and is, generally seen as a middle-class organization with a strong assimilationist orientation (M. García, 1989; also see Chapter 2). It is a reformist organization that clearly works within the system, or in the realm of conventional politics.

Other Latino organizations, including several formed between World War II and the early 1960s, have been notable for combining egalitarian concerns with a service orientation. The G.I. Forum, for instance, was created to assure that Chicano veterans of World War II secured equal treatment and the full benefits that military service gave to other veterans. The group subsequently became involved in other social service activities, such as job-training programs and college scholarships for Latino students.

The Mexican American Legal Defense and Education Fund (MALDEF), created in the late 1960s, has played a role in the Mexican American community similar to that of the National Association for the Advancement of Colored People–Legal Defense Fund (NAACP-LDF) for blacks. A Puerto Rican Legal Defense Fund has also been created. Noting the success of the NAACP-LDF, Latinos saw that litigation could be a useful, and perhaps critical, political strategy. By 1973, the U.S. Supreme Court had handed down decisions in "eight cases in which MALDEF had participated, five of which were amicus curiae briefs filed alone or in conjunction with other organizations" (O'Connor and Epstein 1988, 260). MALDEF sponsored three cases; they involved the constitutionality of at-large election districts, federal government responsibility for the treatment of employees of city jails, and school finance. Other projects addressed voting rights, employment discrimination, and education, including the provision of education to the children of undocumented aliens. In this last concern, MALDEF won one of its major victories (O'Connor and Epstein 1988, 262).

The National Council of La Raza (NCLR), previously the Southwest Council of La Raza (formed in 1968), began as a group oriented toward "community organization and mobilization," including voter registration and research and dissemination of information. Over time, NCLR's efforts have turned to economic development, including small business investment (Barrera 1985, 36).

Other organizations have focused more directly on the electoral arena. The Southwest Voter Research Project (SWVRP) has sought to encourage voter registration and turnout. Increasingly SWVRP has been involved in litigation against factors thought to diminish Latino political participation and electoral opportunities, including at-large elections and the gerrymandering of electoral districts. SWVRP also has conducted numerous studies focusing on actual levels of Latino registration and turnout, and on policy concerns, impacts of public policy, and voting patterns of Latinos.

During the height of the Chicano Movement, from about 1965 to 1975, a number of organizations emerged that "tied together a strong 'communitarian' orientation with an equally strong commitment to equality and anti-discrimination" (Barrera 1985). Among them were the Crusade for Justice, created by Rodolfo "Corky" Gonzales, in Denver, and the Mexican American Youth Organization (MAYO), formed in Texas. There were also other student groups. A major theme of the organizations was cultural nationalism. Explicit and extensive attention also was given to the Indian part of Chicano heritage. There was, similarly, a "very strong focus on culture and the preservation of the Chicano cultural heritage." Programmatically, this often translated into calls for community control of educational, economic, and social institutions (see Chapter 2).

An effort to have a more direct and focused impact in the electoral arena led to the formation of a Chicano political party, La Raza Unida. The party was most visible in the late 1960s, when Chicano candidates swept into office in Crystal City, Texas. There were other successes in some locales, particularly south Texas, but the party split into factions and ceased to exist as a viable electoral mechanism.

Several explanations have been given for the demise of La Raza Unida and the decline of the broader Chicano Movement. Changed circumstances, and the need for different strategies and approaches in different states or regions, led to some splits. Often linked to these factors were major leadership splits that developed from opposing views as to whether electoral, "practical" politics or more radical ideological politics should be pursued. There was also no consistent ideology; the references made to cultural identification, self-determination, and related concepts were generally eclectic and vague. There was a consensus on the problems to be faced. All factions saw Chicanos as an oppressed people and all held the view that the political parties and political system had not been responsive to Chicano concerns. But disagreement existed as to how to go about explaining problems and developing plans to address them. In view of this dissensus, Mexican Americans fell back on liberal reformist approaches (see, e.g., Muñoz 1989). Nonetheless, the impact of the Chicano Movement may have been more real than apparent. The movement produced a group of activists that continues to be politically active and have political clout. Even with the "re-traditionalization" in Mexican American politics— for instance, traditional groups like LULAC have regained standing— groups were affected to some degree by the Chicano Movement.

Several radical organizations, which tended to have a Marxist orientation, split off from other Chicano groups. The overall and direct political impact of these groups was probably minor, but they may have had some philosophical impact. These organizations contended that there was a parallel between the subordinate relationship of Latin American and other Third World countries and the United States that the Chicano situation in the United States replicated. The radicals asserted that Chicanos suffered from internal colonialism and U.S. imperialism in much the same way that foreign countries suffered from (classic) colonialism and imperialism (Barrera 1985). These assertions have been accepted, if only to a limited degree. The greatest impact of the radical perspective has probably been in how Latinos think about certain public policies, particularly immigration. Many, perhaps most, Latinos once supported restrictive immigration policies, but have come to support more permissive policies. The distinction often made by Latinos between undocumented workers and illegal aliens is an instance of where the language and thinking about politics have changed.

Several additional notes about Latino groups bear mention. A large number of Latino groups exist. Martinez (1990, 116–125) lists 114 nationwide Hispanic civic organizations. The Latin American Research and Service Agency of Denver in 1989 published a *Directory of Service for the Colorado Hispanic Community* that lists over 130 agencies and organizations. Not all these agencies serve the Hispanic community solely or even primarily, but many of them do. The majority of the agencies are multifunctional, but few are political by most conventional definitions of the term. A question that is important both theoretically and practically is what impact these service and other "nonpolitical" groups have on politics. Conceivably, they may substitute for, complement, or develop into political interest groups.

_____SUMMARY AND CONCLUSION

The elusive character of attempts to understand Latino politics is evident in issues concerning mass and group politics. Latinos are less likely to perceive discrimination than are other groups, although in some instances "objective" data imply considerable discrimination against them. Latinos (Mexican American) also tend to diverge regarding ethnic self-identification; this presumably indicates, and contributes to, less group cohesion. Despite evidence of a positive orientation to politics, Latino political participation is lower than that of other groups, a pattern that seems to hold even when accounting for socioeconomic status. This may reflect some aspects of Latin culture, for example, language differences and social attachment. It may also be traced to complex voter registration requirements and difficulty in understanding U.S. politics, factors that particularly affect the young, poor, and less educated—characteristics found disproportionately among Latinos.

Latinos are difficult to categorize in terms of self-identification. They seem to be more ideologically diffused than are blacks or Anglos; they tend toward liberal self-identification, but the tendency is not particularly strong. In many respects, Latino policy concerns are not clearly distinct from those of the general population; distinctions are evident on a relatively small number of issues. Although Latinos lean heavily toward the Democratic party, that leaning is not so strong as it is for blacks. As for Latino interest groups, the typology presented here to categorize and describe them should be helpful, but it is only a start.

This chapter underscores that Latino mass and group politics are distinct from that of other groups and are difficult to explain or understand. Conventional explanations, such as pluralism, seem inadequate or incomplete. In order to comprehend the status of Latinos in the political system, we must turn our attention to institutions of the national government. This is the topic of the next chapter.

5

Latinos and the National Government

──────The institutions of the national government—the president and the executive branch, Congress, and the Supreme Court—make policy in the U.S. political system. These institutions have significant general and specific impacts, as well as substantive and symbolic significance, for minority groups. Hence, access to and influence on these institutions is important for Latinos. But, given the absence of research on Latino political roles and activity, the extent of the institutions' influence and impact is hard to ascertain.

Relatively few policies promulgated by these institutions have been in direct response to Latino political activities and initiatives. Major school desegregation decisions by the courts have focused on blacks, for instance, and only later were extended to, or had implications for, Latinos. Similarly, a major bilingual education decision by the U.S. Supreme Court in 1974 was not filed in behalf of Latinos, although they have been the ones most affected by it. This chapter highlights some possible and actual ways in which Latinos can influence the institutions of the national government; it also discusses actions and decisions rendered by federal institutions that have been particularly germane for Latinos.

80

_____THE PRESIDENCY

The presidency is the most important elective position in the U.S. political system. Thus one way that a group can be politically influential is by playing a major role in determining who is elected to that office. People often criticize the method of presidential selection. Yet some observers contend that the long, complex, and fragmented nature of the presidential selection process in the United States actually can provide minority groups with opportunities to influence who ultimately becomes president. According to Henderson (1987, 3), the presidential selection process offers minorities a chance to (1) influence party politics at the state level in presidential primaries; (2) become party delegates and broker with fellow delegates in supporting candidates for the party nomination most supportive of minority policy preferences; (3) express, pursue, and construct planks in the party platform before and during national conventions in a presidential election year; (4) influence national policy issues connected to the presidential campaigns of candidates they support or oppose; (5) become party officials, including candidates or prospective candidates for the presidential or vice-presidential nomination; (6) play major negotiating and brokering roles in both the campaign strategies of presidential candidates in the general election and the formulation and projection of issues associated with the campaign; and (7) influence U.S. Senate and House elections associated with presidential elections.

Little research has systematically examined the frequency or impact of Latino activities regarding the presidential selection process. Nonetheless, the ability of Latinos to influence the process is shaped by several variables. Latinos are concentrated in a few states that are seen as pivotal in presidential elections, including California, Texas, Florida, and New York; this would seem to enhance the possibility of their playing a significant role in electing a president. But even in the late 1980s, Latinos constituted less than 5 percent of the voting electorate for presidential elections. And Republican dominance in presidential elections over the last generation, particularly in several of the states with substantial Latino populations, has diminished the Latino potential to be seen as a "swing vote."

Several conditions seem necessary for Latinos to have much impact in the general election for president. There must be a close election both nationally and within states with large Latino populations; and there must be high levels of registration and voting among the Latino population and strong Latino support for one candidate over the other.

These conditions have not occurred often in the last thirty years or so.

The election of John F. Kennedy in 1960 is generally perceived as one in which Latino votes, especially in Texas, were crucial to the outcome. Since then, the impact of the Latino vote has been less clear, although some believe it was important in the 1976 election of Jimmy Carter. In 1988, it initially appeared that Latino votes might be pivotal. In addition to Latino concentration in key electoral states, the early uncertainty about the outcome—the first presidential election in almost thirty years without a sitting president in the race—pointed to a close race in which groups such as Latinos might prove significant. Within the Democratic party, several candidates, including eventual nominee Michael Dukakis, claimed an affinity and familiarity with Latinos. That Dukakis selected a senator with long-time ties to Texas and an ability to converse in Spanish as his running mate also pointed to recognition of the Hispanic vote. On the Republican side, George Bush noted familial bonds, the fact that one of his sons was married to a Hispanic. During the 1988 Republican convention, then-President Reagan's appointment of a Hispanic (from Texas) as secretary of education also indicated attention to the Latino electorate. But as the campaign progressed and a victory for Republican Bush became increasingly certain, the significance of Latino votes diminished.

The prominence of the president in the U.S. political system makes that person's policy positions particularly significant for minorities. Presidents play various roles in the U.S. political system. Presidents play an important agenda-setting role in terms of the broad issues on which they focus public and governmental attention. Presidents can give, or withhold, attention to specific policies that are germane to minority concerns. Presidents also can play the role of chief legislator, formulating, proposing, and urging the passage of specific bills and programs. Such policies may directly or indirectly, positively or negatively, affect a particular group.

Laws may be viewed differently not only based on their stated goals and purposes but also in terms of their structure. A debate regarding federal government programs affecting the poor and other disadvantaged groups concerns the structure of programs. For instance, should the federal government operate the program, or should it give monies to state and local governments to operate it? If monies are given to state and local governments, who should specify the purposes for which these monies can and cannot be spent? What are the implications for a specific group, such as Latinos, if spending is or is not specified in advance?

The president's role in the budgetary process is important because more or less funding for programs seen as significant by a group may be called for in the president's budget. A president's appointment powers can be used to appoint persons of minority background to major and influential positions. Appointments to high-level positions, such as on the Cabinet, or a federal court, give a group recognition and may make agencies more aware and responsive to the group's policy concerns. Relatedly, as chief executive, the president is responsible for setting the tone of his administration and for facilitating the implementation of government policies. How aggressively programs are proposed and later enforced can be significantly aided by the president.

In short, presidents affect the political and policy concerns of a minority in a number of ways: symbolic recognition, substantive policies, appointments, program structure, level of budgetary commitment, and the vigor with which programs are administered.

PRESIDENTS AND MINORITY CONCERNS: 1960–1988

The 1960 presidential election was especially significant for Latinos. The election of young, charismatic, and Catholic John F. Kennedy generated a level of interest among Latinos that was not evident previously. The Kennedy administration, and the subsequent one of Lyndon Johnson, sponsored a variety of programs aimed at solving problems salient to the Latino population. Johnson's presidency saw the enactment of several laws that were landmarks for minority groups, most prominently the Civil Rights Act of 1964 and the Voting Rights Act of 1965. The 1975 amendments to the Voting Rights Act, with protection of voting rights for "language minorities," were especially crucial for Latinos.

Johnson's War on Poverty was important not only in its substantive focus on poverty but in its community action provisions, which called for the "maximum feasible participation" of those affected by the policies. As interpreted in some locales, the programs gave minority-group members administrative responsibilities and some resources that could be used for social services and, to some extent, for political mobilization. Notably, Rodolfo "Corky" Gonzalez, a major figure in the Chicano political movement, once headed the Denver antipoverty agency.

As part of its domestic policy initiatives, the Johnson administration often favored the use of federal grants to local and state governments. These grants were almost always structured so that monies could be used only for specific purposes; these kinds of grants are referred to as categorical grants. If a categorical grant targets money for purposes that are seen as important to socially disadvantaged minority groups, it increases the likelihood that funds will indeed be used for those purposes and not others. Thus, minority groups are in a much better position to receive the benefits of programs targeted toward low-income, disadvantaged populations than they are when the stated goals and purposes of a grant are broader. This is true because minority groups have little political influence in local and state governments generally, which is also evident in deciding how federal funds will be used.

The Republican administrations of Richard Nixon and Gerald Ford favored "decentralized" decision making in the U.S. federal system. Nixon pursued this by seeking federal grants that gave local elected officials broad discretion in how funds would be used. The General Revenue Sharing (GRS) program, now defunct, is the best example of this policy. Studies of how local governments used unrestricted GRS funds indicate that social programs and minority concerns tended *not* to receive high priority.

The Democratic Carter administration argued that the federal government faced major fiscal constraints and hence stressed the need to target scarce federal funds to the "neediest" populations. The administration's Urban Development Action Grants (UDAGs) directed federal monies to the lowest-income urban areas and sought to encourage the private sector to invest in these socioeconomically distressed areas and therefore "leverage" resources. The problems of poor inner-city minorities were to be addressed through this partnership of the federal government and the city, and through private resources.

The Republican administration of Ronald Reagan has been assessed negatively in terms of policies affecting minority communities. Critics have argued that the Reagan administration reversed many civil rights policies of recent administrations: "Even when making allowances for the differences in civil rights enforcement records of prior Republican and Democratic administrations . . . the Reagan administration's civil rights enforcement record is weaker than the record of all immediate predecessors, including its Republican counterparts" (Amaker 1988, 5). Critics claim that the federal bureaucracy under Reagan manifested a disregard for or even hostility toward civil rights in a variety of areas including education, housing, employment, and voting. The "record is replete with examples of the myriad ways in which the Reagan administration opposed the affirmative action policy of national law in every area of its responsibility" (Amaker 1988, 158). Another study, noting that levels of Hispanic poverty had increased since 1979, attributed at least part of that increase to federal budget cuts in the early 1980s (SWVRI 1988; see also Barker and McCrory 1980).

In addition to securing budget cuts, the Reagan administration had considerable legislative success in enacting its New Federalism proposals. This legislation, which generally reduced the amounts of money provided by federal grants, also changed the way in which the grants were made. There was a heavy emphasis on block grants, that is, grants to be used in specified but broader areas than categorical grants and that thus provide more flexibility to recipients when setting priorities. A second feature of Reagan's federalism approach was that state governments were the primary recipients of block grants. This was a matter of concern for some analysts because the states have often been perceived as insensitive to minority and big-city needs.

Nine block grants, which consolidated fifty-seven previously existing categorical grants, were made during the Reagan years. Notably, bilingual programs, which the Reagan administration had proposed to consolidate into the Education block grant, remained a separate, categorical grant, which was seen by many as a victory for Hispanics. The question of what impact the structure of federal grant programs has on minorities and the poor has been, and remains, an important one. In fact, "no part of the original debate over the [Reagan administration's] block grants generated more controversy than differing speculations about what would happen to the poor, minorities, and those defined as needy under specific federal aid programs" (Peterson 1986, 18).

One study of four Reagan block grants (Social Services, Community Services, Low-Income Energy Assistance, and Health Services) assessed their effects on the poor and on big cities—two categories in which minorities, including Latinos, are disproportionately represented. The evidence from which to draw implications on the use of block-grant funds defies easy categorization. Some evidence indicates that the states tightened the eligibility requirements for some programs so that the very poor received as much, if not more, help and support than previously. But this also meant that those "at the margin of income eligibility" probably lost the financial support or services that previously kept them (barely) afloat (Peterson 1986). Data on Latinos specifically (reported in SWVRI 1988), indicate that increasing num-

TABLE 6
Presidential Appointments of Minorities to Federal Courts

	Reagan	Carter	Ford	Nixon	Johnson
District courts					
Hispanics					
N	14	14	1	2	3
%	4.8	6.9	1.9	1.1	2.5
Blacks					
N	6	28	3	6	5
%	2.1	13.9	5.8	3.4	4.1
Judicial appointments					
Total	290	202	52	179	122
Courts of appeal					
Hispanics					
N	1	2	0	0	0
%	1.3	3.6	0	0	0
Blacks					
N	1	9	0	0	2
%	1.3	16.1	0	0	5.0
Judicial appointments					
Total	78	56	12	45	40

Sources: Sheldon Goldman, "Reagan's Second Term Judicial Appointments," *Judicature* 70, no. 6 (April–May 1987): 328, 331; and Barbara Hinckley and Sheldon Goldman, *American Politics and Government* (Glenview, Ill.: Scott, Foresman, 1990), 385.

bers of the group have fallen through the social safety net; perhaps they were at the margin of income eligibility.

Changes in the Community Services block grant have resulted in "lower proportions of benefits being directly targeted upon low- and moderate-income families." The state Education block grants have also given less support to "big city schools with large minority populations" than did the federal government's categorical grants (Peterson 1986). Moreover, there has been a lessening of the preferential status given to special needs educational programs, such as compensatory education for the disadvantaged and desegregation aid.

Also, big cities, areas that especially affect minority populations, have received substantially less funding than before, although some have argued that big cities previously had received considerably more funding than their proportion of disadvantaged populations (within their respective states) warranted. Therefore, that big cities may now receive less funds may only mean that the poor and needy outside the big cities are receiving a more equitable share (Peterson 1986).

Another indicator of presidential attentiveness to Latino or other minority communities lies in administration appointment practices. Reagan appointed a Hispanic as head of the Department of Education, but he appointed fewer Latinos and blacks to important positions, such as federal court judges, than his predecessor did. Table 6 presents data on presidential appointments to the federal judiciary, the federal district courts, and courts of appeals.

_____LATINOS AND CONGRESS

Congress is the nation's lawmaking body. In addition to making substantive policy, it plays a tremendously important role regarding the power to spend—the power of the purse—as a representative body, a deliberative institution, and in its oversight of the bureaucracy.

In 1988, ten members of the U.S. House of Representatives were of Latino background. There were no Latino senators; the last was Joseph Montoya, a Democrat from New Mexico, who was defeated in 1976. Latinos constitute about 2.3 percent of the House membership, while they represent about 7.5 to 8 percent of the total U.S. population. Using the common notion of representational parity (percentage of officeholders in a body divided by percentage of the total population) suggests a Latino *underrepresentation* in the House of 65 to 75 percent. About twenty-five House districts have a Latino population of 25 percent or more; in addition to those districts represented by Latinos, several districts are represented by blacks. All but two of the district representatives are Democrats.

Generally speaking, Hispanic members of Congress hold "safe seats"; their electoral margin of victory in general elections is comfortable. The percentage of the general election vote received by the ten members of Congress in 1988 averaged about 80 percent. Continuous reelection is central to gaining seniority and hence greater influence in Congress. Several Latino members of Congress were elected in the early 1960s and thus have thirty years of service in the House. Four were elected in the early 1980s, following the redistricting resulting from the 1980 census. Considering their seniority and the advantage of incumbency, the number of Latinos in Congress can be expected to at least remain stable for the next few years. Increases may occur as a result of redistricting following the 1990 census because of high Latino population growth and because Latinos are heavily concentrated in states with high overall population growth status that stand to gain new House seats.

Committees play a major role in the legislative process. Congressional scholars have classified the committees of Congress according to their substantive focus as well as their prestige. Edward Roybal, a Latino Democrat from California's 25th District is on the powerful and prestigious Appropriations Committee. Three Latinos from large urban areas—Esteban Torres from the Los Angeles sector of California, Robert Garcia of the Bronx in New York City, and Henry Gonzalez from San Antonio, Texas—are members of the Banking, Finance, and Urban Affairs Committee. Two are members of the Education and Labor Committee. Thus several Hispanics in Congress serve on committees that, research suggests, can have an impact on substantive policy or policy committees.

Since 1989, Texas Democrat Henry Gonzalez has chaired the Banking Committee, and another Texas Democrat, Kika de la Garza, the Agriculture Committee. The issues that these committees deal with are especially salient to Latinos because of their heavy urban concentration and social policy concerns, such as educational achievement, unemployment, and the like. These policy committees may, in view of the concerns of the Latino community, be similar to a third kind of committee, the "constituency" committee.

CONGRESSIONAL HISPANIC CAUCUS

The Congressional Hispanic Caucus was formed in 1977 with the goal of monitoring legislation and "other governmental activity that affects Hispanics" and to "develop programs and other activities that would increase opportunities for Hispanics to participate in and contribute to the American political system" (Vigil 1987, 65). Nevertheless, according to one analyst, the caucus has not functioned as a unified group within Congress. Instead, it has acted more as a "loose coalition of Congressmen who wield individual power" (Vigil 1987). Their placement and seniority on committees is the source of much of the individual power these congressmen possess.

_____POLICY REPRESENTATION

One central question is the extent to which Congress supports policies that are in accord with the policy preferences of Latinos–Hispanics. A 1984 study examined this question with the assumption that "Hispanics, on the whole [would] be more liberal than Anglos, more likely to favor government intervention in the marketplace and in protecting individual rights" (Welch and Hibbing 1988). The study found that in the 93rd to 96th Congresses (1972 to 1980), Hispanic representatives had voting records nearly thirteen points less conservative (or more liberal), than non-Hispanic representatives. (The study controlled for various factors, such as percentage in poverty and percentage of urban in the district, and party affiliation of the representative.) This pattern was strongest in the southwestern states, where Hispanic representatives "on average, compiled voting records over 23 points less conservative than non-Hispanic representatives" (Welch and Hibbing 1988).

Overall, it was found that there was a (statistically) significant relationship between percentage of *Hispanic constituents* (for all House districts with 5 percent or more Hispanic, regardless of the representative's ethnic background) and less conservative roll-call voting. But that relationship was not very powerful. Welch and Hibbing concluded that Hispanics did not lack influence in the House; "they just lack the influence their numbers warrant."

Based on data presented earlier regarding Latino ideological self-identification and policy preferences, one might question whether the expectation or assumption that Latinos are frequently liberals is entirely appropriate. In any event, it is useful to focus on some data regarding Latinos in Congress. Table 7 suggest that Hispanics in Congress, as measured by their 1986 scores by the Americans for Democratic Action (ADA, a liberal organization), are, on the whole, not particularly liberal. On the one hand, most have high ADA scores, particularly the representatives from California plus Garcia from New York City. On the other hand, Manuel Lujan, at the time of the study the only Republican among the Hispanics in Congress, had a very low liberalism score (5), and several Latino House members from south Texas had middle-range scores (45 to 55).

These data are useful in themselves, and they may aid in examining an important question: To the extent that Hispanics in Congress exhibit a high degree of congruence in voting and issue positions, is it because of similar partisan, ideological, and constitutuency (economic)

TABLE 7
Latinos in Congress, 1988

State and Representative	Percentage Spanish Origin in District	Year Entered House	Committee(s)	ADA 1986 Score	SWVRI 1988 Score
California					
Roybal	57	1963	Appropriations	95	100
Martinez	48	1982	Education–Labor	85	100
			Government Operations		
Torres	42	1983	Banking–Finance–	90	100
			Urban Affairs		
New Mexico					
Lujan (R)	33	1969	Interior	5	47
			Science		
Richardson	37	1983	Commerce	75	93
New York					
Garcia	49	1979	Banking–Finance–	95	100
			Urban Affairs		
			Post Office		
Texas					
de la Garza	66	1965	Agriculture	55	100
Gonzalez	56	1963	Banking–Finance–	95	100
			Urban Affairs		
			Small Business		
Bustamante	51	1985	Armed Services	50	100
			Government Operations		
Ortiz	55	1985	Armed Services	45	67
			Merchant Marine		

Note: Munger (1988) developed a ranking system for House committees as follows: 1./2. Ways and Means, and Appropriations (1.00); 3. Rules (.938); 4. Commerce (.813); 5. Armed Services (.667); 6. Foreign Affairs (.563); 7. Budget (.50); 8. Interior (.429); 9. Banking, Finance and Urban Affairs (.364); 10. Agriculture (.273); 11. Education and Labor (.263); 12. Government Operations (.250); 13. Small Business (.231); 14. Science (.225); 15. Merchant Marine (.20); 16. Post Office (.20); 17. Judiciary (.182); 18. Veterans Affairs (.154); Public Works (.136).

Sources: *Congressional Quarterly* (1989, 1983); SWVRI (1989).

interests, or because they view themselves as "Hispanic politicians," or because of their membership in the Hispanic Caucus? (Vigil 1987, 69). There can be some unity in voting patterns without concerted action.

To assess this and related questions further, I decided to update the 1984 research by Welch and Hibbing on Latino substantive representation in Congress. I examined a measure of congressional voting on Latino issues in the 100th Congress (1987–1988) developed by the Southwest Voter Research Institute (SWVRI), relative to percentage Hispanic in the district and other variables considered earlier by Welch and Hibbing. The SWVRI analysis included votes on several domestic social service issues, such as the homeless, civil rights, and legal services, as well as several foreign policy issues, for example, aid to the Nicaraguan *contras*.

Unlike Welch and Hibbing, I found that the percentage Hispanic among a representative's constituents had no independent impact on congressional voting after the impact of other variables was accounted for. The major variable that explains voting on Latino issues (at least in the 100th Congress) is representatives' political party affiliation; percentage urban and percentage in poverty in representatives' districts also have some impact. That is, to the extent that representatives cast votes consistent with Latino preferences, it is because of these influences, not the proportion of Hispanics in the district per se.

On the other hand, it is notable that the outcome of the fifteen votes in the House of Representatives used to construct the SWVRI Latino support score, were *all* in the manner preferred, or the manner seen as the "right way to vote" by SWVRI. There may thus be responsiveness without representation. Stated otherwise, the substantive representation of Latino concerns was not *predicted* in the way or by the variables that might be anticipated, that is, percentage Latino in the constituency. But there was a "complete" *degree* of substantive representation of Latino concerns in the 100th Congress (Weissberg 1978).

The data also indicate that Latino members of Congress are on the whole more liberal than the average congressperson but less liberal than blacks. And, as a group, Latino representatives' voting patterns suggest less cohesion than is found among blacks. The average score for Latinos on the Americans for Democratic Action (ADA) index, which is an indicator of liberalism, in 1986 was 72.6 (80.1 if Manuel Lujan, the only Latino Republican, is excluded); that for blacks was 91.3. Latinos are also less cohesive, as indicated by the higher standard deviation for Latino representatives than for blacks. The standard deviation for blacks is 6.6, while that for Latinos is 28.2 (it is 16.2 if Lujan is excluded).

———THE FEDERAL COURTS

For some time, particularly from the mid 1950s to the late 1960s when Earl Warren served as chief justice, the U.S. Supreme Court was viewed as a major supporter of minority concerns. In those years the Court handed down a number of decisions that were consistent with the legal and political preferences of civil rights and minority rights groups.

Minorities have often sought to use the courts to champion their cause because legal structures and processes may be more congenial to minority concerns. Minorities focus on courts as important policy-makers for two main reasons. Courts presumably make decisions on the basis of legal arguments, apart from popular beliefs and prejudices. And addressing public policy concerns through the courts often requires fewer, and different, resources than are needed to influence "political" institutions.

Nevertheless, there are limitations to the courts' ability to have their decisions implemented because the courts lack "the power of the purse" and "the power of the sword." That is, the courts often must rely on the executive and legislative branches to enforce decisions. Also, when minorities seek to address collective (i.e., group-based) issues and problems, they generally confront the issue that the Constitution protects *individuals* and individual rights, not *groups* and group-based rights or claims for government benefits or privileges. Indeed, these and related distinctions have been at the center of numerous court decisions.

In seeking policy outcomes through the courts, then, Latinos and other ethnic–racial groups face a dilemma. The political arena generally is a majoritarian one. Success in this arena typically requires the marshaling of electoral or legislative majorities or other forms of coalition building, a particularly difficult task for groups that are clear numerical and political–social *minorities*. The legal arena is generally not majoritarian in the same way because when decisions are based on legal arguments, outcomes may be antimajoritarian. But the legal arena seems best able to address only the most apparent or obvious instances where individuals are denied equal protection of the laws because they are members of a group. Relatedly, the courts have held that only *absolute*, rather than *relative*, deprivation or unequal treatment is necessary to provide judicial relief for minority grievances. These difficulties and paradoxes have been evident in a number of cases.

School finance has been a central focus of Latino legal attention. Latinos and other minority groups have challenged the way that money is raised to support schools. In many states, the major source of school revenues is the property tax. Latinos have challenged this mechanism because it means that the amount of money raised for education depends heavily on the quantity and value of property within a school district. For instance, in San Antonio, Texas, residents of the poor, largely Hispanic Edgewood Independent School District pay a tax of almost $1 per $100 of assessed property. But because the district is poor, and because part of it houses an air force base, which is tax-exempt, the high tax rate translates into only $3,596 per student. In contrast, in another district in south Texas, one that is "oil rich," property taxes are only 8 cents per $100 of assessed valuation, but this generates $12,000 per student.

The U.S. Supreme Court has not agreed with the Latino argument that these revenue mechanisms violate the Constitution's equal protection clause (Fourteenth Amendment). In 1973, the Court ruled in a 5–4 decision (*San Antonio* v. *Rodriguez*) that the Texas system of school finance did "not operate to the peculiar disadvantage of any suspect class." The Court majority asserted that Mexican Americans grounded their case in terms of indigency—being poor—rather than with respect to a "legitimately" suspect classification, such as race. And, the majority opinion added, the poor Mexican American litigants claimed that there was a relative deprivation; there was little or no evidence of absolute deprivation. *Absolute* deprivation, the Court majority suggested, would probably be grounds for overturning the Texas method for financing its schools. The Court also held that funding for education is *not* a fundamental right under the Constitution. (Since this case, the Texas Supreme Court, and supreme courts in a number of other states, have overturned school-financing systems under *state* constitutional provisions.)

School desegregation and bilingual education are other areas where federal court decisions have affected Latinos. There have been several state and federal court decisions, including the landmark *Brown* decision in 1954, but the status of Hispanics regarding desegregation was not clarified until the 1973 *Keyes* decision. As part of that case, the

Supreme Court made an important judgment regarding the definition of a group, deciding that "Mexican Americans were an identifiable minority group and constitutionally entitled to recognition as such for desegregation purposes" (Meier and Stewart 1991, 70).

Despite the *Keyes* decision, Latino groups have not pushed hard for desegregation; instead, they have emphasized bilingual education. In a major bilingual education case, *Lau* v. *Nichols* in 1974, filed on behalf of Chinese students, "the Court found that the failure of school districts to provide non-English speaking students instruction that they could understand denied them their right to equal educational opportunity" (Meier and Stewart 1991, 76). This decision buttressed Latino claims for specific education programs.

Voting rights is another crucial issue for Latinos. A central statute in this regard is the Voting Rights Act of 1965 and its 1975 and 1982 amendments. These laws have brought a number of electoral processes at local government level under federal government scrutiny, requiring local governments to undertake special efforts, such as the provision of bilingual ballots, to assure the protection of "language minorities" (Thernstrom 1987, 50–52). The federal courts also have made determinations regarding local government electoral practices, including at-large elections, the drawing of city council district boundaries, and city annexations that may result in "diluting" a minority's chances in an election. The Supreme Court, for instance, in *Thornburgh* v. *Gingles* (1986) specified factors that it considers relevant to determining when vote dilution is present (see Neighbor 1988, 111). More recently, federal courts decided that the City of Dallas must revamp its election procedure because minorities had tremendous difficulty winning under the system in place, and in California, the districts used to elect the Los Angeles County Board of Supervisors inappropriately blocked the election of Hispanics.

Affirmative action is one more issue on which the courts have rendered decisions significant for Latinos. Although several of these cases have involved situations where blacks were primarily affected, the decisions have direct implications for Latinos. One particularly illustrative case should be discussed at some length.

In January 1989, the Supreme Court struck down a program in Richmond, Virginia, that set aside 30 percent of its public works contracts to be awarded to "minority business enterprises" (defined as businesses that are 51 percent or more minority owned). The city claimed that the program's purpose was "remedial"; that is, the program was created because only about 1 percent of the city's public works contracts had been awarded to minority business enterprises in the years immediately preceding the program's enactment in 1983. At the time, Richmond had a black population of about 55 percent, and five of the nine Richmond City Council members were black.

Writing for the Court majority, Justice Sandra Day O'Connor argued as follows: The rights guaranteed in the Constitution are individual, not group, rights. The Richmond program grants benefits to some and "denies [to other] certain citizens the opportunity to compete for a fixed percentage of public contracts based solely upon their race." Although the city claimed that the program was undertaken to rectify past wrongs, "absent searching judicial inquiry into the justification for such race-based measures, there is simply no way of determining what classifications are 'benign' or 'remedial' and what classifications are in fact motivated by illegitimate notions of racial inferiority or simple racial politics." The simple assertion, or "mere recitation," of benign or legitimate purpose "is entitled to little or no weight." Further, "racial classifications are suspect, and that means that simple legislative assurance of good intention cannot suffice."

The City of Richmond sought to justify the program largely on the basis of the gap between the percentage of blacks in the population (55 percent) and the percentage of contracts awarded to minorities (1 percent). O'Connor viewed this gap as an "amorphous claim," adding that "it is sheer speculation how many minority firms there would be in Richmond absent past societal discrimination" and that to define these gaps as "'identified discrimination' would give local governments license to create a patchwork of racial preferences based on statistical generalizations about any particular field of endeavor." O'Connor was arguing, then, that specific discrimination against particular individuals or particular businesses had not been demonstrated: "The 30 percent quota cannot in any realistic sense be tied to any injury suffered by anyone." Indeed, O'Connor and the justices who concurred in the decision argued strongly that broad claims of "societal discrimination" could not be used as evidence of discrimination to support the Richmond ordinance. Relatedly, O'Connor argued that the remedy, the 30 percent set-aside, was not sufficiently or specifically tailored to the alleged problem in that the policy extended to minority business enterprises outside Richmond and to groups other than blacks; that is, it also applied to Hispanics and other protected class groups that were hardly visible in Richmond.

Part of the grounds for these claims is O'Connor's related assertion that when special qualifications are required to be eligible for a benefit, such as the qualifications presumed necessary to be a business person–contractor, discrimination cannot be inferred simply from numerical or statistical "gaps." If "special qualifications" are not necessary for selection, such as might be true for low- or entry-level government jobs, then large statistical gaps may be sufficient evidence of discrimination. O'Connor also contended that minorities in Richmond were able to protect themselves in the political–governmental arena because blacks constituted a majority on the Richmond City Council. Had the council not been a "majority minority" one, O'Connor might have viewed the policy as at least somewhat less suspect.

Dissenting, Justice Thurgood Marshall criticized the Court majority for "second guessing" Richmond's effort to rectify past discrimination. Marshall also argued that governmental actions intended to help minorities overcome past discrimination should be judged by a more flexible standard, one that takes the country's racial history into account. "A profound difference separates governmental actions that themselves are racist, and governmental actions that seek to remedy the effects of prior racism or to prevent neutral governmental activity from perpetuating the effects of such racism." Marshall also disagreed with the Court majority in terms of the scope and depth of evidence that might appropriately be brought in examining the case. Marshall pointed to various reports by Congress indicating much discrimination in the construction industry nationally, data that had, in fact, been considered by the Court in its decision to *uphold* a federal government set-aside program. (The Court majority deflected this point, suggesting that the federal government, under the Fourteenth Amendment, has powers beyond those of state and local governments to undertake remedial policies.)

Marshall also claimed that there was substantial evidence of discrimination in Richmond in other areas of public policy. He noted that Richmond had been found in an earlier Court case to have discriminated in school segregation and voting rights. Moreover, Marshall contended that the Court was imposing a "daunting standard" on "states and localities contemplating the use of race-conscious measures" to redress discrimination.

A number of cities and states had established policies resembling Richmond's. Denver, Colorado, for instance, with the encouragement of its Hispanic mayor, Federico Peña, had expanded existing minority contracting policies. But the *Richmond* v. *Croson* decision led cities to reassess their minority contracting and perhaps other affirmative action policies. The Richmond case is also important because the Court majority clearly rejected claims of structural or institutional discrimination and was willing to address only specific, clearly identifiable discrimination. This approach, according to Marshall and minority-group advocates, places a difficult burden on those who support affirmative action. And discrimination, if it is primarily "institutional," rather than visible and intentional, is especially difficult to prove. This may be even more true for Latinos, whose historical situation in the United States is quite complex.

It is clear, then, that the federal courts have had a major impact on Latino politics in the role that these courts play in interpreting statutes and the Constitution. According to legal scholars, the federal courts have developed a "multi-tier approach to equal protection analysis" (Ducat and Chase 1988, 634). In the upper tier, where the Supreme Court exercises strict scrutiny, are such fundamental rights as voting and the examination of certain race classifications. The implication of this for Latinos seems to be that because they have not always been defined *racially*, they have been in a difficult position to make certain legal claims and arguments.

Intermediate scrutiny of equal protection is followed in the middle tier: This level of scrutiny has been applied to such matters as race in affirmative action cases (e.g., *Bakke*) and "alienage, where children of illegal aliens are barred from public education" (see Chapter 4 re MALDEF and the *Plyler* case). Finally, with respect to the lower tier, the Court has generally determined that such classifications as indigency are *not* constitutionally suspect and that such "rights" as education, housing, and welfare are *not* fundamental rights. At this level, many, perhaps most, of the substantive policy concerns of minority groups, Latinos and blacks, concentrate. Given the present Court's perception of such policies, Latinos and blacks are almost certain to find the Court an· *unreceptive* avenue to lead to desired political pronouncements.

_____SUMMARY AND CONCLUSION

This chapter has examined the ways and extent to which Latinos have been affected by the institutions of the national government, and vice versa. The text suggested certain conditions necessary for Latinos to have an impact on presidential elections and indicated that those conditions have seldom been met. After pointing out the numerous and important roles presidents play in the American political system, the chapter reviewed presidential policies and activities over the past thirty years. Most carefully assessed were the policies of the Reagan administration; the evidence from major studies suggested that the policies of that administration have probably been detrimental to Latinos.

We examined the degree of "substantive" and "descriptive" representation of Latinos in Congress and considered the status (committee assignments, etc.) of Latinos in that lawmaking body. The proportion of Latinos in Congress is much lower than "parity," and the evidence regarding substantive representation is unclear. That is, the limited evidence available indicates, on the one hand, that there is little or no impact of the percentage of Latinos in a district and voting on Latino issues, on the other hand, evidence (from the 100th Congress) indicates that all the votes thought to be especially important to Latinos were decided in the "preferred" way. Susbstantive representation of Latinos may be high, but it is not well predicted by certain variables.

Finally, we considered the importance of the courts. There are benefits and disadvantages in relying on the courts to make policies in the direction preferred by Latinos. In the past few years, the courts have rendered decisions in several areas of concern to Latinos. *Richmond* v. *Croson* indicates that the Supreme Court has raised the standards of proof regarding, and is less willing to accept arguments concerning, group-based or institutional discrimination.

Overall, the evidence indicates that the Latino presence in institutions of the national government is limited. The evidence also indicates that to the extent that governmental policies are consistent with Latino preferences, those policies do not necessarily result from responsiveness to Latino political influence.

As important as the national institutions are, they are not the sole policymakers in the U.S. political system. The states also make policy; and to state governments we next turn.

6

Latinos and State Politics

_____The federal structure of the U.S. political system places state governments in a major—some would even say primary—role as policymakers and political institutions in the domestic arena of U.S. government. State governments are responsible for drawing district boundaries for the U.S. House of Representatives and their own legislatures. These districts can affect levels of representation. Also, local governments are creatures of the state; they are created and shaped by state governments. How, and whether, local governments are to be created (or "incorporated"); what they can or cannot do once created; the extent of their annexation powers; what procedures must be followed in policymaking; and how much revenue local governments raise are all important aspects of the state government prerogative. In some instances, even local government fragmentation has been attributed to state legislatures' efforts to diminish the political power of ethnic groups (Nice 1983). In a number of ways, both directly and indirectly, understanding local politics requires a knowledge of state politics. In this chapter we consider Latinos and state politics.

There is a vast body of research on politics in the states, but very little of it has specifically addressed whether or how Latinos have shaped state politics or, conversely, the impact of politics in particular states on Latinos. Absent much direct research, this chapter draws on and tries to link the broader research on U.S. state politics and issues of Latino politics. The focus, then, is the socioeconomic environment, the political–cultural context, the nature of state government institutions, and public policies in states with a large Latino population. Also examined are the implications of those factors for Latinos. In addition, the chapter discusses the available research that has specifically examined Latinos and state politics.

—————THE LATINO PRESENCE IN VARIOUS STATES

Five states have a Latino population of 12 percent or more; in several other states, Latinos constitute just under 10 percent of the population. New Mexico has the highest proportion of Latinos, about 38 percent, followed by California and Texas with about 25 percent each. Arizona and Colorado have Latino populations of about 18 and 12 percent, respectively. In sheer numbers, California clearly has the nation's largest Latino population. These states differ not only with respect to the proportion of Latinos in the population but also in the social and political histories of Hispanics in the southwestern states. According to Garcia and de la Garza (1977), the relationship between Chicanos and Anglos in Texas historically has been conflictual; in New Mexico, there has been a more positive relationship (see also Acuña 1988).

Outside the Southwest, Florida and New York both have about 10 percent Hispanic populations, concentrated in Miami and New York City. Florida's population is mostly of Cuban background, while New York's is primarily Puerto Rican.

These broad percentages do not indicate some important points about the Latino populations in these states. There are differences in nationality backgrounds, self-identification, and other characteristics. General differences with respect to group self-identification, discussed earlier, are notable also within states and are in turn related to other issues. Data from late 1988 indicate that in New Mexico, almost two-thirds of Latinos consider themselves of "Other Spanish" national origin, while about one-third consider themselves Mexican (SWVRI 1988). The most common self-identification among Colorado Hispanics is Spanish (26.6 percent), followed by Mexican American (24.8 percent) and Hispanic (22 percent) (LARASA 1989). In California, almost 80 percent say they are of Mexican origin, while only 8 percent consider themselves "Other Spanish." Moreover, it is not clear that Hispanics in New Mexico and California have the same thing in mind when they refer to a "Spanish" or "Other Spanish" background. There are also differences in the several states in the proportions of Hispanics who are native-born. For example, Colorado's Hispanic population is 90 percent native-born; in California, many of the Hispanics are non-citizens.

There are also differences within the states with respect to the presence of other ethnic–racial groups. California has an Asian population of about 6 percent and a black population of more than 7 percent; Texas, too, has a sizable black population (12 percent). Black and Asian populations tend to be small in several other southwestern states; however, Arizona and New Mexico have Native American populations of 6 and 8 percent, respectively. To the extent that the different groups compete politically, or seek to form coalitions, the situation will differ among the states.

————THE SOCIOECONOMIC ENVIRONMENT

Consistent with attention to the broader context within which Latino politics occurs, data regarding the socioeconomic environment in the states with large Latino populations deserve attention. One factor to consider is socioeconomic equality or the lack of it; that is, what is the distribution of wealth among the people in a state, as measured by the gini coefficient, a measure of inequality (see Table 8)? Wealth distribution is important because research indicates that the greater the socioeconomic *inequality*, the more negative is the political setting for minority groups (Dye 1969). Among the southwestern states, overall income inequality is greatest in Texas; income inequality there is well above the average for the fifty states. Inequality in Arizona is also above the fifty-state average. In New Mexico, equality is near the overall average, while in Colorado and California there is greater equality than pertains overall. Of the states not in the Southwest, New York and Illinois have relatively low levels of income *in*equality, while general income inequality is high in Florida.

Table 8 also presents data on per capita income and poverty levels in the states. A great deal of research indicates that a state's general political environment and *policy outputs* specifically are greatly affected by the levels of resources available and the policy needs in the state. By both indicators (income and poverty), New Mexico is the least-well-off Hispanic state. It has the seventh-lowest per capita income of the fifty states and is in the top six ("worst") in terms of poverty levels. Of the other southwestern states, California and Colorado both rank pos-

TABLE 8
General Income Inequality in States with Substantial Latino
Populations

Income Inequality (gini coefficients)		Per Capita Income/Rank among States		Percentage in Poverty Rank among States	
Arizona	.445	$12,795	(28)	31.2	(17)
California	.427	16,065	(5)	11.4	(26)
Colorado	.425	14,812	(9)	10.1	(37)
New Mexico	.440	10,914	(43)	17.6	(5.5)
Texas	.464	13,483	(21)	14.7	(13)
		(lower rank = "better")		(higher rank = "better")	
Five-state average	.432				
Florida	.462	$13,742	(19)	13.5	(14)
Illinois	.423	14,738	(10)	11.0	(27)
New York	.429	16,050	(6)	13.4	(15.5)
U.S. as a whole	.439				

Note: The gini coefficient reported in the first column is an indicator of the degree of *inequality* in the distribution of wealth; thus, the higher the coefficient, the greater the inequality.

Source: Thomas R. Dyer, "Inequality and Civil Rights Policy in the States," from *Journal of Politics*, pp. 1080–1097, 31:4 November 1969. By permission of the author and the University of Texas Press.

itively in levels of per capita income and have fairly low poverty levels. Arizona and Texas lie between the several other southwestern states. Outside the Southwest, Illinois and New York are relatively well-off states, while Florida is somewhat less so. One would expect greater equality and higher levels of wealth (e.g., higher per capita income) to be associated with a context that would be supportive of minority political and policy concerns.

Data comparing the socioeconomic status of the Hispanic population with those of other groups within the southwestern states are presented in Table 9. These data underscore the socioeconomic disadvantage of Hispanics relative to Anglos; they also indicate the lower status of Latinos relative to other minorities with respect to education (percentage of high school graduates).

_____POLITICAL CULTURE

A state's political culture can also help in understanding state politics and policy. Political culture is "the particular pattern of orientation to political action in which each political system is imbedded" and is important as "the historical source of differences in habits, perspectives and attitudes that influence life in the various states" (Elazar 1984, 109–110). According to Elazar, there are three basic political cultures in the American states: individualist, moralist, and traditionalist.

The individualist culture implies a conception of politics as a marketplace, a perception that government is instituted for strictly utilitarian reasons. Politics is "another means by which individuals may improve themselves socially and economically." In this culture, politicians hold public office "as a means of controlling the distribution of the favors or rewards of government rather than as a means of exercising governmental power for programmatic ends" (Elazar 1984, 109–110). That is, the focus of politics is on tangible material rewards, rather than issues and substantive policy concerns.

In the moralist culture, politics "is considered one of the great activities of humanity in its search for the good society . . . an effort to exercise power for the betterment of the commonwealth." Government is considered to be a positive instrument with a responsibility to promote some notion of the general good and general welfare. Issues and substantive policies are central in this political culture (Elazar 1984, 117–118). In the traditionalist political culture, the emphasis is on maintaining the status quo; the role of government is to secure the continued maintenance of the existing social order.

Political culture shapes many aspects of state government, including what are seen as the appropriate spheres of governmental activity; the willingness to initiate and accept new and innovative programs; and the role and purposes of political parties. Few discussions of political culture in the states have addressed the impact of a state's culture on Latinos and politics. And there has been little suggestion in this literature that Latinos have had any significant role in the creation or development of state political cultures (see however, Holmes 1967; Mla-

TABLE 9
Socioeconomic Status of Latinos and Others in Southwestern States, 1980

	Whites	Latinos	Blacks	Native Americans
Arizona				
High school graduates (%)	76.1	44.4	60.6	42.4
Parity with whites	—	.583	.796	.557
Median family income ($)	19,947	15,468	13,724	10,371
Parity with whites	—	.775	.688	.520
Below poverty (%)	6.9	16.8	20.6	15.2
Parity with whites	—	.379	.335	.454
Unemployed (%)	5.5	8.8	11.2	14.4
Parity with whites	—	.625	.491	.382
California				
High school graduates (%)	76.6	43.6	68.5	65.7
Parity with whites	—	.569	.894	.858
Median family income ($)	22,748	16,081	14,887	16,548
Parity with whites	—	.707	.654	.727
Below poverty (%)	6.5	16.8	20.6	15.2
Parity with whites	—	.387	.316	.428
Unemployed (%)	5.8	9.6	11.1	11.8
Parity with whites	—	.604	.523	.492
Colorado				
High school graduates (%)	80.2	48.6	74.4	68.1
Parity with whites	—	.606	.928	.849
Median family income ($)	21,822	15,412	15,732	15,339
Parity with whites	—	.706	.721	.703
Below poverty (%)	6.2	18.4	18.7	19.1
Parity with whites	—	.337	.332	.325
Unemployed (%)	4.6	9.4	8.7	10.7
Parity with whites	—	.489	.529	.430

denka and Hill 1986). Nevertheless, Elazar's (1984) discussion makes it appear that political cultures have developed partly *in response to* the presence of minority groups. The best example of this is that the traditionalist culture has been seen as one heavily focused on maintaining black and other minority subordination in the southern states.

Notwithstanding the scholarly inattention to Latinos and state polit-

TABLE 9–Continued

	Whites	Latinos	Blacks	Native Americans
New Mexico				
High school graduates (%)	73.4	50.6	62.8	74.7
Parity with whites	—	.691	.856	1.02
Median family income ($)	18,429	13,512	12,063	10,826
Parity with whites	—	.733	.655	.587
Below poverty (%)	15.3	29.3	33.8	45.7
Parity with whites	—	.522	.453	.335
Unemployed (%)	5.9	9.3	13.1	14.6
Parity with whites	—	.634	.450	.404
Texas				
High school graduates (%)	65.7	35.5	53.0	63.2
Parity with whites	—	.540	.807	.962
Median family income ($)	20,955	13,293	13,042	17,302
Parity with whites	—	.634	.622	.826
Below poverty (%)	12.1	33.3	31.8	18.6
Parity with whites	—	.363	.381	.651
Unemployed (%)	3.4	6.4	6.9	5.8
Parity with whites	—	.531	.493	.586

Source: U.S. Census Bureau, *1980 Census of Population, Detailed Population Characteristics* (Washington, DC: Department of Commerce, 1983), selected states.

ical culture, the descriptions of political cultures summarized here would lead to the expectation that the moralist culture is the most conducive and most receptive of minority groups because of its presumed concern for the good of all. The traditionalist culture would seem the most detrimental to Latinos, and to blacks, because it stresses maintaining the status quo, a social order that generally has been hostile toward these groups. Finally, the individualist culture would probably lie somewhere between the moralist and traditionalist in its expected effects on minority-group politics.

What are the political cultures of the Latino states? According to Elazar, Colorado has a moralist political culture and California has one that is primarily moralist with individualism as a secondary influence. Both New Mexico and Texas are categorized as primarily traditionalist

TABLE 10
Political Ideology in "Latino" States

	Average Score	% Liberal	% Moderate	% Conservative
Arizona	.195	17.2	41.0	35.5
California	.041	25.4	38.5	29.2
Colorado	.089	22.9	40.7	31.4
New Mexico	.156	21.8	34.8	36.3
Texas	.225	16.4	37.5	36.8
Five-state average	.141	20.7	38.5	33.8
Florida	.149	20.3	38.3	34.1
Illinois	.122	19.6	41.9	30.9
New York	.056	25.2	37.6	30.4
Fifty-state average	.124	20.6	39.1	32.0

Note: Lower average score indicates more liberal.

Source: Gerald C. Wright, Robert S. Erikson, and John P. McIver, "Measuring State Partisanship and Ideology with Survey Data," from *Journal of Politics* 47, no. 2 (May 1985): 469–489. By permission of the authors and the University of Texas Press.

with secondary individualist tendencies, and Arizona's culture is primarily traditionalist with secondary moralist influence (Elazar 1984, 135). Florida and New York are described as having traditionalist–individualist and individualist–moralist cultures, respectively.

Generally, these contexts alone, that is without respect to the proportion of the population that is Latino, would lead to the expectation that the most favorable settings for Latino political influence would be Colorado and California, with relatively less influence possible in New Mexico, Texas, and Arizona. Although this is important, it should also be noted that the states vary in their proportion of Latino populations.

_____POLITICAL IDEOLOGY

Somewhat related to political culture is political ideology. We can examine the states in terms of the ideology of state residents, that is, residents' self-identification on a liberal–conservative continuum (Wright, Erikson, and McIver 1985). As seen in Table 10, people in California and Colorado self-identify toward the liberal end of the political spectrum, considerably more so than the fifty-state average. People in the other three states with substantial Latino populations are more conservative than the fifty-state average, especially Texans. These patterns generally are consistent with those regarding political culture as discussed by Elazar and would, again, imply that Colorado and California might be the states most receptive to minority political influence. New Mexico would rank third in this group, and then Arizona and Texas. Outside the Southwest, New York ranks as highly liberal, Illinois as moderate, and Florida as relatively conservative.

Along with the overall ideological pattern, another item in the table is worthy of note. Not only are Texas and Arizona the two most conservative states overall, the liberal–conservative split is also greatest in these two states. In Texas, 21 percent more of the population identify themselves as conservative than liberal; in Arizona, the spread is more than 18 percent. In contrast, the liberal–conservative spread in California and Colorado is 3.8 and 8.5, respectively. In short, there are not only overall differences but the dispersion of ideology also is quite different among the states. There are no directly comparable data on Latino ideological identification for the same time period, but some recent evidence would suggest that in California, New Mexico, and Texas, Mexican Americans tend to be more liberal or moderate than the non-Latino population. Again, patterns may be found to be somewhat different within the individual states.

—————PARTY COMPETITION AND ITS POLICY RELEVANCE

Scholars have theorized that for social and political have-nots to obtain real influence and desired political outcomes in state politics, two conditions are necessary: There must be significant levels of competition between the political parties, and party competition must be "policy relevant." "Only if the parties reflect different class constituencies, the party activists are concerned with policy issues, and the party of the have-nots gains control of state government, can we then expect party politics to result in increased welfare expenditures" (Dye 1984,1114). The assumption is that have-not groups favor welfare expenditures as a way of alleviating social and economic problems. The have-nots include the poor and Latino and other minority groups, particularly Mexican Americans and Puerto Ricans. This body of thought has implications for Latino politics.

Let us look more closely at the necessary political conditions. First, the two major political parties (Democratic and Republican) must be competitive; that is, control of the major institutions of state government—the governorship and state legislature—must be seriously contested and not dominated by one party or the other. Second, for the have-nots to gain political influence, the parties must reflect different social-class constituencies. Ethnic–racial constituencies would also seem to factor in here, for the data examined earlier clearly indicate that minority groups are disproportionately represented among the poor and otherwise socioeconomically disadvantaged. Finally, party competition must be *policy relevant;* that is, it must revolve around programs and issues and not be solely a question of patronage.

We can draw a party and policy profile of the states with substantial Latino populations from Dye's 1984 study. The study indicates that of the five southwestern states, only California has *both* competitive and policy-relevant political parties. Colorado's party competition is not fully competitive—it is "mixed"—and party competition is not policy relevant. Arizona, New Mexico, and Texas have both *noncompetitive and non-policy-relevant parties.* Thus, with the exception of California, and possibly Colorado, political party and policy processes in these states do *not* appear conducive to policies that would be generally perceived as directly salient for poor and minority groups. Outside the Southwest, New York and Illinois both have competitive but non-policy-relevant parties, and Florida has neither party competition nor policy-relevant parties (Dye 1984).

STATE LEGISLATURES
LATINOS IN THE LEGISLATURES

Another factor to consider is the degree of Latino presence, or "descriptive" or "sociological" representation (see Chapter 5) in state governing bodies. Table 11 indicates the numbers, percentages, and parity ratios for Chicanos in state legislatures (percentage in the legislative body is divided by percentage in the state as a whole) in 1987 and 1973. Latinos in New Mexico have achieved parity, while Latinos in the other states fall short in either or both chambers of the state legislature.

TABLE 11
Latinos in State Legislatures, 1987

	House			Senate			Overall Parity, 1973
	N	%	Parity	N	%	Parity	
Arizona	5 of 60	8.3	.50	5 of 30	16.7	1.03	.59
California	5 of 80	6.3	.33	3 of 40	7.5	.39	.27
Colorado	5 of 65	7.7	.65	3 of 35	8.6	.73	.31
New Mexico	26 of 70	37.1	1.01	13 of 42	30.9	.84	.85
Texas	19 of 150	12.7	.60	6 of 31	16.1	.77	.30
Five-state average			.62			.75	.46

Sources: 1987 data calculated by author from Arthur Martinez, *Who's Who: Chicano Officeholders, 1987–1988.* Overall parity for 1973 calculated from Garcia and de la Garza 1977.

Notably, the largest parity deficit is in California, a state that might be expected to be much closer to representational parity based on its ostensibly supportive political environment, as indicated by political culture, ideological patterns, and low levels of socioeconomic inequality. While research at this point does not provide a definitive answer, several factors may explain the disjunction between expectations and actual outcomes in descriptive representational parity. California's Latinos are most heavily concentrated in the southern part of the state, which is generally considered to be more conservative than northern California. Also, allegations of ethnic–racial gerrymandering in southern California are legion. These allegations primarily have been made regarding *local* elections, and a 1990 federal court found that there had indeed been gerrymandering in Los Angeles County. Gerrymandering at the local level would certainly be expected to have broader and longer-term implications at the state level, since candidates often follow a path from local to higher (i.e., state) office. A final point to be noted in the table is that the level of Latino presence in these state legislatures increased considerably between 1973 and 1987.

_____THE QUALITY OF THE LEGISLATURES

The representativeness of a state legislature is indeed an important dimension to consider, but other aspects are also relevant. Research has examined the quality and professionalism of state legisla-

TABLE 12
Legislatures in "Latino" States: Overall Ranking and FAIIR Rankings

Overall	State	FAIIR Rankings				
		Func-tional	Ac-countable	In-formed	Inde-pendent	Repre-sentative
1	Calif.	1	3	2	3	2
11	N.Mex.	3	16	28	39	4
28	Colo.	21	25	21	28	27
38	Tex.	45	36	43	45	17
43	Ariz.	11	47	38	17	50
2	N.Y.	4	13	1	8	1
3	Ill.	17	4	6	2	13
4	Fla.	5	8	4	1	30

Sources: The Sometimes Governments: A Critical Study of the American Legislatures, 2d ed. (Kansas City, Mo.: Citizens Conference on State Legislatures, 1973); J. Grumm, "Legislative Professionalism," in Hofferbert and Sharkansky 1971.

tures based on the assumption that these factors affect the legislatures' ability to function as viable governmental institutions. One early study, calling itself FAIIR, sought to ascertain the degree to which state legislatures were *F*unctional, *A*ccountable, *I*nformed, *I*ndependent, and *R*epresentative (Citizens Conference on State Legislatures 1973); the patterns it identified then apparently have not changed much over time. Table 12 shows the rankings of the "Latino" states. California scored very high, as did the states outside the Southwest. New Mexico scored somewhat lower, but rather higher than the other southwestern states.

_____INFLUENCE IN THE LEGISLATURES

Several studies have considered Latino *influence* in state legislatures. Mindiola and Gutierrez (1988) examined the activities and degree of success of Chicanos in the Texas state legislature during 1981 in introducing and having enacted bills that were relevant to Chicanos. They concluded that "in terms of what was attempted, the legislators examined have a better than average record. In terms of success, however, based on the 67th session, the record is less than impressive, since only nine bills which had exclusive concern for Chicanos passed" (p. 360). In short, this study found the Latino influence in the Texas state legislature to be not very strong.

A study of southern state legislatures found that Mexican Americans (and blacks) in the Texas legislature have formed a relatively cohesive voting group (Harmel, Hamm, and Thompson 1983). Prior to the election of many Mexican Americans to the Texas legislature, the state's urban areas had spawned numerous legislators who were liberal on both racial and socioeconomic issues. To the extent that *"racial* issues [as opposed to simply socioeconomic issues] are prominent in Texas politics, it might be argued" that the addition of Mexican Americans and blacks to the liberal block "may have introduced a new dimension to liberal voting." The study concludes that "it remains unclear what the long-term impact" of minorities will be, or "even if the minority members will remain as cohesive as their numbers increase or as more of them are integrated into the leadership ranks. Long-term consequences remain a subject for future research" (Harmel, Hamm, and Thompson 1983,191).

_____LATINO STATE INTEREST GROUPS

A recent, comprehensive study of interest groups in the various states has noted that minority groups and public interest groups are more identifiable and more common now than they were twenty years ago. But, the study claims, the presence of mass-based, nontraditional groups, such as Latinos, in state politics has *not* meant any major power shifts. While outward appearances have changed, the hallmarks of political success in the state interest-group arena remain in the possession of those with important resources, particularly financial resources (Thomas and Hrebenar 1990). Given the low social status of Latinos, it is not surprising that Latino interest groups are not identified as very important in state politics in the southwestern states.

_____STATE POLICIES

Many political observers argue that how and why political processes occur as they do is less important than the actual policies that governments "produce." We should therefore examine actual state *policies,* or outputs. Yet it is difficult to determine the degree to which state policies directly address the policy concerns or needs of

Latinos. For example, a state may allocate a great deal of funding for education, which generally is considered to coincide with the goals of, or be responsive to, Latinos. But without information on the specific allocation of funding to certain school districts and particular educational programs, the degree of responsiveness is less clear.

These caveats aside, general-level data suggest that social and political environments do indeed have the impact on state policy activities that theories and hypotheses would predict. One study examined policy liberalism in the states, based on programs in these policy areas: education (public education spending per pupil); Medicaid (the scope of Medicaid support); Aid to Families with Dependent Children (AFDC, the scope of eligibility); consumer protection; legalized gambling; ratification of the equal rights amendment; and tax progressivity. Overall, California had among the most liberal policies of the fifty American states; Colorado ranked second highest of the five southwestern states we have been considering (and seventeenth overall), well above our other southwestern states, but clearly below California. Texas, New Mexico, and Arizona, in that order, were clustered together and ranked fairly low overall, in about the bottom third of the fifty states (Wright, Erikson, and McIver 1987).

This information on policy liberalism, while useful and important, is limited in several respects concerning Latino politics. It is unclear where Latino public opinion and preference might stand on the specific policies that make up the policy liberalism measure, although one might expect liberal attitudes regarding most of the policies. That ostensible liberalism among Latinos might reflect their socioeconomic status as much as their ethnic background, however (De Leon 1988; Dyer and Vedlitz 1986). Also, the measures of policy liberalism used may not adequately control for the "effort" a state may make, in general or in particular fields. That is, a state may have a low ranking on policy liberalism and yet make a substantial effort relative to its resources. The research on state policy liberalism presented here does not factor in effort. It is unclear what such factoring would mean in terms of state rankings.

New Mexico is an interesting example in this respect. As we noted earlier, New Mexico has the nation's highest percentage of Hispanics and the highest Hispanic representation in a state legislature. Yet it is an economically poor state with a traditionalist–individualist political culture and low and non-policy-relevant political party competition. Finally, it ranks low in policy liberalism generally. Yet it ranks high (sixth in the nation) in per capita expenditure for elementary and secondary education. And if one considers its education spending relative to its per capita income (spending divided by income as an indicator of effort), New Mexico's spending on education is even more significant. There apparently has been no systematic analysis seeking to *explain* why New Mexico is exceptional in its education policies; thus, it is not clear what impact, if any, the state's history, and its Latino presence, has had.

One of the more extensive discussions of Hispanics in New Mexico concludes that Hispanics "have traditionally been well integrated into the political system, even though Hispanics earn only about two-thirds the income of Anglos." But such social factors as less education and weak economic power have combined "to prevent them [Hispanics] from using politics to increase their economic position" (Garcia and Thomas 1987).

A second point is that the policy measures used to assess a state's liberalism do not consider some policies that are particularly salient to the Latino community. For instance, in 1986, California, liberal by most indicators and with a substantial Latino population, became the first state to vote in favor of an Official English measure, and the measure passed by a wide margin. In 1988, Colorado, another liberal policy state according to the policy areas studied, also handily passed an Official English measure through popular vote. Arizona and Florida, too, conservative by the parameters used, passed Official English measures, but by smaller margins; the Arizona measure, a highly stringent one, barely passed. Texas and New Mexico, both ostensibly conservative states, have *not* enacted Official English measures. The reason for the different outcomes may be largely internal state factors; neither Texas nor New Mexico has an initiative process.

Texas and New Mexico are also notable for the number of elected and appointed Latino officials in both states. Almost half, 48 percent (1,920 of 4,004), of all Latino elected and appointed officials in the United States are from Texas, although Texas accounts for about 21 percent of the U.S. Hispanic population. New Mexico, a sparsely populated state, accounts for only about 1 percent of all U.S. Hispanics, yet 17 percent of Latino elected and appointed officials are from that state. Arizona and Colorado also have somewhat more Latino officials (7 percent and 5 percent of the total, respectively) than their Latino population (less than 4 percent and 2 percent of the nation's total, respectively) would predict. In contrast, California, where 34 percent of U.S.

Hispanics reside, accounts for only 14 percent of all Latino elected or appointed officials. And New York and Florida have only about 20 percent of the nation's Latino officials that their Latino populations would predict (National Association of Latino Elected and Appointed Officials 1990a).

These patterns are difficult to explain. The most likely reason for the large number of Latino officials in Texas is that there are many opportunities for election. Texas has 243 counties; California, with a substantially larger population than Texas, has fewer than 70 counties. The large number of Texas counties, along with the different political traditions of south Texas (and New Mexico), may explain why these states have produced proportionally many more elected officials than other states. But why Florida, with a relatively affluent Latino population, has produced so few Latino officials is not clear. Perhaps politics in Florida has not been seen as a desirable or necessary avenue for group well-being, as it has elsewhere.

A final aspect of state-level policy is the employment of Hispanics in state and local governments in the southwestern states. We can examine this in two ways: total employment (numbers and percentages relative to percentage in the state's population) and salary (median Hispanic salaries relative to salaries in the white–Anglo population). Overall, census data indicate that Hispanic employment in state and local governments is essentially proportionate to the percentages in the population; an exception is New Mexico, where Hispanics are substantially *overrepresented* in state and local employment. When one examines salary levels, a different pattern emerges. In Texas, Hispanics average 77 to 82–85 percent of the median salaries of whites; Hispanics are thus concentrated in low-level jobs with lower salaries than whites.

—————SUMMARY AND CONCLUSION

The situation of Latinos in the politics of various states is somewhat paradoxical. On the whole (with the possible exception of New Mexico), Latino political presence and influence in formal decision-making bodies seems rather low. Even in New Mexico, with its large and long-present Hispanic population, political influence and policy outcomes do not appear to be particularly responsive to Latino concerns. The broad political environment and public policies of several states, such as California and Colorado, would seem conducive to Latino political and policy concerns. Some general evidence on policy liberalism supports this view. Yet, in those two states, Latinos have been underrepresented in the state legislature and other governing bodies, and Official English measures have been enacted by comfortable electoral margins. Hispanics are generally proportionately represented in state and local employment, but their salaries are lower than those of whites, probably because of a concentration in lower-level jobs.

Pluralism's assertion that multiple access points permit groups to be influential at one level of the U.S. political system if they do not succeed in another does not seem to be supported with respect to Latinos and state politics. There is little evidence that, on the whole, the substantial numbers and proportions of Latinos in some states has offset their low socioeconomic status and lack of political resources to translate into much political clout. Several states show some "descriptive representation" of Latinos, with little evidence of policy responsiveness or substantive representation; in other states, the situation is reversed. The meaning of this is not entirely clear. But the erratic nature of the relationships does not appear to be the stuff of pluralism. It seems that contextual–environmental characteristics of the *states*, as much as the Latino population's qualities, explain policy outcomes, if not political processes.

The ambiguous relationship between Latinos and their group resources, political institutions–processes, and policy outcomes implies that perspectives in addition to, or other than, "standard" pluralism are plausible. There are, nonetheless, other dimensions of the U.S. political system to consider. The urban political arena, with its possibilities and limitations for Latinos, is examined in the next two chapters.

7

The Elections of Federico Peña

_____The political integration of ethnic–racial and minority groups at the local level has been viewed as a prerequisite for those groups to achieve political influence in the larger U.S. political system. At the same time, certain interpretations of U.S. politics, including pluralism, attach considerable significance to elections and related political activities. The opportunity for election and the actual meaning of elections by Latinos to major city government positions are important factors to consider. In this context, how a Latino was elected to a powerful position in a city with a relatively small Latino–minority population warrants attention. This chapter addresses the election of Federico Peña as mayor of Denver. While Peña's election is itself significant for Latino politics, it also is the only election of a Latino mayor that has been the subject of extensive statistical analysis (see Hero 1987; Hero and Beatty 1989).

In 1983, a Mexican American, Federico Peña, was elected mayor of Denver; in 1987, he was reelected (he did not seek reelection in 1991). His election is notable for several reasons. Peña's election in a citywide race was among the first such outcomes for Latinos in a major U.S. city. Yet Denver's Hispanic and minority populations are not especially large. Hispanics constitute about 18 percent of the city's total population and about 10 percent of the voting-age population; blacks make up about 12 percent of the total population and about 9 percent of the voting-age population. Also, Denver has a "strong mayor" system; indeed, the mayor of Denver holds what many observers in Colorado

116

perceive to be the state's most powerful elective office. Compared to other large cities with Hispanic mayors, or to most other cities, the Denver mayor holds considerable formal authority.

_____THEORETICAL DISCUSSION

The electoral response to minority candidates, research suggests, is influenced by such factors as the composition of the constituency in which they are running, the strategies they pursue, and the particular circumstances of the election (Hahn, Klingman, and Pachon 1976). Minority mayoral candidates have employed several different strategies based on these conditions. Holloway (1968) described three kinds of coalitions between minority and white voters: the "conservative coalition," the "independent power politics" approach, and the "liberal coalition." The conservative coalition links the minority community with powerful white business and financial interests. In independent-power politics, the backing of white voters is either not needed to secure a majority or is seemingly impossible to obtain. The liberal coalition seeks to unite ethnic–racial minorities with low-income whites, labor unions, and white or Anglo liberals from the business and professional world.

A 1984 study found that the major factor leading to the election of minorities in a group of northern California cities with small minority populations was the emergence of liberal coalitions (Browning, Marshall, and Tabb 1984). These coalitions generally included ethnic–racial minorities, the poor, and white liberals (particularly Democrats). De la Garza (1974), however, found that despite the bicultural image of El Paso, Texas, Anglos were reluctant to vote for Mexican American candidates in state and local elections, especially when the Mexican American candidates made "ethnic appeals" (Hahn, Klingman, and Pachon 1976; Vigil 1987).

Bullock and Campbell (1984) found considerable evidence of racial, as distinct from racist, voting in city elections in Atlanta. "Racial" voting occurs when whites, as well as blacks, are likely to vote for persons of their own race unless they see compelling reasons to do otherwise. For example, candidates' positions on issues are often an important factor in leading citizens to vote for candidates of another racial or ethnic background.

A study of a number of Texas cities found that in order to be elected to citywide office, Chicano candidates had to receive "dual validation."

That is, they had to be "validated by," or acceptable to, *both* the minority (Chicano) and majority (Anglo) community. Certain characteristics of a Chicano candidate might make the office seeker more acceptable to Anglo voters than would otherwise be the case. Age was important; Chicano candidates between thirty-five and forty-five years of age were most successful at the polls. And involvement in civic activities, being of higher socioeconomic status, and having a moderate political ideology and a relatively minor "ethnic" emphasis in campaigns and activities, seemed to be more attractive to voters than were militant political stands (Baird 1977).

It appears, therefore, that when minority candidates run for office in a city where the minority population does not constitute a majority or near-majority of the electorate, they most frequently seek to create a liberal coalition; that is, they tend to make broad-based and issue-oriented appeals and do not emphasize ethnic concerns, which might imply redistributive policies (Hahn, Klingman, and Pachon 1976; de la Garza 1974). Also, in the absence of compelling reasons—such as strong issue agreement, candidate image, or personality factors—voters generally support candidates of their own racial–ethnic background. These findings would appear to be significant for what kinds of viable minority candidates emerge in the first place, what kinds of campaigns they run, and, if elected, what kinds of policies they pursue or do not pursue. The following section considers the implications of these points in the first Peña elections in 1983.

THE 1983 ELECTIONS
THE CAMPAIGN

The Peña strategy to get elected in 1983 had several components. First, the Peña campaign sought to generate an exciting, dynamic contest, one that would increase turnout from the 50 to 55 percent range common in Denver mayoralty races to 70 percent or more. Campaign strategists believed that a higher turnout would benefit Peña and would offset the slim margins by which the incumbent had won in the past. Another part of the Peña election strategy was to undertake a drive to register Hispanics and the poor, who had the city's lowest registration rates (Muñoz and Henry 1990). Peña had previously worked for the Mexican American Legal Defense and Education Fund (MALDEF) and the Chicano Education Project. And as a member of the state House of Representatives, he had been a visible supporter of efforts to provide more equitable funding for education, a particular concern for Mexican Americans and blacks. With this background of support for minority concerns, Peña was viewed as a "natural" for minority constituents. Also, as a result of his activities and voting record as a state legislator, Peña had built strong ties with labor, neighborhood organizations, environmentalists, the handicapped, young professionals, and the elderly.

The 1983 Peña campaign themes did not emphasize his ethnic heritage (see, e.g., *Denver Post*, April 26, 1983; June 12, 1983). But Peña's obviously ethnic name and previous record as a proponent of minority concerns were important. His major campaign themes focused on issues and leadership, emphases that served several purposes. First, they helped put Peña's views on record and attract the news coverage deemed essential, given Peña's relatively meager financial resources. They also helped establish an image of Peña as a forward-looking, bold leader and play down any talk of a single-issue, namely, minority-oriented, candidate (*Denver Post*, April 26, 1983; Hahn, Klingman and Pachon, 1976; cf. Baird 1977).

Along with these and other concerns, Peña issued a number of detailed position papers dealing with such matters as airport expansion, neighborhood preservation, economic development and job creation, bringing a major league baseball team to the city, and the city's financial future. The campaign's strategy and themes were geared toward building an aggregate of electoral support similar to what has been described as a liberal coalition. Also, campaign themes had a nondivisive, "distributive," or "developmental" policy flavor to them (see Chapter 8).

Several other circumstances should be noted about the Peña campaign. Denver mayoral elections are held in odd-numbered years and thus are separate from national and state elections; this is consistent with the prescriptions of the turn-of-the-century reform movement. The elections are nonpartisan, although all the major candidates in 1983 were Democrats. The 1983 elections required a runoff because no candidate received a majority in the general election.

Peña received a number of endorsements, most prominently from labor groups, including the American Federation of State, County, and Municipal Employees (AFSCME), the Denver Area Labor Federation, and the local chapter of the International Brotherhood of Electrical Workers. Peña was also aided by the Southwest Voter Education Project's substantial effort to register Mexican American voters.

TABLE 13
Percentage of Voter Turnout in Denver Mayoral Elections,
1975–1987

Year	Election	%
1975	General election	53.4
	Runoff election	51.2
1979	General election	53.3
1983	General election	63.5
	Runoff election	71.7
1987	General election	48.6
	Runoff election	53.8

Source: Author's calculations based on data from Denver Election Commission.

Peña surprised most observers by not only making it into a runoff but by leading the field in the general election. Analysts attributed Peña's success to several factors: his early entrance into the race and his relentless campaigning; his very well-organized campaign, which had large numbers of volunteers; the number of new voter registrants and the high voter turnout (see Table 13); and the highly effective use of relatively scarce money in the media campaign (*Denver Post*, May 18, 1983). Peña won the runoff election by a narrow 51.4 to 48.6 vote. The election was notable not only for the election of Denver's first Mexican American mayor but also for its record turnout.

──────────AN ANALYSIS OF ELECTION RESULTS

This section provides an assessment of the 1983 Peña campaign strategy. Tables 13 and 14 present registration and turnout figures (see data in the tables pertaining to 1983) indicating that the 1983 elections had considerably higher levels of registration than did the 1979 election. Turnout among registered voters for the general election in 1983 was a full 10 percentage points above that for any of the 1975 and 1979 elections. The runoff election turnout was a record for city elections in Denver.

Table 14 more specifically attempts to assess the extent to which precinct-level registration and turnout correlate with the precinct-level vote for Peña. These data suggest that increased registration was quite

TABLE 14
**Simple Correlation (*r*) between Percentage Registration and
Turnout and Percentage Vote for Peña, 1987 and 1983 (by precincts)**

	% for Peña in General Election		% for Peña in Runoff Election	
	1987	1983	1987	1983
Registration between general and runoff elections	.105	.706	.106	.595
Registration between early in election year and runoff election	.144	.368	.131	.452
Turnout, general election	−.308	−.054	−.314	−.119
Turnout, runoff election	−.244	−.049	−.280	−.185

important to Peña's ultimate victory (Muñoz and Henry 1990). The strongest relationships are those of registration between the first election and the runoff election and the vote for Peña. Increases in registration during the three-day period between the general and runoff elections were strongly positively related (.706) to the vote for Peña in the general election; that is, the registration between elections was greatest where Peña had done best in the general election. Also, the simple correlations between percentage of Spanish and new registrations for the several time periods that are specified in Table 14 are .214, .739, and .361.

Table 14 also shows negative, although weak, relationships between turnout and the vote for Peña. These findings must be seen in the context of the considerable new registration and the overall higher levels of turnout. While high levels of turnout at the precinct level are not positively related to the vote for Peña, the precincts that had historically turned out at the highest levels were relatively conservative areas—and presumably not supportive of minority candidates. Thus, if turnout in these affluent areas remained the same or increased somewhat, and the minority areas increased their turnout considerably— remembering that registration in these minority and poor areas had also increased considerably—a negative relationship between turnout

TABLE 15
Simple Correlation (r) of Percentage of Vote for Peña with Independent Variables (by precinct)

Election Variables (precinct level)	% for Peña in General Election		% for Peña in Runoff Election	
	1987	1983	1987	1983
% Spanish (18+ yrs)	.628	.654	.571	.519
% Black (18+ yrs)	.542	−.199	.582	.537
% Nonminority (18+ yrs)	−.855	−.359	−.841	−.776
Median income	−.170	−.178	−.138	−.133
Median value of housing	−.096	−.006	−.071	−.004
% Unemployed	.658	.456	.638	.586
% Some college	−.594	−.327	−.601	−.468
% Registered Democrat	.528	.363	.579	.743
% Registered Republican	−.723	−.808	−.768	−.516
% Unaffiliated	−.299	.197	−.282	.081

and vote for Peña is less surprising, particularly when those negative relationships are weak. And data support this speculation; the simple correlation between percentage of new registration from the general to the runoff election and percentage of *non*minority is −.54 (Muñoz and Henry 1990). Also notable is that the positive relationship between registration and vote for Peña is stronger than the negative relationships between turnout and vote for Peña.

The simple correlations among various demographic characteristics and other variables and the vote for Peña shown in Table 15 indicate a liberal coalition. The correlation between percentage of Spanish and vote for Peña is rather strong for both the general and runoff elections. While the relationships between Peña's vote in the runoff and percentage of Spanish and black voters are strong, they are not as strong as one might expect. Based on aggregate, data, however, Muñoz and Henry claim that 96 percent of Hispanics and 86 percent of blacks who actually voted in the runoff supported Peña. The reason that the aggregated numbers do not translate into stronger statistical correlations in the table seems to be related to differences between groups in levels of registration and turnout. Even though minority registration had increased substantially over previous city elections, it still lagged behind that of other groups (Muñoz and Henry 1990; Lovrich and Marenin 1976).

The relationship between the vote for Peña and the percentage of black voters is rather strong and positive for the runoff election. The weak negative relationship between vote for Peña and percentage of black voters in the general election is probably the result of the presence (and strong showing among black voters) of a black candidate in the general election.

The simple correlation between the vote for Peña and the percentage of nonminority voters is negative for both elections and is particularly strong in the runoff election. Muñoz and Henry's aggregate analysis found that Peña received about 42 percent of the white–Anglo vote in the runoff. These and subsequent data indicate considerable racial voting. Despite the lack of explicit emphasis in his campaign on ethnic concerns, Peña's name and record, along with several endorsements, brought him strong minority-group support. There is also considerable evidence of racial voting among nonminorities, which, as we see shortly, was modified by several factors.

The negative relationship of vote for Peña with percentage of voters with some college and the rather strong relationship with percentage of unemployed voters provide further evidence that Peña did relatively well among less-educated and lower-status economic groups. Some further, although tentative, evidence of the liberal coalition is that the relationships between vote for Peña and measures of income, median income, and median value of housing are weak. That these relationships were not strongly related to the Peña vote suggests some success in gaining the support of professionals.

While Denver elections are nonpartisan and all the major candidates in both elections were Democrats, Peña clearly did better in areas of the city where voters identify themselves as Democrats than in areas where Republican affiliation is high (Browning, Marshall, and Tabb 1984). This pattern, particularly notable in the runoff election, is important because Democrats constitute about 15 percent more of Denver's registered voters than Republicans do.

The data also suggest some lack of cohesion among Hispanic voters related to education levels. Minority voters who did not support Peña were probably those with higher levels of education; among whites, education has a negligible or slightly positive effect overall on the vote for Peña.

—————PEÑA'S FIRST TERM

During his first term, Peña tried to address the diverse expectations and concerns implied in his broad electoral coalition, but he placed greater emphasis on economic development—with the expectation that the benefits of economic development would spill over to minorities (Judd and Ready 1986; author interviews). Some of the specific priorities of Peña's first term were the building of a new convention center and a new airport. Peña also sought improvement of the city's economic development operations in the hope of making these efforts better coordinated and more effective.

Peña's most direct overtures to minority and neighborhood groups took several forms. He appointed more minorities to city boards and commissions, and was sensitive to the hiring of minorities to visible city offices (author interviews; also see Chapter 8; Saiz 1988). In conjunction with some city council members, he expanded the policy of awarding city contracts to minority contractors (see, e.g., *Denver Post*, February 18, 1988). To increase input from neighborhood groups, Peña began a series of town meetings in each council district. Peña increased the size of the neighborhood planning staff from three to eight people and ordered a traffic study of the one-way streets running through the neighborhoods toward downtown.

Writing in the midst of Peña's first term, Judd and Ready (1986, 225) observed:

> An interesting political experiment is being conducted in Denver. Can conflicts be managed by implementing an economic development program that justifies downtown revitalization by its potential spillover effects into neighborhood and minority communities? Is this repackaging of progrowth politics what may be expected by minority mayors who are elected by broadly based coalitions? Certainly, the coalitions that elect Peña will begin at some point to expect more than openness and symbolic sharing of power. Until then, Denver's program provides a glimpse into what may become a familiar development strategy in cities all across America: a reworking of familiar progrowth politics by minority and "reform" mayors to make downtown development palatable both to domi-

nant business interests and to minority and neighborhood constituencies.

Others also have questioned whether economic development can be compatible with the social service or redistributive policy needs presumably sought by minority groups (Lovrich 1974; Peterson 1981; Flores 1989). The Peña administration contended that economic growth and development were necessary to generate revenues to maintain basic services, as well as to provide money for other purposes, such as social services (Judd and Ready 1986; author interviews).

How did the various elements of the Denver electorate evaluate the Peña administration? In 1987, Peña sought reelection; the issues raised in that campaign along with voting behavior probably offer some clues to this question.

_____THE 1987 ELECTIONS

Despite conflicting expectations of what seemed to be a fragile electoral coalition, and despite what appeared to be considerable dissatisfaction with Peña's performance during his first term (see, e.g., *Denver Post*, April 5, 1987; May 17, 1987), important elements of Peña's constituency continued to support him. For example, the Denver Chamber of Commerce, claiming that Peña had laid the groundwork for important projects, endorsed him relatively early in the campaign (*Denver Post*, April 7, 1987). And newspaper stories suggested that Hispanics would support Peña "warts and all" (*Denver Post*, March 15, 1987).

Nevertheless, there seemed to be a perception, and resultant criticism, that Peña's administration had not accomplished much and that he had not made good on his 1983 promise to make Denver "a great city" (*Denver Post*, June 7, 1987). These views are manifested in the general election results. Peña received 37.1 percent of the vote, enough to make it to a runoff, but he trailed the sole Republican, a corporate lawyer, who garnered 41.7 percent of the vote.

There were several disconcerting features for Peña in the general election. Beyond the obvious point that he did not receive the most votes, evidence suggested that much of the vote for his opponent was a vote *against* Peña (*Denver Post*, June 7, 1987). Also, the enthusiasm and turnout among groups, especially minorities, that had been important to Peña's 1983 election seemed notably weaker than it had been in the

TABLE 16
**Results of Regression Analysis of Vote for Peña in Runoff Elections,
1983 and 1987, with Ethnicity, Party, and Increased Turnout
(controlling for education)**

| Independent Variable | 1983 | | 1987 | |
(percentages)	b	β	b	β
Hispanic	.53	.44	.32	.26
Black	.58	.44	.27	.21
Democrat	− .40	−.32	.30	.23
Republican	− 1.10	−.78	− .76	− .49
Increase in turnout, May–June	.15	.09	.10	.06
Some college	.18	.21	.83	.09
Adjusted R²	.766		.895	

Key: b = unstandardized regression coefficients; β = standardized regression coefficients.

Note: All coefficients are significant at p < .001. The partisan affiliation data are different for the two years. For 1987, the data are from February of that year; for 1983, the data are actually from late 1982.

earlier election (*Denver Post*, June 12, 1987). Nevertheless, Peña was able to rally his electoral coalition and won reelection by a slim margin.

Table 16 examines the importance of a number of variables as predictors of a vote for Peña in both the 1983 and the 1987 runoff elections. As suggested earlier, Peña's mayoral victory in 1983 depended heavily on the support of Hispanics and blacks (as indicated by the relatively strong relationships, beta = .44 for both variables) and was related to the increase in turnout in the runoff election (beta = .09). Although the simple correlation between percentage of Democrats and percentage of the vote for Peña for precincts was strongly positive in 1983 (*r* = .74), when the effects of other variables are accounted for, the effect of percentage of Democrats is negative. Because Peña's runoff opponent in 1983 was also a Democrat, party impact should be less decisive than in a race with a Republican candidate. On the other

TABLE 17
Average Percentage for Peña in Selected Precincts

	1983	1987
Five most heavily Anglo precincts	38.3%	35.6%
Five most heavily Hispanic precincts	89.3	84.8
Five most heavily black precincts	84.5	87.8
Socioeconomic Characteristics		
Median Income		
Lowest five precincts	73.0	73.2
Highest five precincts	48.1	47.1
Percentage with some college		
Lowest five precincts	85.0	81.2
Highest five precincts	31.2	33.5
Percentage unemployed		
Highest five precincts	78.4	79.6
Lowest five precincts	39.2	36.4

Note: The five most heavily Anglo districts in both 1987 and 1983 were all 99 percent or more Anglo. The five most heavily Hispanic precincts ranged from 61.9 to 72.8 percent Hispanic in 1987 and 61.2 to 73 percent in 1983. Comparable ranges for most heavily black districts for the two years were 65.2 to 76.4 and 58.2 to 76.1, respectively.

hand, the level of Republican affiliation has a clear negative impact on the vote for Peña (beta = − .78).

In 1987, the independent variables produce a *different* constellation of effects. Hispanic and black support remained strong in 1987, although its relative importance declined between 1983 and 1987. Again, turnout increases between the general and runoff elections seemed to be to Peña's advantage, although the impact was slightly smaller than in 1983. Overall, Peña's reliance on ethnic minority support was slightly greater in 1983 than in 1987, when party affiliation worked in his favor among Democrats.

Estimating the percentage of each ethnic–racial group voting for Peña suggests that Anglo support for Peña in both runoff elections (1983 and 1987) was about 40 percent; Hispanic and black support for Peña was above 90 percent, probably approaching 100 percent for both runoff elections. To examine the ethnic vote further and to consider further the nature of the Peña coalition with respect to voters' socioeconomic characteristics, selected precincts were chosen for analysis. Examined were the five precincts with the highest concentrations of Hispanics, blacks, and whites (Anglos) plus the precincts that ranked highest and lowest on a variety of socioeconomic characteristics (median income, value of housing, education, and unemployment). The results of the analysis, shown in Table 17, seem to support the estimates noted, as well as offering some other evidence (Muñoz and Henry 1990).

The average percentage for Peña exceeds the percentage of minority voters (Hispanic or black). On average, Peña received between 85 and 89 percent of the vote (in 1987 and 1983) in the most heavily Hispanic precincts, although these precincts were at most 73 percent Hispanic. Similarly, Peña received over 84 percent of the vote in both years in the most heavily black precincts, though none of these precincts exceeded 77 percent black. In contrast, Peña received less than 40 percent of the vote in the most heavily (99 percent plus) white or Anglo precincts. Also, Peña did substantially better in both years in less socioeconomically advantaged precincts. This is evident for all four socioeconomic variables considered, but it is most substantial regarding education (percentage with some college) and unemployment.

In 1987, Peña defeated a Republican in the runoff election (in 1983 his runoff opponent was another Democrat), and the effects of party reflect the two-party campaign. Republicans supported the Republican candidate, not Peña (beta = − .76), while Democrats supported Peña (as indicated by the beta = .30). Also estimated was the percentage voting for Peña among Democrats, Independents, and Republicans. In 1983, Peña's support among Democrats was strong, estimated at about 85 percent, but it did not reach the virtually unanimous level of support estimated for 1987. A much more striking difference can be seen in the support of Independents across the two years. In 1983, Independents strongly supported Peña (an estimate of about 72 percent), while estimated Independent support for Peña fell to 40 percent in 1987. Republicans, in both years, were quite strong in their opposition to the Peña candidacy.

SUMMARY AND CONCLUSIONS

This chapter has illuminated the roles of ethnicity, party affiliation, and increased voter turnout in the 1983 and 1987 Federico Peña mayoral elections. It shows fairly decisive evidence of what has been referred to as racial voting—both minorities and nonminorities tend to vote "for their own." Although Hispanics and blacks were a critical element of Peña's electoral base, they constituted only a third of that base. Anglo–white support for Peña was weaker than that among Hispanics and blacks, but notably stronger than white support for black candidates in other cities, such as Chicago and Philadelphia. Under certain circumstances, citizens do cross ethnic–racial lines when they vote in city elections. Even though the Denver elections described took place in a setting of formal nonpartisanship, party affiliation had a clear impact, particularly in 1987, when the two candidates were of different parties. This speaks to the nature of nonpartisan city elections; apparently they can be quite partisan when party affiliation becomes an issue in the campaign. Voting estimates by party indicate that while Peña solidified his Democratic support in 1987, he lost ground with Independents when he faced a Republican opponent. In addition to ethnicity and party, Peña's strategy of actively attempting to increase minority voter turnout appears to have been effective and, in fact, been the deciding factor in his victory.

What are the implications of the findings regarding the necessary conditions for electing minority candidates in cities that do not have large concentrations of minority voters? First, almost unanimous support from minority voters is critical. Peña accomplished this without stressing that he was a "minority" candidate. Instead, he addressed minority needs indirectly; that is, he spoke in general or abstract terms about "neighborhoods" and "openness," notions that have general appeal but are particularly attractive to Denver's minority communities, which historically have been outside the political mainstream. Peña maintained, for example, that redistributive and developmental policies need not be mutually exclusive and can be linked.

Second, Hispanic candidates probably have to make extraordinary efforts to appeal to nonminority voters for their support or to lessen electoral opposition from them. The Peña experience suggests that this can be done in one of two ways. The more likely way is through a broad appeal, emphasizing "unitary" or citywide concerns. The other way requires the right partisan circumstances, for example, where partisanship can be introduced as an important factor and where partisan affiliation patterns are favorable, as they were in Denver. It also seems that efforts to develop winning coalitions can benefit from an increase in voter turnout among selected groups.

At the same time, the data suggest that unless the nonminorities who gave Peña their electoral support were very supportive of minority-group concerns, it would have been difficult to address the social service or redistributive policies that minorities would be expected to favor (Lovrich and Marenin 1976). Peterson's (1981) arguments in the upcoming chapter imply that addressing redistributive concerns is inherently difficult in city elections. And Stone (1986) has claimed that even where minorities are an electoral majority, minority mayors are highly constrained by the need to form effective *governing* coalitions (see Chapter 2 regarding coalitional bias and Chapter 8). Given the situation in Denver, the fragile nature of Peña's electoral coalition would seem to lower the chances that we will see major departures from existing city policies. In any event, it is not evident that Peña sought to make such departures (de la Garza 1974). Issues of urban governance are more directly and extensively assessed in the next chapter.

8

Latinos and Urban Politics

_____The study of Latinos in local politics in the United States is especially important for several reasons. Over 85 percent of Latinos live in urban areas, a higher percentage than among the U.S. population as a whole (Moore and Pachon 1985). Because of this urban concentration, the political significance of Latinos is likely to be greatest in local government. In fact, more than 75 percent of the 4,004 Latino elected and appointed officials in the United States hold positions in various local governments, such as municipalities, counties, special districts, and school districts (National Association of Latino Elected and Appointed Officials 1990b). The structure and operation of government in the United States, its federal structure most specifically, means that local governments are significant political and policy institutions. At the same time, urban governments are constrained by their "place" in the U.S. political economy.

Urban governments generally have similar legal relationships to their state government—they are creatures of the state government—and to the national government. This status is significant for urban politics. But local governments, including municipalities and counties, are not alike internally. These differences make a difference for politics in urban settings. Political, ecological, and structural factors are important in providing a background and context for understanding Latino politics, but they have not been extensively examined in previous work relating to Latino politics.

131

This chapter discusses the implications for Latino politics of the similarities and differences in and among local governments. It also examines these issues with specific reference to cities with large Latino populations. The most focused attention is on cities that have been closely studied in political science research, if for no other reason than that much more is known about these cities.

Before turning to specific issues and specific cities, however, urban politics in earlier periods as it dealt with other ethnic groups should be reviewed. This history deserves consideration because much of the scholarly expectations and understandings regarding Latinos and contemporary urban politics are shaped by the understanding of earlier periods of urban–ethnic politics.

CHALLENGE TO THE RAINBOW MYTH

A widely held view argues that urban politics often was a major avenue for ethnic-group social and political integration, incorporation, and mobility. That is, the conventional wisdom says that old-style urban political machines, such as those found in northeastern and midwestern cities in the late nineteenth and early twentieth centuries, created multiethnic coalitions (of the Irish, Italians, and other white ethnics) by rewarding these groups with jobs drawn from a sizable urban government sector. In turn, the perception is that these jobs led to substantial economic well-being for the ethnic groups. This view of white ethnic groups has been called the "rainbow myth" (Erie 1985, 250).

From the standpoint of the rainbow myth or theory, the concentration of Latinos in urban areas is a politically favorable sign for the group. Despite the acceptance of the rainbow view in popular and academic circles, however, recent studies suggest that the actual historical situation substantially departs from it. With few exceptions, even white ethnic groups faced staunch opposition when they tried to influence urban governments (Erie 1985). Only grudgingly were groups such as the Irish and Italians accommodated in the urban political arena in the early twentieth century. Nor did their success in that arena lead to success or upward mobility in their social and economic life. For instance, despite long-time dominance in urban politics, a substantial Irish middle class did not exist until after World War II (Erie 1985, 254–256). A study of politics in New Haven, Connecticut, similarly reveals that "politics has not been the path to equality for the ethnics in social and economic life." In the late 1950s and for many years before that, New Haven's three major ethnic immigrant groups were "overrepresented in political positions and drastically underrepresented in the city's social and economic elite" (Wolfinger 1974, 67).

Also, according to some observers, urban ethnic politics has historically "inhibited the development of class consciousness" by diverting attention from fundamental class-based issues and toward symbolic concerns (Erie 1985, 254; Wolfinger 1974, 61–63). The real consequence of ethnic politics, this interpretation suggests, has been tangible rewards for a few, generally in the form of patronage and government contracts, and symbolic gratification for the rest, in the form of "recognition" by election or the appointment of ethnics to official positions (Wolfinger 1974).

Increasingly, research shows that politics in urban America was substantially less "open" to white ethnic groups, even where "machines" dominated, than has generally been perceived. Similarly, the social and economic benefits for those ethnic groups were less extensive than is generally thought. Slow and delayed incorporation of ethnic immigrant groups into urban politics seems to be the norm. The perception of "rainbow coalitions" in earlier periods of urban ethnic politics is largely a myth.

Yet the perceived parochial and corrupt quality of ethnic politics engendered reform movements around the turn of the century, and many observers believe that "reform" has made it more difficult for today's ethnic minority groups, such as Latinos and blacks, to influence city politics. The political structures and associated bureaucratic agencies that emerged from the reform movements have not been politically neutral, as they once claimed to be; "they are only independent" of popular control (Lowi 1967).

Despite the mounting evidence from the historical record, and despite observations that contemporary urban governments and bureaucracies may not be especially responsive to minority concerns, urban politics continues to be perceived as an avenue for ethnic-group upward political and social mobility. A fuller understanding of urban and Latino politics requires an awareness of the historical reality and what it may mean for Latinos.

Nevertheless, assuming for a moment that urban politics can be an important route by which ethnic groups can achieve political recognition and influence (disregarding the social and economic significance of that influence), other questions remain as to what this might mean for Latinos. For instance, at what point in a group's presence in an urban area might we expect the group's influence to become manifest? According to some scholars, ethnic-group voting is likely to be greatest in the first generation, when a group is new to the city, and assimilation has not yet taken place. According to others, ethnic voting is greatest in the second and third generations, not the first, because middle-class status, which takes several generations to develop, is a "virtual prerequisite for candidacy for major office; an ethnic group's development of sufficient political skill and influence to secure nomination also requires the development of a middle class" (Wolfinger 1974, 49).

It is difficult to decide this issue as it concerns Latinos, for several reasons. First, we would have to choose the appropriate time from which to calculate a group's "arrival." Should it, for example, be when significant numbers of a group first enter a nation, or should it be when a group becomes more visible in a particular city? Mexican Americans, for instance, entered the nation in the 1850s, immediately following the "conquest" by the United States; and in the early 1900s, there was a massive emigration from Mexico coincident with the Mexican Revolution. Should these be our signposts, or should we choose some other time, such as when a group becomes *predominantly* urban? If the latter, how substantial must the group's proportion be within cities, or within specific cities, and relative to the group's population as a whole? Again, what should we use to measure a group's having developed a middle class; and where must that middle class develop— within the nation as a whole, within some cities, or within most cities? Moreover, Erie (1985) implies that it took more than three generations for the Irish, supposedly among the more successful ethnic groups politically, to develop a substantial middle class. Should we look to third-generation Latinos to measure "success"? These questions indicate the difficulty in developing standards by which to gauge Latino political success in urban or, for that matter, any domain of U.S. politics. These questions are further complicated by arguments that cities are increasingly constrained and dependent entities in the U.S. political economy.

The historical background indicates the problems in applying certain theoretical views to Latinos. We must first examine contemporary circumstances and see how they are similar to, and different from, those of earlier periods.

URBAN POLITICS IN CONTEXT

In the past decade or so, writers on U.S. urban government have suggested that there are significant similarities among urban governments that result from their place in the U.S. federal system and the related U.S. political economy. These similarities make urban politics distinct from politics in other arenas of the system. Yet there is also variation in the political economy of cities because of their different historical and economic circumstances (Stein 1989; Elkin 1987). To place Latino politics in proper theoretical perspective, these similarities and differences regarding urban politics are important.

THE PETERSON FRAMEWORK

Paul Peterson (1981), in a highly influential book on U.S. urban politics, argued that there are three kinds of public policies with which urban governments are involved: developmental, redistributive, and allocational. According to his theory, cities emphasize economic development, or *developmental* policies, because they must compete with one another to attract industry, because they are compelled to protect their tax base, and because such policies are thought to provide net economic benefits to cities that everyone living in the cities benefits from. Major development projects, such as roads, bridges, and sewers are generally viewed favorably by city officials. The larger U.S. political economy virtually dictates this emphasis.

Redistributive policies supposedly "take from the rich and give to the poor." These are such policies as welfare, low-income housing, and health care for the indigent. Redistributive policies are avoided by cities because there are clear net economic losses associated with them, and because such policies make cities less attractive to industry when monies are spent for "unproductive" purposes. *Allocational* policies include various activities of the caretaker or housekeeping sort, such as public safety (police and fire), trash collection, and snow removal; these are generally neutral in their economic consequences for cities.

The Peterson theory has several implications for Latinos and urban politics. First, urban governments are unlikely to undertake redistributive policies, even though Latinos may see urban government as a vehicle for the amelioration of various social problems through such policies. If they are undertaken at all, redistributive policies are most likely to be initiated elsewhere, such as at the national level. Yet Latino political influence is not likely to be very great at this level of government (see Chapters 5 and 6). Second, the theory seems to assume—and many political officials seem to act on the assumption—that economic development policies are not only beneficial to cities as a whole but are essentially *equally* beneficial to all individuals and groups in a city. Yet there are theoretical and real reasons to ask whether the benefits derived from economic development are distributed equally and, if benefits are equal, whether such equality can be shown in absolute or relative terms (Sanders and Stone 1987; Flores 1989; Elkin 1987). In short, cities are unlikely to pursue the policies thought to be most salient to poor and minority groups, and even policies presumed to be beneficial for "everyone" in a city, that is, developmental policies, may not necessarily benefit socioeconomically disadvantaged groups very much.

The situation is ironic: Latino political influence is most likely to be greatest in urban politics, which is probably the political arena that is least willing and least able to pursue policies beneficial to Latinos. In contrast, because of their supposed economic neutrality, allocational policies, which include city public employment practices, might be open to minority penetration (Elkin 1987, 89; Wolfinger 1974, 69). And so it is not surprising that cities have focused on these policies in addressing minority-groups concerns (see Chapter 10).

————OTHER THEORETICAL MODELS

A study by Stephen Elkin (1987) also argues that cities share basic similarities in the political and economic circumstances they confront, but posits some variations as well. "Entrepeneurial cities" or entrepenurial political economies have in common "a relatively unimpeded alliance composed of public officials and local businessmen, an alliance that is able to shape the workings of political institutions so as to foster economic growth." Elkin further suggests that there is little evidence that such growth does much for minority populations. In the post–World War II period, entrepeneurial political economies have been dominant in southwestern cities. This region is, of course, one in which Chicanos are concentrated, and it is in this period that Chicanos became a heavily urban population (Elkin 1987).

Pluralist and federalist political economies are most often found in large northeastern and midwestern cities, respectively. The entrepreneurial political economies differ from pluralist and federalist ones in that the "behavior of public officials in the entrepenurial version is *not as much shaped by the building of electoral organizations and political coa-*

litions" (Elkin 1987, 81; emphasis added). Others have made similar claims about southwestern cities (see Perry and Watkins 1977). This suggests that Latinos are less likely to have an impact even in the more mainstream or visible aspects of politics (e.g., voting or interest-group participation), to say nothing of broader dimensions of urban politics.

We can note other characteristics of southwestern cities and their policy emphases and outcomes. Southwestern (and southern) cities are often newer than cities of the Northeast and Midwest, and they emerged mostly during a postindustrial era. The *formative building phase*—that period when a city "really becomes" a city—seems crucial in considering the kinds and levels of government programs initially undertaken and maintained. In the Northeast, nonnative Europeans predominated during the formative period. A native white middle class dominated the growth period of most southwestern cities. This native white middle-class dominance led to a consensual, nonpartisan city politics that in turn produced a minimal level of social services and a narrow range of local government services. And that history of minimal social services (redistributive policies) continues to this day, as does the tendency in northeastern cities toward a more extensive range of local government services (Stein 1989).

As an urban population group, Chicanos were numerically and politically overwhelmed during the formative stage of southwestern cities, and even if their numbers had been greater, several mechanisms would have limited their political impact. In any event, the precedents set in the formative period of these cities continue to shape or, more specifically, constrain the provision of social services. Historical developments in the urban arena in this century have had important implications for Latinos and urban politics. This is a significant point that has not been adequately recognized in theoretical models that try to explain Latino politics.

Another aspect that is important in understanding urban government is its heavily service-oriented and bureaucratic nature. Much of what urban governments do is provide services directly to people; officials who provide these services—police officers, teachers, welfare workers, and so on—have been referred to as "street-level bureaucrats." Typically, street-level bureaucrats have considerable discretion in how programs are implemented and are thus important policymakers. Street-level bureaucrats often treat members of minority groups less well than other groups, and bureaucratic processes generally may have negative effects on minorities (Lipsky 1980; Nivola

1978; Stone, Whelan, and Murin 1986; but see also Mladenka 1980; Goodsell 1985). Indeed, one of the most direct and comprehensive efforts to examine an especially important urban service—elementary and secondary education—contends that there is substantial discrimination in urban government (see Chapter 9).

That urban politics is heavily bureuacratic in nature has also affected how citizens participate and interact with urban institutions. Citizen contact with bureaucratic officials has come to be seen as an important form of political participation. That is, citizens bring specific concerns, problems, or grievances to local government agencies. While there has been little research on this matter that has paid specific attention to Latinos, the existing evidence indicates that persons of minority background are *less* likely to contact urban officials (Hero 1986b; Verba and Nie 1972). This is important because citizen contact may alter the allocation or distribution of public services. A factor that affects the amount of minority citizen contact of government officials, including city council members, is the presence of minority council members holding district-based seats (Heilig and Mundt 1984).

DIFFERENCES IN LOCAL GOVERNMENTS

Although there is a general context that shapes urban politics and policy, differences within cities also have significance for urban politics. A major dimension on which urban governments differ is their formal governmental system. At the broadest level two formal governmental systems have been delineated: reformed and unreformed. The terms are meant to indicate historical occurrence, not necessarily normative evaluation, although normative connotations are often implied. Generally, the most reformed structures have a council–manager system and at-large and nonpartisan elections. Reformed structures suggest that cities should be structured and run like businesses; they place an emphasis on efficiency and consensus. Other elements of the reform package typically include a professional, merit-based (rather than patronage-based) bureaucracy and staggered terms, as well as long terms in office for council members. The unreformed or least-reformed structures have a mayor–council system with district-based and partisan elections. The government structure of any particular city may vary.

City government structure has been extensively examined in terms of two major questions: Why do cities have particular structures in the first place? And what political and policy implications do the various structures have?

Why cities have a particular structure is an important question because of the policy effects associated with the different kinds of structures (discussed in the next section) and because of the basic political importance for groups of playing a role in *creating* institutions, that is, in establishing the basic structures and processes that guide political discussion, activity, and the like. Banfield and Wilson (1966) claim that government systems could best be explained by the ethos or ethics of groups within a city. That is, groups prefer government systems that reflect the particular group's view of government.

According to Banfield and Wilson, ethnic groups of western and northern European background have a "public regarding" political ethos, one that emphasizes the good of the community as a whole. At-large and nonpartisan elections, along with council–manager systems, exemplify that ethos. Groups of southern and eastern European background are said to have a "private regarding" ethos, one that views government actions in terms of what is good for oneself, one's family, or one's group. The private-regarding ethos is viewed as having little concern for the larger community. District and partisan elections along with a weak mayor–council system exemplify this ethos.

There are several implications in Banfield and Wilson's ethos theory. First, Latinos are not discussed at all in their theory, which was developed in the mid 1960s. This underscores how Latinos have been overlooked in studies of U.S. politics until recently; it also is suggestive of the Eurocentric, or "Atlantic immigration" focus of U.S. political science (see Chapter 1). Based on what is suggested by ethos theory, however, it can be inferred that Latinos would hold a private-regarding perspective on politics and would thus prefer *unreformed* local political systems.

As we have indicated, Latinos are concentrated in cities that are more, rather than less, reformed. The few studies that have systematically examined ethos theory with specific attention to Hispanics (Hero 1986a) and to the western United States (Wolfinger and Field 1966) have found little or no support for the theory. Clearly, Latinos historically have had little or no influence on the creation and structuring of local government institutions in the United States.

THE POLICY SIGNIFICANCE OF URBAN POLITICAL SYSTEMS

A substantial body of research indicates that unreformed structures have been more responsive to the concerns of relatively disadvantaged groups. That is, cities with reformed structures tend to spend less money for social services, that is, on redistributive policies (Lyons 1978; Lineberry and Fowler 1967; see also Morgan and Pelissero 1980; Stein 1989). Latinos are concentrated in cities with reformed structures, which would seem to work against their presumed policy preferences.

But recent research has challenged the assumption that unreformed structures are more responsive to Hispanics. Using level of Latino public employment, rather than tax and spending policies, as a measure of policy responsiveness, has shown that "reformed governments with professional city managers and civil service bureaucracies are actually more hospitable environments for Hispanic job aspirants than unreformed governments" (Mladenka 1989). This is true, Mladenka speculates, because "although unreformed local institutions may enhance responsiveness to *groups in general,* they may not operate to the advantage of *Hispanics in particular.* More groups may be heard in an unreformed environment. However, only the *more resourceful* will likely be heeded. In fact, there is no guarantee that the greater sensitivity to diverse groups allegedly found in unreformed communities will imply equality of response" (Mladenka 1989, 404; emphasis added).

Mladenka seems to be suggesting that because of their receptiveness to group pressure generally, unreformed cities have a bigger overall "pie"; but how the pie is actually distributed depends on group political resources and political mobilization. Reformed cities have smaller pies, but because they are more professionalized, they may respond only to legitimate, properly channeled needs and pressures.

This is an important argument, but it needs to be kept in perspective. First, the public sector in southwestern cities (cities that are among the most heavily Hispanic) tends to be smaller than the public sector in northeastern cities to begin with. Second, given that allocational policies—which would include public employment—are economically neutral, the viability of public employment as a measure of responsiveness is questionable by some standards (Peterson 1981; Elkin 1987; Wolfinger 1974; Barrera 1979; see also Chapter 10). Moreover, the claimed responsiveness of reformed structures may simply be an artifact of the group setting in cities with substantial Hispanic populations. That is, it may be easier to give jobs to Hispanics when there is little competition from other ethnic–racial groups for those jobs.

Several ideas have been put forth to explain the different impacts on policy of different governmental structures—with, again, the most common finding being that reform structures and processes are *not* beneficial to minority interests. District, rather than at-large, election of council members seems to be an advantage in the election of minority council members for several reasons. First, to the extent that a group is residentially segregated, district elections increase the likelihood that a minority candidate will be elected because the minority population may be a majority or near-majority within the district. Also, the cost of running for a district seat is less expensive than running for at-large, citywide seats; and as much evidence indicates that Latinos are generally less affluent than Anglos, district seats offer another advantage to a Latino seeking election.

But some research indicates that district elections may not be as advantageous for Latinos as they are for blacks (Welch 1990; Taebel 1978; Zax 1990). This is so because Latinos generally have been less residentially segregated than blacks. On the other hand, research on the election of Latinos to *school boards* stresses the importance of district elections for equitable Latino representation on those bodies (Meier and Stewart 1991). Other research indicates that the *size* of the Latino population is the most important factor for Latino council election and that district elections have only a marginal impact (Bullock and Mac-Manus 1990). This last study also claimed that at-large elections may not be as detrimental to the election of Latinos as has been thought.

The Bullock and MacManus research, however, overlooks the fact that there may be differences in the *kinds* of Hispanics elected under different systems. Council members elected from districts tend to be more assertive spokespersons for their constituents. And council members elected from districts are more likely to play constituent service, casework, or ombudsman roles (Heilig and Mundt 1984). This can be important to Latinos when they are dealing with bureaucracies, which are such an important part of government, particularly local government (as the earlier discussion on citizen contact suggests). In any event, should Latinos become more residentially segregated, and there is some evidence that this might be occurring, district elections might have a greater impact than they have at present on the election of Hispanics (Bullock and MacManus 1990).

The most recent research on the impact of district or at-large or mixed electoral structures finds that electoral structure has little or no impact on the election of Hispanics to city councils (Welch 1990). Moreover, whatever conclusions are reached about "the relative efficacy of district and at-large elections in promoting equitable Hispanic representation, it is very clear that *no matter which electoral form is used Hispanics are represented at a much lower ratio* relative to their population proportions than are blacks" (Welch 1990, 1067, emphasis added; see also Bullock and MacManus 1990).

By the removal of a candidate's political party affiliation as a cue for citizens in making voting decisions, *nonpartisan* elections increase voter "information costs." Presumably, this has the greatest impact on relatively less educated groups, such as Latinos, who may have ready access to less political information. On the other hand, nonpartisan elections may *increase* the salience of ethnicity in local elections because a candidate's ethnicity, as evidenced by her or his surname, becomes more noticeable in the absence of party identification.

A number of other mechanisms may have a detrimental impact on the election of Latinos to city council seats. These include majority-vote requirements, anti–single shot rules, staggered terms, the number of seats on a council, and the length of council members' terms. The most comprehensive study of these issues, however, found that these mechanisms have little impact on Hispanic election to city councils (Bullock and MacManus 1990).

The council–manager system places chief administrative responsibility in the hands of an appointed, rather than elected, official: the city manager. This diminishes the public accountability of the city's chief executive and, along with other mechanisms, insulates city government from certain kinds of political pressures. Indeed, the increasing bureaucratization of local government, including greater role for staff agencies over line agencies, is a development whose implications for Latinos and urban politics more generally has not been adequately explored (Stone, Whelan, and Murin 1986). Yet it seems important, given that Latinos frequently claim that an obstacle to greater participation is an inability to *understand* government (Vigil 1987).

LATINO POLITICS IN U.S. CITIES: SOME EXAMPLES

Urban politics has been discussed in general terms to this point; a consideration of politics in a number of cities is useful to provide greater detail. Research on Latinos in urban politics is relatively scarce; the research that does exist has not necessarily focused on the same issues or taken the same approaches. This section summarizes

TABLE 18
Hypotheses and Findings of Factors Related to Minority Political Influence in Urban Politics

Factor or Variable	Expected Relationship
Size of minority population	+
SES resources of minority population	+
Political resources outside group	+
Organizational development through demand–protest	+
Group competition—and modeling	+
Resistance of dominant coalition	−
Size of city	+
Socioeconomic inequality	+
Structure of government (unreformed)	+

Key: + indicates positive relationship; − indicates negative relationship.
Source: Browning, Marshall, and Tabb 1984.

some of the major work that has been done. Two Colorado cities, Denver and Pueblo, are given extensive focus because they have been studied more extensively than other cities with substantial Latino populations. And the research approach used to study Denver and Pueblo was the same as that used in a study of cities in northern California.

NORTHERN CALIFORNIA

A major study examined ten cities in northern California to assess the "struggle of Hispanics (and blacks) for equality in urban politics" (Browning, Marshall, and Tabb 1984; also see Chapter 10). The cities were Berkeley, Daly City, Hayward, Oakland, Richmond, Sacramento, San Francisco, San Jose, Stockton, and Vallejo. Hispanic populations in these cities in 1979 averaged 14.4 percent; they ranged from 5.1 to 22.1 percent.

"Nine factors of resources, opportunity and incentive" that might help explain levels of local political mobilization among minorities were specified (Browning, Marshall, and Tabb 1984, 81–84). They are delineated in Table 18 (the discussion earlier in this chapter suggests a number of these points). Browning, Marshall, and Tabb also pointed to various preconditions to minority influence: the growth of minority populations and Democratic majorities on the city council. The study then examined levels of representation, incorporation, and policy responsiveness.

Hispanic *representation*, or officeholding on city councils, was well below equality or parity; parity was defined as having representation on councils or as being mayor in proportion to overall Hispanic population. For the period from 1975 to 1978, the average Hispanic parity score in the ten cities was about one-third, or .35 (1.00 would indicate equality of representation; Welch 1990). *Political incorporation*, the extent to which a minority group is "represented in coalitions that dominate city policy-making on minority-related issues," was quite low for Hispanics. Finally, and not surprisingly, given the findings on representation and incorporation, there was little *policy responsiveness* to Latinos. Policy responsiveness was measured in terms of public employment, minority membership on city boards and commissions, the establishment of civilian police review boards, the distribution of federal grants, and minority-contracting programs. There was little or no evidence that these policies, which are thought to be especially important to minorities, were adopted in response to Hispanic influence.

Notably, blacks did much better than Hispanics in the politics of these ten northern California cities. Blacks achieved fairly high levels of representation, incorporation, and policy responsiveness. Nonetheless, there is little evidence that the general social or economic status of blacks improved.

The Browning, Marshall, and Tabb study is the most rigorous and extensive examination of a number of cities with substantial Latino populations. Whether the political situation of Hispanics in these northern California cities is indicative of the situation in other cities is a question that deserves consideration (Browning and Marshall 1986).

———————COLORADO CITIES

Another study (Hero 1990), adopting the analytic approach of the Browning, Marshall, and Tabb study, examined two Colorado cities with substantial Hispanic populations, Denver and Pueblo. It compared and contrasted these cities with each other as well as with the ten northern California cities.

Denver and Pueblo rank somewhat differently on the various aspects of the social and political environment suggested in Table 18. In some respects, Pueblo's would seem to be a more supportive environment; overall, however, Denver's sociopolitical environment would lead to the expectation of higher minority political mobilization than in Pueblo. Pueblo's Hispanic population (34 percent) constitutes about twice the proportion of that city's population as does Denver's Hispanic population. Also, the socioeconomic resources of the Hispanic population in Pueblo are higher than in Denver. For example, in 1980, Hispanics in Pueblo had slightly lower levels of poverty than Hispanics in Denver (21 to 23.9 percent), higher levels of per capita income ($4,677 to $4,510), higher educational attainment (12 to 11.1 median school years completed), and a larger percentage in managerial–professional occupations (13.5 to 11 percent) (Hero 1990, 32). Whether these differences are sufficiently large to be of major consequence is unclear.

Most of the other factors would point to a greater Hispanic political mobilization in Denver than in Pueblo. There appears to be greater support for and political resources outside the minority (Hispanic) group in Denver; indicative of this is the electoral support for a Hispanic mayor (Federico Peña) from white liberals and from blacks (see Chapter 7; also see Hero 1987; Hero and Beatty 1989). Some evidence suggests that "demand–protest" activities, which may be precursors to other political activities, have been somewhat more extensive in Denver.[1] Competition with, and modeling after the activities of, other minority groups, such as blacks, is more likely and feasible in Denver, where there is a substantial (12 percent) and active black population, than in Pueblo, which has a small (2 percent) black population.

While it is difficult to measure precisely the "resistance of the dominant coalition,"[2] the factors of size, socioeconomic inequality, and government structure lead one to hypothesize a greater mobilization in Denver. Denver is substantially larger than Pueblo (492,000 to 101,000 population in 1980). There also is greater socioeconomic *inequality* of Hispanics relative to Anglos or the general population in Denver than in Pueblo in terms of the measures suggested earlier (that is, poverty levels, per capita income, education, and the like; see Hero 1990). The assumption is that inequality spurs political action.

Denver's government structure is relatively unreformed, with a strong mayor–council system; is heavily district based; and has a relatively large council (eleven of thirteen council members are elected from districts), albeit with a nonpartisan elected council. In contrast, Pueblo's government stucture is generally reformed with the council–manager system, a numerically smaller council ($N = 7$), and a smaller percentage of council members elected from districts (four of seven, or 57 percent, versus 85 percent in Denver).

_____PRECONDITIONS TO POLITICAL MOBILIZATION

Certain preconditions or contextual variables that may be important (Browning, Marshall, and Tabb 1984) deserve consideration before we consider Hispanic representation in Denver and Pueblo. A first precondition to minority political mobilization is growth in minority population. Both cities have shown substantial relative growth of the Hispanic population in the last generation. Hispanics constituted about 8.7 percent of Denver's population in 1960, 16.8 percent in 1970, and 18.8 percent in 1980. The comparable percentages for 1960, 1970, and 1980 among Pueblo's Hispanics were 17.2, 31.5, and 34.4. In comparison, the average Hispanic population for the ten northern California cities was 10.6 percent in 1970 and 14.4 in 1979 (Browning, Marshall, and Tabb 1984).

Despite the formally nonpartisan nature of the California cities, "new Democratic majorities among voters and on the council" seemed to be another precondition for minority political mobilization (Browning, Marshall, and Tabb 1984). That is, where larger portions of the electorate, and its elected officials, identified themselves as Democrats, more support for minority concerns was found. Since at least 1963, Denver has had a majority of Democrats on its city council; since the mid 1970s, the majority has exceeded 60 percent. Democrats seem to have been overrepresented on the city council in proportion to registered Democratic voters. At the same time, it should be noted that Republican membership on the Denver council exceeded Republican registration in every year except the more recent ones. Both parties are overrepresented on the city council partly because of the substantial number of self-identified Independents among registered voters.

In Pueblo, Democratic council members have long dominated and are overrepresented in proportion to the city's registered voters. And while Republican identifiers constituted a majority of the Pueblo City Council for only the earliest year for which data were collected (1964), Republicans were on average, more heavily overrepresented from 1964 to 1987 in proportion to Republican registered voters than were Democrats.

_____COMPARISONS OF COLORADO AND CALIFORNIA CITIES

Comparing Denver and Pueblo with the California cities as far as partisan competition is concerned is difficult but is worth trying. It appears that in the early to mid 1960s, Denver and Pueblo had slightly more Democratic council membership than was the average for the northern California cities. In the late 1970s, the average Democratic membership for the California councils was higher than that for Denver and Pueblo. The Democratic partisan affiliation of voters in the California cities is and has generally been higher than the percentages in Denver and Pueblo, which are themselves substantial (Browning, Marshall, and Tabb 1984, 35).

_____HISPANIC REPRESENTATION AND INCORPORATION

Findings on the relative *representational parity* of Hispanics in Denver and Pueblo, that is, being represented on the city council or in a mayoral position in proportion to population numbers in the city as a whole,[3] indicate that since the early 1960s, Hispanics in Denver generally have been been underrepresented or below parity in proportion to their numbers in the general population. Before 1975, there was no Hispanic representation on the Denver City Council despite the presence of an all-district (nine-member) council before 1971 and the expansion of that council to thirteen members (eleven from districts and two at-large), in a way that was supposed to enhance the likelihood of Hispanic representation (Lovrich and Marenin 1976; Taebel 1978). In recent years, however, representation has been above parity, generally supporting the expectations indicated earlier.

Hispanic representational parity on the Pueblo City Council has generally been low—lower in fact than in Denver—averaging only about half the Hispanic proportion since 1963. It has also been erratic. The basic relationships and their erratic quality are caused partly by the impact that the presence or absence of one Hispanic council member can have when the total number of councilors is small (seven). Nonetheless, the drop from three Hispanics on the city council in 1976 to none between 1983 and 1987 is substantial.

Hispanics in both Denver and Pueblo had substantially higher scores—more than double—on representational parity during the mid to late 1970s than was the average for Hispanics in the California cities over the same period. Indeed, the average proportional ratio for Denver and Pueblo from the mid 1960s to the mid 1980s, which includes several years in which there was no Hispanic representation in the two cities, is somewhat greater than the average for the northern California cities from 1975 to 1978.

Political *incorporation* here refers not only to representation but also to the position of minority representatives in relation to the dominant coalition on the city council. Incorporation measures the extent to which Hispanic minorities are represented in "coalitions that dominate city policy-making on minority-related issues" (Browning, Marshall, and Tabb 1984, 25, 18). Estimates of Hispanic incorporation[4] (developed by the author based on interviews; see notes) indicate that Denver's incorporation score in 1984 and 1987 is fairly high and is well above that for any of the California cities (the highest of which was 3, in 1978); also, Denver's 1976–1980 score of 2 was well above the average (.5) for the ten northern California cities in 1978. Incorporation in Pueblo is generally much lower than in Denver, but the average score from 1976 to 1980 (1.5) compares favorably with the average in the California cities (.5) in 1978. In short, and as anticipated, Hispanic incorporation is higher in Denver than in Pueblo. Also, the two Colorado cities have greater minority incorporation than do the ten California cities.

At least two variables seem significant regarding the higher representation and incorporation in Denver and Pueblo compared to the California cities, but these variables were not considered in the Browning, Marshall, and Tabb (1984) study. Residential segregation can foster minority representation on a council (Vedlitz and Johnson 1982). Council representation is a prerequisite for incorporation—and in turn, policy responsiveness—in the explanatory model developed by Browning, Marshall, and Tabb. Denver Hispanics are more residentially segregated than are Hispanics in Pueblo and, indeed, in the northern California cities. Mexican–Anglo segregation in 1970 in Denver was 52.8; it was 41.7 in Pueblo and averaged 37.3 in five northern California cities for which data were available (see Lopez 1981).

Second, Denver's largely unreformed government structure also has a somewhat more professionalized council than does Pueblo or the northern California cities studied by Browning, Marshall, and Tabb. Research on U.S. state politics has shown that legislative professionalism may affect policy outputs (Carmines 1974). Professionalism may also play a significant role in institutionalizing influence, including minority influence, at the urban level because it provides resources for councilors to give more time and attention to their legislative and related activities. Members of the Denver City Council are substantially better paid ($18,675 in 1982) than councilors in Pueblo ($2,400) or the California cities studied (*Municipal Yearbook* 1982). Denver councilors also have more staff, and the council appears to have a more formalized committee structure than does Pueblo and the California cities. These factors would, in turn, be expected to have implications for questions of policy responsiveness.

_____POLICY RESPONSIVENESS

Representation and incorporation are important in themselves, but they must also be considered relative to policy responsiveness (Browning, Marshall, and Tabb 1984). The northern California study expected, and found, that greater incorporation is related to greater policy responsiveness. The study used several measures of policy responsiveness, and we replicate the major ones here for Denver and Pueblo.

CITY GOVERNMENT EMPLOYMENT.   One measure of policy responsiveness is the proportion of minority employment in city government. When all city government occupations are considered, Denver is, and has been since at least 1973, above the proportion based on population; Pueblo has been and remains below it. The average Hispanic employment parity in California cities in 1978 was .62 (Browning, Marshall, and Tabb 1984, 196, 266). Denver's Hispanic employment parity was about twice that average in 1978, while Pueblo's was very near that average.

In both Denver and Pueblo, however, Hispanics are heavily concentrated in low-level positions and occupations (Hero 1990). In high-status positions, "officials and administrators," in 1987, Denver's parity score for city employment was .62; Pueblo's was .43. Data for the ten northern California cities in 1978 indicated an average of .45; at about the same time, Denver was somewhat higher (estimate .57), while Pueblo was considerably lower (estimate .26).

CONTRACTING POLICIES.   Another indicator of responsiveness focuses on minority contracting. Several measures evaluated city policies to enhance the opportunities of minority businesses to receive city contracts. First was an assessment as to whether the cities had adopted such contracting practices (cf. Browning, Marshall, and Tabb

1984, 161, 284–285) as "specifically targeting minority entrepreneurs in advertising its contracting needs" and having an ordinance "that permits giving preference to local or minority contractors even if they are not the lowest bidders." Interview responses revealed that of six such practices identified,[5] Denver had adopted essentially *all* of them, while Pueblo had adopted none. And interview responses suggested that the actual *implementation* in Denver of these policies was moderately aggressive. In Pueblo, of course, there was no policy to implement.

Another way to measure minority contracting policies deals with the Community Development Block Grant (CDBG) program, a federal program created in the mid 1970s that allocates monies to cities. CDBG legislation calls for cities to identify the ethnic–racial background of owners of firms that receive contracts to carry out work under the program. Estimates from 1983 to 1987 indicate that, relative to the overall Hispanic population, Hispanic businesses in Denver and Pueblo received .64 and .42 of the contract dollars that parity would imply (based on my calculations and estimates from CDBG data obtained from HUD Regional Office, Denver). While below parity, these percentages are comparable to the average for the northern California cities at an earlier period, 1978 (see Browning, Marshall, and Tabb 1984, 162).[6]

MEMBERSHIP ON CITY BOARDS AND COMMISSIONS. Appointments to city boards and commissions "enable elected officials to reward supporters, to give at least symbolic representation to groups, and to give ambitious activists the opportunity to gain visibility for future political candidacies" (Browning, Marshall, and Tabb 1984, 156–157). As with the other measures of policy responsiveness, Hispanics in Denver are considerably better represented than those in Pueblo, with a proportional score of .91 versus .54 (based on my calculations from city data).[7]

CIVILIAN POLICE REVIEW BOARD. Civilian police review boards have been seen as one way of dealing with concerns surrounding the treatment of minorities by the police. Therefore, the presence or absence of a review board has been used as a measure of policy responsiveness (Browning, Marshall, and Tabb 1984, 152–155).

Neither Denver nor Pueblo has established a civilian police review board, although the creation of a board was discussed with some frequency in Denver during the late 1970s and early 1980s. Interestingly, the election of Federico Peña as Denver's mayor in 1983 dampened discussions on the matter (Browning, Marshall, and Tabb 1984, 155–156). According to interviews I conducted, Peña's election as Denver's chief executive, with the power to appoint the head of the Department of Public Safety and the police chief, allayed minority concerns about police treatment.

————————IMPLICATIONS

The Denver and Pueblo findings suggest that the variables specified by Browning, Marshall, and Tabb are probably important ones in understanding Hispanic political mobilization. Government structure in particular appears significant in explaining the different levels of political mobilization of Denver's versus Pueblo's Hispanic community. It may also explain the considerably higher political mobilization of Denver Hispanics versus comparable figures in the California cities. At a minimum, the findings on the Colorado cities are important in that they indicate that the low levels of Hispanic representation and incorporation, and the resulting low policy responsiveness found in the California cities, are *not* universal. Denver's Hispanic community in particular has obtained political influence well beyond that found in the northern California cities. And the political achievements of Pueblo's Hispanics, while modest relative to Denver's, nonetheless are greater than those in the northern California cities.

Why this is true cannot be explained with any certainty at this point, but we can speculate about it. Regional or state differences may play a role. Garcia and de la Garza (1977), for instance, have claimed that the "Chicano political experience" has been different in the various southwestern states, and Sanchez-Jankowski (1986) has noted the importance of different urban environments for political attitudes. Similarly, the "real" nature and degree of nonpartisanship may differ between northern California and the Colorado cities.

Probably more important is that the role of governmental structure may be greater than the Browning, Marshall, and Tabb study indicated. The potential impact of government structure cannot be systematically or extensively examined in the northern California cities because the ten cities are all basically reformed; thus there simply is not sufficient variation between the cities for purposes of analysis. It is notable that in Denver, with an unreformed structure, including a strong-mayor system—and a Hispanic mayor from 1983 to 1991—political representation, incorporation, and responsiveness are so much greater than in the northern California cities and in Pueblo. Residential segregation and legislative professionalism may also play a role.

Much speculation, and considerable research, has contended that Hispanics are politically acquiescent (Lovrich and Marenin 1976), that they are not very active politically or very effective when they act (Browning, Marshall, and Tabb 1984). The evidence regarding Denver shows that that is not always valid. Clearly, more inquiry into Hispanics in the urban political system remains to be done (see Chapter 10).

———OTHER CITIES

No other cities with substantial Latino populations have been the subject of an examination comparable to that of the northern California cities or the two Colorado cities discussed here. The descriptions and discussions that have been undertaken are summarized briefly in this section.

———SAN ANTONIO

The population of San Antonio is about 55 percent Mexican American. "San Antonio is a unique city. It is unique in being the only 'Mexican' large city in the United States" (Muñoz and Henry 1990, 180). San Antonio received much attention in terms of Latino political development after the election of Henry Cisneros as mayor in 1981. Originally elected to the San Antonio City Council as a candidate of the Anglo and business-dominated Good Government League, Cisneros received considerable electoral support as a mayoral candidate from the Anglo community—and overwhelming support from the city's Hispanic community. Yet evidence indicates that the Cisneros election left the general political standing of Hispanics little changed.

The elections of Cisneros did not translate into Mexican political power for at least two reasons. First, the mayor of San Antonio has little power to make changes: "City government is a weak mayor–strong city council system with a city manager." Second, outside the Mexican American community, Cisneros did not promote either his Mexican American background or the specific interests of the Mexican American community (Muñoz and Henry 1990, 183). His public policy focus was on economic development, but he placed little emphasis on policies explicitly or directly targeted toward poor and minority communities. And research findings indicate that the economic development policies undertaken in San Antonio were not of much benefit to Chicanos (Flores 1989).

————LOS ANGELES

Latinos constitute more than a quarter of the population of Los Angeles, but their representation in city government has historically been well below their proportion of the population. One reason for this disparity is the gerrymandering of electoral districts (Regalado 1988). Also, Latinos fare poorly in Los Angeles on certain measures of policy responsiveness. In 1984, Latino representation on city boards and commissions was .582 of parity. Their overall representation in the city workforce was .611, but in the better job categories—those of "officials and administrators" and "professionals"—Latino parity scores were .262 and .324, respectively (Regalado 1988).

————NEW YORK CITY

Despite New York City's liberal image and a number of structural characteristics that would make the city seem open to minority political influence, Latinos are poorly represented among major decision-making bodies. Latinos make up about 20 percent of the city's population, yet only three City Council members (8.6 percent) are Latinos. Part of this underrepresentation reflects internal division. Although Puerto Ricans constitute the largest portion of New York City's Latino population, theirs is a declining share. Additionally, there are "tensions between natives and immigrants, between different ethnicities, and between the traditional black and Latino minorities and more recently arrived groups" (Mollenkopf 1990, 84). In contrast, minorities, including Latinos, have achieved some level of policy responsiveness, at least as measured by public employment.

————MIAMI

Hispanics have had a rapid political ascendancy in Miami. But in order to understand Latino politics in Miami, some distinctive features of the local situation need to be recognized. Miami's Hispanic population is predominantly Cuban; and what is more important, it is generally wealthier than Latino populations in other cities. Hispanic economic incorporation has significantly facilitated political incorporation. Also, Hispanic incorporation has "preceded rather than followed the incorporation of blacks"; Hispanic incorporation is "widely perceived as not benefiting blacks." Finally, the political incorporation of Hispanics in Miami "has generally not been associated with the building of more liberal coalitions, but has generally had the effect of complementing rather than challenging the agenda of downtown business elites" (Warren, Corbett, and Stack 1990, 172).

_____**SUMMARY AND CONCLUSION**

Latinos are a largely urban population, and urban politics has often been seen as an avenue for the upward mobility of disadvantaged groups in the United States. But, contrary to the rainbow theory, a theory that has come to be seen as a myth regarding earlier white ethnic groups, Latinos have not had a major influence on U.S. urban politics. There are a number of reasons for this, including the historical development, politicoeconomic circumstances, and government structural characteristics of cities. U.S. cities with substantial Latino populations seem not to be tending toward minority-group empowerment.

9

Latinos and Public Policies

————*Public policy* can be defined as the sum of activities of governments—whether the governments act directly or through intermediate institutions or other agents—as it has an influence on the lives of citizens in a society. Public policy includes *policy choices*—decisions regarding the use of public power to affect the lives of citizens; *policy outputs*—policy choices put into action; and *policy impacts*—the effects of policy choices and policy outcomes on citizens (Peters 1986, 4–5). Public policy is formulated in a variety of arenas and is carried out through various mechanisms or instruments. The most common instruments are laws, court decisions, government services, and money, although any one policy may use several of these instruments simultaneously. The impact of public policies may be direct or indirect, intentional or unintentional, short term or long term. These points about public policy are important to keep in mind generally and are particularly significant for Latinos and public policy.

The choices that government bodies make, the "things" that governments actually do, are important in understanding whether and how governments respond to citizen pressure and citizens' needs. How public policy affects groups and what governments do about, for, and to groups in a society are important to examine. Understanding public policy as it affects Latinos and other minority groups may be especially important because these groups are more often acted upon by govern-

155

ment; they are often unable to shape the policies that governmental institutions adopt and implement.

Before we examine the issue of Latinos and public policy, we should ask a couple of pertinent questions. Are there government policies that have uniquely significant implications for Latinos? Or do Latinos simply have the same concerns as others (especially low-income minority groups), but to different degrees? It is noteworthy that the answer to *both* questions is probably yes. Several concerns do seem unique to Latinos; language policies such as Official English and bilingual education policies are examples that come quickly to mind. Latinos, for example, are particularly concerned about and *opposed* to the enactment of Official English or English Only measures. But Latinos have numerous concerns in common with other groups, although Latinos may be especially affected by them because of their relatively low socioeconomic status. Education in general, tax policy, and affordable housing are common examples.

This chapter focuses on several policies that have a special significance for the Latino community. We are constrained somewhat in our discussion by those aspects of the policy process (formulation, implementation, outcomes, impact, etc.) where there is available political science research on the issues. Most research has focused on the outcomes and impacts of policies on Latinos; seldom has the research detailed the particular processes leading to those outcomes and impacts (see, however, Lipsky 1980).

_____EDUCATION

Education is and long has been a central public policy issue. There is a strong belief in the United States that education is vital to the proper functioning of democracy, national economic development, and social stability. At the individual level, we view educational achievement as crucial for upward social mobility, and we recognize that education affects "life chances" in such areas as employment, income, quality of housing, and access to health care (Meier and Stewart 1991). Moreover, education clearly is a leading public policy concern among Latinos (see, e.g., LARASA 1989). Despite this, Latino educational achievement lags behind that of Anglos and blacks.

Education plays a pivotal role in socioeconomic well-being, but for many years recognition of that fact was coupled with the notion that education policy should be apolitical or nonpolitical. Education was viewed outside politics, as "above" politics; it was largely a task consigned to expert professionals. Only in the last generation or so has education come to be seen as political because it consumes enormous amounts of public funds and plays a major role in what social and political values are considered important, appropriate, and legitimate. Because education is so significant, understanding its impact is critical in understanding the political status of Latinos.

For many years, children of different ethnic–racial backgrounds were segregated in separate schools. Considerable efforts toward school desegregation came in the wake of several U.S. Supreme Court decisions in the 1950s. Yet Latinos did not push for desegregation to the same extent as blacks did (Meier and Stewart 1991). Instead, Latino groups placed greater emphasis on bilingual and bicultural education programs as mechanisms to improve educational outcomes. In any event, it came to be recognized that students can be, and often are, segregated *within* schools. Several studies have explored how this happens, what factors influence the extent to which resegregation and differential treatment of students takes place, and the consequences of these processes.

The term *second-generation discrimination* has been used to describe the differential and negative treatment that minorities may experience in schools after formal desegregation. Second-generation discrimination is a form of institutional discrimination, a process that occurs "when the rules or procedures of an organization are such that the neutral application of these rules and procedures results in a disproportionate impact on minorities" (Meier and Stewart 1991, 205–206). Second-generation discrimination has various aspects and forms. In one form, individuals are placed in different groups on the basis of alleged ability, through curriculum tracking, special education, compensatory education and their ability to comprehend English. "Through the arbitrary and capricious selection and subsequent placement of Hispanic children in certain types of classes, Hispanic children can be denied access to quality education" (Meier and Stewart 1991, 16–23).

Disciplinary practices, if applied differently to students on the basis of their ethnic–racial background, are another form of second-generation discrimination. The two practices—ability grouping and differential discipline—in turn may have implications for educational "outputs" in terms of dropout rates, graduation rates, students losing interest in school, or students not receiving the same quality of education as other children (Meier and Stewart 1991, 23–26).

A comprehensive study of the politics of Hispanic education examined 142 local school districts in the United States with at least five thousand students and at least 5 percent Hispanic enrollment to ascertain whether second-generation discrimination in fact occurs and, if so, its extent. Data covered the 1970s to 1987 (Meier and Stewart 1991). A major finding of the study was that Hispanics were overrepresented in undesirable and underrepresented in desirable academic groupings. Specifically, Hispanics were significantly overrepresented in classes for the "educable mentally retarded" and, to a lesser degree, "trainable mentally retarded"; they were underrepresented in classes for the "gifted." Hispanics also were dramatically overrpresented in bilingual education classes. Although this latter finding may seem entirely logical and thus theoretically unimportant, the potential reasons for, and consequences of, this overrepresentation are noteworthy both theoretically and practically, and are discussed later in the chapter.

Regarding disciplinary practices, Hispanics are significantly more likely to be suspended and expelled than Anglo students. In earlier days, Hispanic students were more likely to suffer disproportionately from corporal punishment; this is no longer evident. In terms of educational achievement, "Hispanic high school graduation rates are only about three-fourths the size that one would expect given their numbers in the student body. Anglo graduation rates are twenty percent and more above expected percentages" (Meier and Stewart 1991, 134–135). Hispanic dropout rates in 1976, the only year for which these data are available, were about 27 percent above what would be expected statistically and were significantly higher than the white dropout ratio.

Overall, the patterns and intercorrelations of education outcomes are sufficiently consistent and strong that Meier and Stewart (1991) feel that "discrimination" is an apt characterization of the educational situation faced by Hispanics. Moreover, their study affirms that second-generation discrimination results from political representation, race, and social class, rather than other factors. Other possible explanations—specifically, school district resources, language problems of Latinos, and the recency of immigration—do *not* explain second-generation discrimination (Meier and Stewart 1991, 158–162).

Another notable finding of this study is the difference between three Latino groups in the extent and kind of discrimination. Academic grouping into lower-ability groups affects Mexican Americans more than Puerto Rican or Cuban American students. Cuban American disciplinary treatment is fairly similar to that for Anglos. Mexican Americans and Puerto Ricans suffer disproportionately on several measures of disciplinary practice, but the former are disadvantaged with respect to suspensions, while Puerto Ricans are highly overrepresented in terms of expulsions. *None* of the three Latino groups has much access to gifted classes.

There are related patterns regarding educational achievement. Cuban American achievement is comparable to that of Anglos. Mexican Americans do worst in terms of dropouts and have low graduation rates; Puerto Ricans have the lowest graduation rates, although their dropout rate is less than that for Mexican Americans (Meier and Stewart 1991, 135–138).

What factors relate to the general degree of second-generation discrimination against Hispanics? Different explanatory factors are significant for different dimensions of discrimination. The factors most consistently related to the several kinds of discrimination (i.e., ability grouping, discipline, and achievement) are the proportion of black students in a school district and the size of the school district. Higher proportions of black students in a district are associated with *less* discrimination against Hispanics. The speculation is that, because Hispanics are seen as more similar socially to Anglos than blacks are, Anglos are more willing to be supportive of Hispanics than blacks and to discriminate against the latter. Large district size appears to correlate with less discrimination against Hispanic students because district size is associated with "more professional" school districts, as well as with greater visibility to government agencies responsible for monitoring discrimination (Meier and Stewart 1991, 156–157).

Hispanic representation in official capacities, such as teachers and administrators, was also found to be important. It resulted in fewer Hispanic students being placed in remedial classes, more Hispanic placements in gifted programs, fewer Hispanic enrollments in bilingual programs, higher Hispanic graduation rates (Meier and Stewart 1991, 257–258).

Overall, interrelated processes seem to be at work. Along with school size and the size of a school's black population—factors beyond the control of the Hispanic community—an increase in the proportions of Hispanic teachers (i.e., representation) produces less second-generation discrimination. And increased numbers of Hispanic teachers are linked to increased numbers of Hispanic administrators; in turn, the number of Hispanic administrators is linked to Hispanic membership on school boards. And finally, school board membership is linked to

Hispanic social and political resources. Thus, in places where Hispanics have the greatest resources, as indicated by higher levels of education in the local Hispanic community, second-generation discrimination decreases. Hence, it is not surprising that Cuban Americans suffer the least second-generation discrimination, for they are better-off than other Latinos, but still probably less well-off than the general population. At the same time, Mexican Americans have the highest level of political representation *relative to their socioeconomic status*.

The general message is that Hispanics suffer second-generation discrimination, although it is not, on the whole, as great as that of blacks. Educational discrimination regarding Hispanics may also differ in *form* from discrimination against blacks, for example, in bilingual education programs, which are an important mechanism for Latinos. Second-generation discrimination also differs between Latino groups. From the standpoint of the broader political process, a central conclusion of this study is that the "political process model" of second-generation discrimination does not explain the situation of Hispanics as well as it does that of blacks. "Political models of Hispanic discrimination do not predict as well as black models . . . because Hispanics do not have the same political clout that blacks do" (Meier and Stewart 1991, 156–158). Hispanics have fewer political resources—representation on school boards, Hispanic administrators and teachers. Second-generation discrimination is lessened by greater political resources and their effective use.

The Meier and Stewart study presents another argument. Building on the work of other scholars, they test the "power hypothesis" that as a result of greater social similarities between Hispanics and Anglos than between Anglos and blacks, Hispanics are preferred over blacks when it comes to political alliances. Relatedly, where there are high concentrations of poor Anglos, Hispanics are looked on favorably, are seen as desirable coalition partners, and, indeed, suffer less damage from second-generation discrimination (Meier and Stewart 1991).

This seems to be another form of coalition-bias argument, and it also suggests two things further: (1) Social class and ethnic background may not be related quite so simply as the coalitional bias theory implies—*which* minority groups one is talking about may be another important factor (Stone 1986); and (2) social similarity or social distance is the primary criterion that groups consider when choosing coalition partners. The implication here is that social distance outweighs other factors, such as how politically cohesive or well mobilized a group is, when groups are assessing political strategies.

Nevertheless, if the "power hypothesis" suggests that middle-class Hispanics are preferred over lower-class Anglo candidates, an important point may be overlooked. There are probably few circumstances in which a viable candidate for office, of whatever ethnic–racial background, is *not* of middle-class or at least upper-working-class, background (Wolfinger 1974; Baird 1977). In any event, despite some ostensible advantages of Hispanics over blacks, Hispanics are most underrepresented in educational bureaucracies.

_____PUBLIC EMPLOYMENT

Public-sector employment historically has been perceived as a major means to upward mobility for ethnic minorities (Wolfinger 1974; Erie 1985; and see Chapter 8). Government jobs presumably provide income and security, and may be more readily available to ethnic–racial minorities than private-sector employment. Minority representation in government jobs is also important from the standpoint of descriptive and substantive representation. Some observers claim that it is appropriate, desirable, and necessary that government bureaucracies represent, or mirror and reflect (are "descriptive of"), the general population. Also, because the social background of public servants may affect their behavior toward and treatment of citizens, the composition of the bureaucracy may have substantive implications.

Since the early 1970s, the national government has in various ways encouraged the hiring of minorities for public-sector jobs and has monitored itself and state and local governments regarding levels of minority employment. The outcomes of these policies—more specifically, the levels of Latino public employment—and what factors seem to explain the patterns found, deserve attention.

There have been few studies of Latino public-employment patterns; nonetheless, the findings are generally consistent. First, Hispanics are underrepresented in public-sector bureaucracies in the United States; second, they are largely concentrated at the lower-income and -occupational levels of the bureaucracy.

_____FEDERAL JOBS

Latino representation in the federal bureaucracy in 1986 was about 70 to 80 percent of parity; this indicates an increase from 1982, when the parity ratio was .60 to .70. Latino employment was greatest in low-level jobs; at GS 1–4 positions, Latino presence was near parity (.97) in 1986. Latino presence decreases considerably as one moves up the occupational and income scales. For the higher-paying (GS 13–15) positions, the parity ratio is .34; and in executive positions, the parity ratio is .17. The ratio for executive positions is lower than the 1982 ratio of .19.

Meier and Stewart (1991, 105) reported Latino parity in federal public employment in 1989 as follows: .58 for "all federal employees," .69 for GS 1–4, .57 for GS 5–8, .46 for GS 9–12, .25 for GS 13–15, and .17 for executives. These data indicate a *decline* in Latino public employment in the late 1980s.

The data from the mid 1980s permit comparison with blacks. In 1986, black employment in GS 1–4 positions was more than twice parity, 2.23. At higher levels (GS 13–15), the black parity ratio was .46; in executive positions, it was .38. Thus, in terms of the federal bureaucracy, blacks have substantially higher parity ratios than Latinos. Still, both groups fall well short of parity in middle- and higher-level positions.

———————STATE AND LOCAL JOBS

According to a study of state and local governments, Hispanics accounted for 3.3 percent and 3.8 percent of all state and local government employment in 1973 and 1976, respectively (Sigelman and Cayer 1986). By 1980, the rate had increased to 4 percent, for a parity ratio of about .61. Another study reported similar findings; it also underscored the concentration of Hispanics in lower-level positions. Hispanic representation ratios were .65 for all employees, .48 for technical and professional employees, and .37 for managers (Dometrious and Sigelman 1984). By 1989, Latino representational parity among state and local employees was as follows: administrators–officials, .35; professionals, .47; technicians, .62; protective services, .65; paraprofessionals, .64; clerical, .84; skilled craft, .81; and service–maintenance, 1.08 (Meier and Stewart 1991, 105).

We can also look at data on salaries. Using the salary levels of white males as a standard (i.e., 1.00), in 1980 the salary index for Spanish-surnamed males was .87, up from .81 in 1973. For Spanish-surnamed females, the 1980 index was .70, up from .66 in 1973. Thus, in 1980 the salaries of Latino males were about 13 percent less than those of white males, and Latinas were about 30 percent less. We can also compare Latinos to other groups. The Latino male salary index of .87 in 1986 was lower than that for all groups of males (white, 1.00; Asian, 1.25; and Indian, .92) other than black males (.79). Similarly, the salary index for Spanish-surnamed females (.70) was lower than that for all groups of females (white, .74; Asian, .91; Indian, .73) other than black females (.69).

The Browning, Marshall, and Tabb (1984) study of ten northern California cities (see Chapter 8) found a Hispanic parity ratio of .65 in 1978 in public employment in those cities, up from .32 in 1966. My study of two Colorado cities, Denver and Pueblo, found that in Denver, for all occupations, Hispanics were represented above parity (1.18) as early as 1973 and that the ratio had increased to 1.47 by 1986. In employment among officials and administrators in Denver, the parity ratio was .25 in 1973 and .62 in 1986. In Pueblo, Hispanic parity for all occupations was .64 in 1973 and .75 in 1986; for officials and administrators it was .17 in 1976 and .43 in 1986 (Hero 1990). A 1989 study of twelve hundred cities in the United States found the following parity scores for Hispanics: .782 for total jobs, .356 for officials–administrators, .447 for professional positions, and .582 for protective-service positions (Mladenka 1989).

Hispanic representation among teachers and school administrators in the 142 school districts studied by Meier and Stewart (1991) was also very low. The parity ratio for Hispanic teachers was .38 in 1986, but this ratio is about double what it had been in 1968. The ratio for Hispanic school administrators in 1986 (.39) indicates a 61 percent underrepresentation (no data are available for earlier years).

Another study, of cities in the Southwest with at least a twenty-five-thousand population and a 10 percent Spanish-surnamed population in 1970, found that, overall, Hispanic presence in city bureaucracies was near parity, although Hispanic males were substantially overrepresented and females were dramatically underrepresented (Welch, Karnig, and Eribes 1983). The same study also presented salary data. "In general, Hispanic males are paid less than Anglo males, although by 1978 near parity existed in the professional and clerical occupations." In clerical positions, Hispanic females are nearly equal in salary to others, but "lag far behind the Anglo male pacesetters in every other occupation."

What factors can help "explain" levels of Hispanic representation in public employment? One study that systematically examined that question focused on local governments because at the local level there were enough cases to permit consideration of a number of variables. Welch, Karnig, and Eribes (1983) found that Hispanic public employment in city jobs is most strongly and consistently related to the proportion of Hispanics in a city's population. The locale or state also seems important. Cities in New Mexico and Texas tend to have higher levels of Latino employment; Colorado and California tend to have relatively lower levels. Also, there is a negative relationship with the presence of large black populations; as the size of the black population increases, Latino employment decreases for males, but not for females. City-manager, rather than mayor–council, systems have a small positive effect on Hispanic employment in the professional category, but not for other categories of employment.

A 1989 study of twelve hundred cities with over ten thousand population in the United States found that when examining all cities without respect to the proportion of Hispanic population, the proportion of the Hispanic population is the dominant factor in explaining Hispanic public employment in cities; Hispanic representation (on the city council or as mayor) is also important (Mladenka 1989). When only those cities with 10 percent or more Hispanic population were examined, the size of the public sector became an important factor: the larger the city's public sector (i.e., government employees per 1,000 population), the larger the proportion of Hispanics in municipal employment (see Chapter 8 on urban politics). Also, Hispanics have higher levels of public employment in *reformed* than *unreformed* cities, a finding that runs counter to earlier theorizing and research regarding the impact of government structure on urban politics and policy outputs. In addition, public-employee unions have only a limited detrimental impact on Hispanic efforts to secure public employment; public-employee unions have a negative effect on blacks, although blacks do much better overall than Hispanics in terms of public employment relative to their respective shares of the population (Mladenka 1989).

In discussing the findings about the impact of government structure—more specifically, city-manager systems—Mladenka speculates that if a city manager is sensitive to minority aspirations, "he may well be in a better position than the mayor in an unreformed system to increase the Hispanic share of public jobs. As the Hispanic presence on council increases, the manager will likely be more receptive to minority demands" (Mladenka 1989, 404; cf. Lyons 1978). Regarding city public employment, the "prognosis for Hispanics is good" because as a result of "reduced levels of social isolation and residential segregation, they are likely to experience fewer obstacles on their way to continued political progress" (Mladenka 1989, 405).

The Browing, Marshall, and Tabb (1984) study of northern California cities also found low Hispanic public-employment parity, lower than that for blacks. Of the variables examined, the only one that seemed related to levels of Hispanic public employment was size of the Hispanic population. In none of the ten cities studied had "Hispanics generated the combination of demand-protest and incorporation" found to lead to substantial levels of public employment for blacks. This study suggests that political activity can indeed generate policy responsiveness, including public-employment opportunities. The claim is that Hispanics have not engaged in those activities to a degree that will produce policy responsiveness.

The Meier and Stewart (1991) study of Hispanic education found that Hispanic population and school board membership are most strongly related to the level of Hispanics holding positions in school district *administration* (also see Dye and Renick 1981). When we examine levels of Hispanic public employment among *teachers*, the presence of Hispanic administrators is the most related variable. Also, when Mexican Americans are the predominant Hispanic group, employment ratios (parity) for administrators is higher than when Cubans and Puerto Ricans are the predominant Hispanic group.

In summary, studies examining Hispanic employment in cities tend to find that the size of the Hispanic population, the size of the local public sector, and Hispanic representation in elected and administrative positions are the three most important factors. Findings that reformed systems (rather than unreformed) and city-manager cities (rather than mayor–council) are environments more conducive to Latino public employment are also noteworthy.

LANGUAGE POLICY

The status of one's language in a society can have an impact on individual self-esteem and raise "deeper issues of group worth" (Citrin et al. 1990). Issues of language policy were very visible in the United States during the mid to late 1980s, particularly in the form of measures for Official English or English Only. The vast majority of Latinos opposed these measures, probably because they perceived them as aimed at their community. Despite Latino concern and opposition, Official English has been adopted in a number of states, including several states with large Hispanic populations. We should discuss this movement for several reasons. Among the questions worth examining are these: What accounts for the emergence, or reemergence, of an Official

English movement? Where have such measures been enacted, and what factors have been associated with those enactments? What might Official English measures mean for Latinos in American society and politics?

During much of the nineteenth and early twentieth centuries, language diversity was generally tolerated in the United States. After World War I, however, the "liberal tradition of tolerance for bilingualism was in remission. The symbolic defense of English was one element in the effort of dominant ethnic groups to repulse a perceived threat to their values and customs" (Citrin et al. 1990, 536–538). Language issues receded from the public agenda after the mid 1920s, but they have reemerged. Several reasons have been offered to explain that reemergence.

In the 1960s, new laws regarding immigration brought dramatic increases in the numbers and percentages of Latin American immigrants, particularly Mexicans. Because all immigrants initially maintain their native language, this aroused much concern about the new immigration. Also, various government policies *supported* those minorities wishing to retain their native languages. Bilingual education programs, court decisions, and administrative regulations in the 1970s seemed to favor the use of languages other than English. But some research indicated that bilingual programs did not work to improve English proficiency or academic achievement; instead, they led to classroom segregation of Hispanic children (Citrin et al. 1990).

These developments led to a concern among people who eventually came to support Official English. They felt that the failure to promote a common language would produce social and political disunity and unrest. After failing to secure action in Congress, proponents of Official English focused their attention on the states. Since 1981, all but four states have considered the enactment of Official English laws or the question of an official language on initiatives (Citrin et al. 1990).

Supporters of Official English deny that they harbor hostility toward minorities. Instead, they claim to be concerned only with political cohesion and stability. They say that they do *not* want to negate existing programs that may have encouraged the use of languages other than English; their focus is on checking the further spread of these programs, which they believe undermine a common national identity. Moreover, they claim that they are interested in the well-being of the minority community; that is, they feel that minorities benefit by learning the English language (Citrin et al. 1990).

Opponents of Official English measures see them as insulting, perhaps racist, and probably unnecessary. Those who oppose the measures argue that English is and has been the de facto official language of the United States; there is no need to affirm or reaffirm that language use through laws. Indeed, opponents of Official English say it implies a distrust of Spanish speakers and an implicit devaluing of the Spanish language and Spanish culture. Official English measures are particularly decried in view of the evidence that Hispanics develop English proficiency as rapidly as have other ethnic groups historically. The reason Hispanics are seen as not learning English rapidly enough probably reflects the continued Hispanic immigration; that is, the newly arrived are not immediately proficient in English (Citrin et al. 1990).

By the early 1980s, only three states had decreed that English was their only official language; by 1989, that number had grown to sixteen. A number of state legislatures passed such measures. Four states with substantial Latino populations—California in 1986, and Arizona, Colorado, and Florida in 1988—passed constitutional amendments through popular initiatives. The form and the strength of Official English measures differed considerably. In a number of instances, the measures consisted of simple declarations; other measures were more stringent and detailed, and would probably have more substantive impact.

The constitutional amendment in Arizona, among the most stringent measures, specified that English would be the "official language . . . is the language of the ballot, the public schools and all government functions and actions." The amendment applied to (1) the "legislative, executive and judicial branches of government; (2) all political subdivisions, departments, agencies, organizations, and instrumentalities of this State, including local governments and municipalities; (3) all statutes, ordinances, rules, orders, programs and policies; and (4) all government officials and employees during the performance of government business." It also gave state residents the right to sue in order to enforce the amendment in court. A federal district court struck down the measure.

Several Official English measures have been subject to court interpretation. The California Supreme Court has found the California amendment to be primarily "symbolic"; its substantive impact, therefore, will probably be limited.

What kinds of states have adopted Official English measures? According to one analysis, adoptions through the *state legislature* have occurred primarily in southern states with negligible numbers of Hispanics or other foreign-born populations (Citrin et al., 1990). In states in which 10 percent or more of the population spoke a language other than English, state legislatures have *not* enacted language policies. Nevertheless, in the four states with the highest concentration of non-English speakers, immigrants, Hispanics, and Asians, voters have used the *initiative* process to add English-language amendments to the state constitution (Citrin et al., 1990).

Where Official English measures have been put to a vote, in general voters have supported them rather strongly, although Hispanics, and to a lesser degree Asians, are decidedly opposed. An analysis of the voting on the 1986 California proposition, which passed with 73 percent approval, found that "having a Hispanic or Asian background, a college education, being registered as a Democrat and identifying oneself politically as liberal rather than moderate or conservative" were significantly related to voting against the measure (Citrin et al. 1990). In Arizona, an estimated 80 percent of Hispanics voted against the English Only amendment, although the measure narrowly passed (51 to 49 percent). In the precincts that were most heavily Hispanic, opposition was almost universal (Hero 1989). In Florida, too, there was overwhelming Hispanic opposition (about 80 percent), but strong white and black support (more than 70 percent) passed that state's initiative (Citrin et al. 1990).

The popularity of and support for Official English measures among the general population occur because such support represents a positive statement about, or a symbolic affirmation of, identity with the nation. The general public seems to view the ability to speak English as among those characteristics essential to defining "what it means to be an American." "Feelings of nationalism are a principal source of the mass appeal of 'official English'; patriotism is a key symbolic issue raised by language policy" (Citrin et al. 1990, 557). Concern that the newcomers may threaten one's economic well-being, as well as ethnic resentment, are plausible explanations for support of Official English measures, but these factors do not seem to be especially important (Citrin et al. 1990).

————HOUSING

Housing is important not only because of the basic need for shelter but also because it is often linked to other dimensions of physical well-being—for example, health, safety, and transportation—

which in turn are related to employment, educational, and larger economic opportunities (Lopez 1986). Governments at the national, state, and local levels can affect the availability of housing through such mechanisms as the tax structure, programs that provide low-interest housing loans, and public housing. Government can affect the quality and availability of housing through zoning policies and the provision of various public services to houses and neighborhoods, including housing inspections. Government can also affect housing patterns, that is, who lives where, to the extent that it encourages or discourages people of different social and ethnic–racial backgrounds from living in greater or lesser proximity to one other.

With its emphasis on equality without respect to race, ethnicity, and so on, the United States would be expected to have residential housing patterns that are mostly affected by income levels. But evidence suggests that "while income differentials may explain some location differences they fail to account for significant disparities in group distribution" in housing patterns (Lopez 1986, 129). Latinos are more residentially segregated than would be expected based solely on socioeconomic status.

The federal government's tax code encourages homeownership through its provision for home mortgage deductions, a benefit that can be received by anyone who can afford to purchase a house in the first place. This in an instance where an ostensibly neutral policy has a differential impact on individuals and groups based on their socioeconomic conditions. Given the data regarding the socioeconomic status of Latinos and other minorities, one would expect that Latinos would be somewhat less likely than others to be homeowners. And in 1980, 43.3 percent of Hispanics, compared to 68.5 percent of non-Hispanic whites, owned their own homes.

Several programs seek to assure equal housing opportunities. The 1977 Federal Community Reinvestment Act, for example, prohibits lending institutions from racial discrimination in their home-lending practices. Yet studies in a number of cities have found that "race—not income—appeared to determine home-lending patterns" at savings and loans institutions (*Denver Post*, October 1, 1989).

————IMMIGRATION POLICY

The federal government's immigration policy has had the greatest impact on Mexican Americans because of the long, shared border between the United States and Mexico. Puerto Ricans, who are already U.S. citizens, have not been affected by immigration policy, and Cubans have been most affected by government policies regarding refugees (Moore and Pachon 1985, 135).

Immigration policy in the Western hemisphere has been "an endless struggle between racial and cultural prejudice—and economic opportunism" (Moore and Pachon 1985). Following a long period of minimal restrictions on immigration, policies became more restrictive about 1875. Despite attitudes that were racially biased against Mexicans, when the "national origin" quota system was enacted in the mid 1920s, Mexicans and other Western hemisphere immigrants were treated as exceptions because of "strong pressure from border state ranchers and employers who made a powerful case for the continuing need for Mexican labor" and "the ideology of pan-Americanism as an overriding and traditional policy" (Moore and Pachon 1985, 136).

During most of the 1900s, the flow of Mexican immigrants was managed through administrative controls. As circumstances warranted, that is, as the need for cheap labor increased or decreased, the administration of policy was adjusted accordingly to encourage or discourage Mexicans. Also, during most of the period between 1942 and 1964, Mexican workers were recruited to work in the border states under the Bracero, or contract labor, program.

Policy changes in the mid 1960s, especially the termination of the program that had favored northern and western Europeans, along with other developments, changed the national-origin composition of immigrants from predominantly European to predominantly Latin and Asian. Illegal immigration from Mexico and other Latin American and Caribbean countries also grew during the 1970s and 1980s. Increasingly, the "U.S. public perceived that illegal aliens were a 'problem'" (Bean, Vernez, and Keely 1989, 21–22).

Concern over illegal immigration eventually led to the enactment of the Immigration Reform and Control Act (IRCA) of 1986. A primary purpose of IRCA was to reduce illegal immigration; major mechanisms to achieve this end were employer requirements and sanctions, making it illegal to hire undocumented workers, and increased border-patrol inspections and other enforcement activities. Advocates of ethnic and religious groups had strong enough support in Congress to block passage of the employer sanctions bill unless it included the legalization of undocumented aliens already residing in the United States. The legalization provisions, which were controversial, instituted two programs. One pertained to "general legalization for those illegally resident in the country since January 1, 1982" and the other was a special program for workers in the agricultural sector (Bean, Vernez, and Keely 1989, 25–26).

Other IRCA provisions, also pushed by advocates for ethnic groups, were antidiscrimination safeguards "designed to prevent employment discrimination against foreign-looking and foreign-sounding citizens and legal aliens." Existing prohibitions against employment discrimination based on national origin were expanded under IRCA to prohibit discrimination on the basis of citizenship status. The law also mandated an annual report from the General Accounting Office to Congress "to determine if a pattern of discrimination based on national origin is resulting from employer sanctions" (Bean, Vernez, and Keely 1989, 27).

The implementation of IRCA has been questioned on several grounds. Some observers have claimed that the registration fees required of those seeking legalization are extremely high. Other criticisms have been directed at the alleged inadequacies of formal outreach and public information programs, lack of uniformity in administration and regulation across regions and districts, and the large number of applications for temporary residence that have not been processed (Bean, Vernez, and Keely 1989, chap. 4). Assessments of IRCA's impact have noted several consequences. A major question concerns discrimination; some early evidence indicated that the concern about employer sanctions leading to discrimination against those, such as Latinos, who are "foreign-looking" and "foreign-sounding" was well founded. As a result, several Latino groups have called for the repeal of employer sanctions (*Denver Post*, November 14, 1990). Latino groups and others have also argued that there are major disincentives to participation in IRCA's legalization program. These include fear of the Immigration and Naturalization Service (INS), documentation requirements, the cost of the application process, complex eligibility requirements, and the exclusion of family members from legalization unless they are eligible in their own right (Bean, Vernez, and Keely 1989, chap. 5). Latino groups have been concerned that the structure and administration of IRCA may make it a "restrictive," rather than a "regulatory" program, and have thus monitored the law's impact.

SUMMARY AND CONCLUSION

The policies that governments enact and implement, and their impact on Latinos, have been the focus of this chapter. The scant evidence available indicates that, with few exceptions, Latinos have not had much impact on the formulation of policies. And the policy outcomes for Latinos have been quite negative. This is most evident in the highly significant area of education policy. Second-generation discrimination in education exists and is attributable to the low ethnic–racial and socioeconomic status of Latinos, not to language problems or recency of immigration. Latino status regarding public employment indicates a fairly high level of employment, but in low-status and low-paying jobs. And Official English measures, which are seen as symbolically, if not substantively, detrimental to Latinos, were adopted in a number of states during the 1980s. In other policy areas, Latino concerns seem to be, at most, only partly addressed.

10

The Study of Latino Politics: Questions and Issues

————The *study* of politics, no less than politics itself, is an inherently normative enterprise, involving a variety of theoretical and normative assumptions, choices of what questions to study, how to study those questions, and so on (Rocco 1977; Shapiro 1981). The recognition of the normative biases of political and social science research, in fact, gave impetus to the development of alternative theoretical frameworks, such as internal colonialism, to study Latino politics, and to the creation of alternative professional scholarly organizations, such as the National Association of Chicano Studies (NACS) and similar groups (Muñoz 1989).

We have discussed a great deal of research on Latinos and politics in the United States. To this point, most of that research has been essentially accepted as accurate and appropriate; with few exceptions, the foci, assumptions, findings, and conclusions of the research have not been questioned. It is important now to examine that body of work more carefully and critically.

What biases might there be in academic research regarding Latinos and other minority groups? Evidence exists that bias does occur, although that evidence has itself largely been ignored in political science circles. We can talk about two forms of bias: one of omission, that is, the absence of significant research on many issues of Latino politics; and one of commission.

A study comparing the number of articles on race, gender, and eth-

173

nicity in selected political science and sociology journals from 1964 to 1988 noted a paucity or even an absence of such articles by political scientists (Avalos 1989). The three most prestigious journals in the field of U.S. politics (*American Political Science Review, American Journal of Political Science,* and *Journal of Politics*) collectively published only one article focusing on Hispanics over this twenty-five-year period. Another scholarly journal, *Western Political Quarterly,* generally perceived as somewhat less prestigious than the top three, published nine articles on Latino politics in this quarter-century. In contrast, the three most prestigious sociology journals (*American Sociological Review, American Journal of Sociology,* and *Social Forces*) published significantly more articles (forty) during this time than the political science journals.

It is certainly difficult to specify, or even to establish normative or quantitative criteria for specifying, how much research (*published* research) there might or should be regarding Latinos and U.S. politics. Yet that the three major sociological journals published four times as many articles (forty versus ten) on Hispanics as did four major political science journals is difficult to explain.

How can we explain the absolute and relative absence, in political science, compared to sociology and other disciplines, of articles on Latinos and U.S. politics? Several explanations have been offered. First, the historical development of political science and sociology were different; studies of race and ethnicity in sociology date back to the early 1900s, including the work of early urban sociologists (Avalos 1989, 14). But this partly begs the question. That is, the explanation does not address why political science has a tradition that seems to ignore or neglect certain research topics. Notably, however, when political science first developed as a distinct academic discipline, it had a rather strong "prescriptive" flavor. For instance, some of its early scholars were major advocates for reformed urban government structures.

Avalos (1989) suggests that a second reason for the dearth of political science research on Latinos may be "the domination of somewhat more narrowly defined topics in mainstream political science journals as opposed to the more varied range of topics found in sociology journals." More specifically, "over the last twenty-five years . . . the single most important topic of publication" in the three major political science journals "has been in the area of elections and voting behavior." Yet very few articles published in these journals examine the political behavior of Latinos or other minority groups, nor do they use race or ethnicity as important variables in their analyses. This in large part "may be due to the fact that the primary data used for these analyses, the National Election Survey (NES) has *never* oversampled any minority group . . . so that analysis of ethnic electoral behavioral could be done" (Avalos 1989, 15).

A third explanation offered by Avalos is "the reluctance on the part of the discipline of political science to accept critical (or radical political economy) theory as a legitimate model of analysis of political phenomena." Scholars who are themselves Latinos have been disproportionately involved in research on Latino politics, and "a number of Latino scholars, especially those trained in the late 1960s and early 1970s, have adopted a critical theory approach to the study of Latino political phenomena . . . yet they have very few journals available for submission of their research," and few if any of these journals are considered to be political science journals (Avalos 1989).

This assessment of research on Latino politics is in many respects similar to that of another scholar regarding the study of *black* politics; his contentions seem applicable to Latinos and politics. Wilson (1985) finds that sociology journals and history journals have been much more likely to publish research on minorities (blacks) than have political science journals. This may be due partly to how the disciplines define their domain.

> It may be . . . that history and sociology are more universal in what they claim as their field of study, since the latter bases its legitimacy on the study of all society; the former makes the same claim for longitudinal analysis—all that has happened is its legitimate domain. By contrast, perhaps, political science is restricted to a single area of social or historical activity, "the political," which may admit to many definitions, some inclusive and others exclusive. (Wilson 1985, 605)

Implied is that the dominant definitions of politics in U.S. political science have been fairly exclusive and have tended not to give adequate attention to (thus deemphasizing) the study of minorities (also see Lindblom 1982). Wilson goes further, implying that the definitions of politics most commonly used have been not only rather narrow but also that political science has not studied blacks, and by implication other minority groups, for the following reasons:

> A. Political science typically studies elites and "decision makers," the users and uses of influence and power, especially as expressed through formal channels (voting, legislative behavior, etc.).

B. [Minorities] have historically been deprived of elite status and hence rarely are involved in authoritative decisions; they are more frequently the objects or victims of the use of power; politics, as such, often involves the creative design or adaptation to disenfranchisement and economic domination through reliance on nonformal channels like the church.

C. Therefore, political science doesn't study [minority] politics. (Wilson 1985, 604)

Thus, minority politics, including Latino and black politics, receives little attention from political science, less attention than given by several related disciplines. Scholars who are not themselves of ethnic–racial minority background have made similar, perhaps even stronger, assertions recently (see Barber 1990; see also Chapter 11). The disciplines of sociology and history seem inherently, by their self-definition, better able to address these issues; political science's dominant self-definitions seem less receptive. But that self-definition is neither inevitable nor necessarily desirable. In short, there is a "politics of politics" or a "politics of (professional) political science." Beyond the question of disciplinary self-definition of domain, there is some agreement regarding other explanations for the almost total absence of minority studies in political science.

————THE BROWNING, MARSHALL, AND TABB (1984) STUDY

In addition to omissions in the study of Latinos and politics, there are problems of commission. Although the study of minority politics has not been a major (or even minor) focus of political science research, scholarly work increasingly has sought to address such issues carefully. In several ways, Browning, Marshall, and Tabb's *Protest Is Not Enough: The Struggle of Blacks and Hispanics for Equality in Urban Politics* (1984) is a benchmark in the study of minority politics, both in its approach and in its substantive findings. It is worth examining this book, particularly as it pertains to Hispanics and urban politics.

Treating this study (hereafter referred to as *Protest*) as a primary example of mainstream political science research into minority politics is appropriate for several reasons. First, and at the most general level, the book exemplifies the approach of much mainstream, or behavioral, political science to the study of Hispanic and black political activity (Lindblom 1982). Second, *Protest* has been seen as a major development in the study of minority politics. And third, the book has not previously, to my knowledge, been subject to extensive critical scrutiny.[1]

Several points indicate that *Protest* has been received as a major contribution to minority studies. The book was published by the highly prestigious University of California Press. It won two awards from the American Political Science Association as the best book published in 1984 in the fields of ethnic and cultural pluralism (the Ralph Bunche Award) and U.S. public policy (the Gladys Kammerer Award). Moreover, the book's ideas served as a reference point for a symposium (and a subsequent book) on "Minority Power in City Politics" (*PS* 1986; Browning, Marshall, and Tabb 1990). In short, the approach to and the findings of *Protest* were taken very seriously by political scholars. And since its publication, the book has been frequently cited in scholarly research.

Because *Protest* is seen as mainstream political science research on minority politics at its best (and deservedly so) we should examine it closely. This carefully prepared work is sympathetic to the minority pursuit of social and political equality. To the extent that it manifests certain assumptions, and perhaps shortcomings, much other mainstream research on Latino (and minority) politics might also be expected to share similar assumptions and shortcomings. And as the remainder of this chapter and the following chapter make clear, those assumptions and related perspectives are important aspects in understanding U.S. politics generally and Latino politics in particular.

We begin with a brief summary of *Protest*, then proceed to address several major points: What do the approach and findings of this work "really" tell us about the place of minorities, particularly Hispanics, in contemporary urban politics? And what might this suggest about the assumptions underlying much political science research?

Browning, Marshall, and Tabb subtitled their work as the "Struggle of Blacks and Hispanics for Equality in Urban Politics." They centered their specific concerns on several questions: (1) How open are urban political systems? (2) How does political incorporation occur? (3) Does the political incorporation of minorities make a difference for policy?

Browning, Marshall, and Tabb examined the political activities of, and responsiveness to, blacks and Hispanics in ten northern California cities over the twenty-year period from 1960 to 1980. They drew on an impressive array of data including numerous structured and unstructured interviews, city council election results, city budget and employment figures, program data, newspaper clippings, and so forth. Indeed, their comprehensiveness and quantitative–methodological rigor are formidable and probably have few parallels in the study of minority politics in the United States.

They delineate several levels or kinds of political activities: demand–protest, electoral mobilization, representation, and incorporation. As the title of their book suggests, protest is not sufficient to bring about policy responsiveness. What is crucial is *incorporation*, that is, minority participation in liberal coalitions in city government. Incorporation itself depends on electoral mobilization, which in turn is often preceded by demand–protest. Policy responsiveness, as measured by four individual indicators and an aggregate indicator, is largely determined by levels of minority incorporation (see Chapter 8). This approach provides useful insights into minority politics. At the same time, the approach and its findings and implications have to be kept in perspective.

THEORETICAL AND NORMATIVE ISSUES

Despite specific reservations expressed about the Browning, Marshall, and Tabb study the general findings are significant and worthy of attention and consideration. Nonetheless, those findings and their significance may be questioned, in terms of underlying assumptions and related issues, from broader theoretical–normative perspectives. These questions focus not so much on the accuracy of the findings as on the approach to the study of minority politics, and especially, for present purposes, Hispanic politics, on its *adequacy* and *appropriateness*.

APPROPRIATENESS OF THE APPROACH.   Perhaps the first shortcoming of the Browning, Marshall, and Tabb approach has to do with historical and political perspective. Questions and criticisms of the approaches and assumptions of what can be called mainstream or empirical political science's examination of ethnic politics, especially black and Hispanic politics, have been raised by a variety of scholars for some time (e.g., Moore 1970; Blauner 1969; Hirsch 1972; Rocco 1970; Garcia and de la Garza 1977; Morris 1975). The *Protest* approach acknowledges that the historical situation of Hispanics (and blacks) is and has been different from that of other white ethnic immigrant groups (Browning, Marshall, and Tabb 1984, 9, 244). But it does not, and may have had difficulty trying to, incorporate that knowledge into its analysis. Instead, the difference is treated as a given, as "unproblematic" (Shapiro 1981, 92).

The methods used in the approach are partly longitudinal in nature, but that is not the same as adequately recognizing the apparently lasting historical significance of the means by which Hispanics (Mexican Americans) and blacks "became" members of U.S. society (Browning, Marshall and Tabb 1984, 6, 10). It appears, in fact, that the pluralist approach, which *Protest* uses, is ahistorical (as suggested in Chapter 2). Not only is the essential distinction between longitudinal data and an appreciation of history an issue, but there is a related irony: The unique condition of Hispanics and blacks is what makes this kind of study *possible* in the first place. If, indeed, blacks and Hispanics were but two more ethnic groups, one suspects that the focus and findings of *Protest*, and similar studies, would not have been deemed so necessary or have received so much attention. This irony seems to have been overlooked, which is particularly notable when cities with such obviously Spanish names as San Francisco, San Jose, Sacramento, and Vallejo are included in the study.

An ostensibly related tendency is to dismiss other views of the Hispanic (and black) situation that scholars have developed. Other explanations, variations of colonial or internal colonial models (discussed in Chapter 1), may also provide some understanding about the Hispanic situation, but they are not raised in *Protest* or in similar research (see Morris 1975, chap. 2; Lindblom 1982). Yet the political situation of minorities in a majority of these California cities ultimately is *not* well explained by the Browning, Marshall, and Tabb theory (as discussed later in the chapter). The approach of *Protest* seems to have ruled out a consideration of other perspectives without ever discussing whether their approach is superior (Garcia and de la Garza 1977; Lindlbom 1982).

QUESTIONS OF ADEQUACY. Several issues lead one to wonder about the *adequacy* of the study's questions and approach. Literature on urban politics has witnessed major debates regarding how pluralist or elitist local political systems are. Browning, Marshall, and Tabb touch on this issue, suggesting that

> our work does not attempt to provide a global assessment of power dispersion in our cities. Instead this book examines the change in the political position of two groups (blacks and Hispanics) vis-a-vis city government and its policies. It asks . . . whether the dispersion of power to these groups increased over time and what factors were associated with the changes. Whether the dispersion of power prior to these changes or after was great enough to warrant the pluralist label is not addressed. (Pp. 8–9)

This comment and some of the analysis that follows it are confusing, probably inconsistent, and need to be questioned if research in minority politics is to become more meaningful. It is difficult to claim that the potential or actual dispersion of power *to* blacks and Hispanics does not have implications for the overall power distribution (i.e., "away from" other groups) and across a range of issues in the cities studied (Browning, Marshall, and Tabb 1984, 9–10). Indeed, if the political activities of blacks and Hispanics have little or no significant implications except for blacks and Hispanics, what does it mean for the politics of equality and the redistribution, which the study claims to address, or for politics generally? And why would or should "resistant" coalitions, which the study finds to be major obstacles to minority political influence, be concerned about minority political activities that have so little significance? Stone (1980, 979–980) contends that "few would quarrel" with the position that power relationships are not only interpersonal but also *intergroup*. In the above quotation, however, Browning, Marshall, and Tabb seem to question that point.

The questions just raised also suggest that the Browning, Marshall, and Tabb approach is narrow in that it implicitly, if not explicitly, focuses largely on one kind of power relationship. Stone argues that four kinds of intergroup power relationships, shaped by elements in the relationship, can be identified in the urban political arena: (1) Where power is used *intentionally* (openly) and political competition or conflict is *direct*, the power relationship is "decisional"; (2) a power relationship of "anticipated reaction" results when power is exercised through the "logic of the situation," or larger contextual forces, and is, again, *direct*; (3) where power is used *intentionally* and conflict occurs *indirectly*, there is a relationship of "nondecision making"; and (4) "systemic" power occurs where conflict is *indirect* and the "logic of the situation," rather than clear-cut intentions, are determinant (Stone 1980, 980).

Browning, Marshall, and Tabb focus primarily on decisional relationships. There is, at most, only scant attention paid to anticipated reaction, nondecision making, and (least of all) systemic power. Several points in particular support this contention. One is the assertion, noted earlier, that the study "examines the change in the political position of . . . (blacks and Hispanics) vis-a-vis city government and its policies." This suggests that the *intergroup* political competition being examined is *indirect*. Stone (1980, 980) comments that "systemic power appears as that type of power *furthest* removed from open competition (*direct* power relationships) and purposive activity involving a conscious (*intention*) among individuals (*interpersonal*)." Emphases on protest, elections, representation, and, to a lesser degree, incorporation are examples of overt and intentional political activities and thus are of the decisional variety. To be sure, a focus on minority access is useful and significant; nonetheless, it is a limited focus. There is much more to politics than this one dimension.

A decisional focus is ostensibly part of an approach that has been referred to as "politics is what we see" and can readily measure. While this approach is common, it has been strongly challenged (Lindblom 1982; Shapiro 1981; Rocco 1970). And the approach seems especially problematic regarding a study of groups outside the political mainstream. For this reason, too, the Browning, Marshall, and Tabb study may not be fully adequate.

Another instance where the adequacy, as distinct from the accuracy, of the approach can be questioned concerns what it takes as "policy responsiveness." Although different from the issue of the kinds of power relationships noted, this question is closely related. Peterson (1981), whose contentions Browning, Marshall, and Tabb directly speak to, argues that there are several policy arenas in local government: developmental, allocational, and redistributive (see Chapter 8). The policies examined in the study focus most heavily on allocational policies, albeit in their most redistributive aspects.

The policy responsiveness measures deserve closer attention (Kahn 1985). Two of those measures are the existence of a police review board and minority membership on boards and commissions. These are somewhat related in that any board must first exist before its membership becomes an issue and can be measured. But only the presence or absence of a police review board is treated as of great significance in the study. Also, the policy impact of the *existence* of and *membership* on boards and commissions requires substantiation if the measure is to be used as a significant indicator of policy responsiveness. That impact is not shown convincingly (see Browning, Marshall and Tabb 1984, 284). Indeed, it is suggested that board appointments may be more symbolic than substantively significant (Browning, Marshall, and Tabb 1984, 156–157). Consistent with this questioning of the study, Lipsky and Olson (1976) had argued that commissions created by various cities to study racial violence in the 1960s generally "processed" racial crisis but did not address significant questions.

The levels of employment and the distribution of minorities em-

ployed in city government are used as another measure of policy responsiveness. Again, however important this may be, from the standpoint of other theoretical standards (e.g., Peterson's), it is not clearly of
great consequence. In fact, an implication that can be readily drawn
from Peterson's argument is that affirmative action in employment is
where "minority concerns" might be most easily addressed. This is so
because the allocational arena is supposedly neutral in its economic
impact, and affirmative action hiring thus would impose little, if any,
additional absolute economic cost on city government. Browning,
Marshall, and Tabb (1984, 169–170) recognize that Peterson views
minority employment as an "allocational" issue, but suggest that, over
the long term, affirmative action hiring has redistributive consequences. That may or may not be so.

Seen from various perspectives, such as those of Stone and Peterson
(and see Wolfinger 1974), affirmative action may be equally well understood as "action which affirms" existing political and social relationships. It may bring about greater acceptance of the "durable features of the larger socioeconomic system" despite that system's overall
ostensibly deleterious consequences (Stone 1980, 980; Eisinger 1980;
Saiz 1988; see Chapter 11).

Using minority employment as an indicator of government responsiveness also fails to recognize the fact that public-sector work has
lower prestige, and may be seen as less desirable in certain other ways,
than employment in the private sector (Pursley and Snortland 1980,
253). It may be, then, that heavy minority reliance on government for
employment reinforces an image of group social dependence (Welch,
Karnig, and Eribes 1983; Eisinger 1986; Mladenka 1988; Moore
1981). For example, Erie (1980) speculates that there may be a "prole-
tarianization" of minorities through such programs.[2]

Similar comment may apply to minority contracting as a measure of
policy responsiveness. Minority-contracting policies that have been initiated by cities (as distinct from those required as part of federal grant
programs) seem interesting in ways beyond those implied in the research. Such contracting programs may link the minority business
community (to the extent that one exists) and the broader minority
population (to a lesser degree) to cities' overarching economic development imperatives. Thus minorities may become strong proponents,
or at least are less likely to become opponents, of economic development, even if the benefits to the broader minority community are not
especially great or if the development leads to considerable housing

displacement (Flores 1989; Anderson 1967) or is not seen as an appro-priate means to the "good life." A prominent black political columnist has questioned the significance of contracting policies because "that's only getting a little bit of the action *after* the deals have *already been shaped*" by others (see Raspberry 1987; emphasis added).

Questions concerning the significance of employment and contract-ing point up another potential flaw in the interpretation that Brown-ing, Marshall, and Tabb offer. That is, there seems to be an assumption that cooptation of minority groups occurs only through electoral poli-tics or the federal poverty program arena when minority groups are (clearly) pitted against one another for the resources of social programs (see Browning, Marshall, and Tabb 1984, 46, 53–61). As has been suggested, cooptation may occur implicitly rather than just explicitly. And what some choose to refer to as responsiveness may, at another level, based on other assumptions, be interpreted rather differently—as conflict management, for example. These assumptions need to be con-sidered and integrated into future research.

The major point of this section is that two of the major measures of policy responsiveness used in the Browning, Marshall, and Tabb ap-proach are in the allocational arena, an arena that does not, according to some theoretical perspectives, have much consequence for equality or redistribution. Because of this focus on one arena, research ade-quacy can be questioned. Moreover, not only does the research focus primarily on one arena, but it focuses only on its most obvious and measurable aspects and thus addresses the decisional aspects of alloca-tive policy. Again, this approach addresses certain questions carefully and rigorously; but it is only a small sampling of questions. And it is not clear that those questions are the most important ones or, indeed, actually address redistributive issues, which is claimed to be the major research concern.

Finally, we can question whether the policy measures are as salient to minorities as claimed. Browning, Marshall, and Tabb indicate that the measures of policy responsiveness were chosen because of their importance to minorities. And research has found that social services are important to Hispanics and blacks in Denver (Lovrich 1974). But it is not clear that the measures that have been used really "get at" those social service concerns; at best, the measures may capture only some aspects of concern. For instance, while employment opportunities are probably important to minorities, it is not altogether clear that *govern-ment* jobs, and city government jobs in particular, are all that important. Those jobs may be the ones that are most accessible to minorities, but that may say as much about the social and political system as it does about minority preference. Furthermore, evidence indicates that a variety of concerns that are somewhat different from those considered relative to policy responsiveness are of greater salience. For example, in 1987 one group, Hispanics of Colorado, published its *Hispanic Agenda: 1990 and Beyond* (LARASA 1987). The issues emphasized in that agenda do not square well with those used in Browning, Marshall, and Tabb's research as indicators of policy responsiveness.[3] Research must be careful not to "impose" definitions of policy salience.

——————RELATED ISSUES

Although it is not altogether clear that Browning, Marshall, and Tabb focus on redistributive policies, let us assume for the sake of argument that they do. By implication, then, the arenas of minority and redistributive politics (or the redistributive aspects of allocational politics) are one and the same. Yet Peterson and others have argued that cities are generally averse to redistributive politics. Browning, Marshall, and Tabb modify, but do not really refute, that contention. If this line of reasoning is correct, minority politics seems largely marginal. To imply that minority politics is virtually synonymous with redistributive politics seems to relegate most (legitimate) minority political actions to a small part of the (urban) political arena. That is, it limits their range of activities to a politics of *need*, rather than more broadly "purposive" politics. It may limit minorities to "pre-politics," rather than more common notions or practices of politics.[4] To draw an analogy from labor economics, minorities are relegated to a secondary, rather than primary, political (labor) market (see Chapter 11).

Two other issues are unclear in the study: What is meant by political equality and, related to an earlier question, is political equality seen as a beginning, as an end, or as both? At times, Browning, Marshall, and Tabb seem to imply that if there were proportional representation and incorporation, and/or complete parity as measured by their policy responsiveness indicators, equality would be achieved. But what if there were proportional representation and incorporation but *not* parity in responsiveness, or vice versa. Would this be sufficient? More important, is parity in terms of the measures of government responsiveness deemed the achievement of equality? It is unclear, for nowhere is it specified "what (full) equality would look like." Yet the use of the particular measures suggests that parity in those areas might be "enough."

Also, should representation–incorporation and responsiveness (relative to the measures used and, perhaps, some additional ones) be defined as the goal of minorities, or is this just a beginning? Would minorities have to be full participants in dominant coalitions that influence policy formulation and government responsiveness in power relationships *beyond* the decisional and allocational—or, as the authors of the study claim, some redistributive—domains? These points are unclear and seem to require more attention if the findings are to speak more meaningfully to the issues of equality that the study poses as significant.

In the process of describing and explaining the minority political situation, the Browning, Marshall, and Tabb approach of necessity posits *standards* for judging minority politics. These standards often seem somewhat low, and ostensibly low standards probably would not be applied to other groups in U.S. society. Yet the standards are seldom met in the cities studied. The research is underlaid by normative political assumptions, as has been shown in a number of ways (Shapiro 1981), despite the claims that it is (only) an "empirical" study that "also develops a [positive or descriptive] theory of urban political change, a theory of political incorporation and policy responsiveness" (Browning, Marshall, and Tabb 1984, 6; cf. Rocco 1970, 90). These normative assumptions may or may not be deemed appropriate and acceptable, but the assumptions are present and should not be ignored, as they have been in much of the research, especially the mainstream research, on minorities and politics.

Another point is the seemingly major disjunction between an optimistic theory and pessimistic findings. Despite what some have seen as Browning, Marshall, and Tabb's "optimistic" conclusions (Sonenshein 1986, 582) that electoral activity is crucial and can translate to incorporation, which in turn leads to responsiveness, the data in the study do show "improvements," but also starkly portray tremendous immobilization, underrepresentation, nonincorporation, and unresponsiveness (see, e.g., Browning, Marshall, and Tabb 1984, 21, 30, 165). The data indicate that mobilization, incorporation, and responsiveness are generally quite low.[5] And if the arguments made earlier are correct, not only do the necessary conditions for political influence seldom occur, but they take place within relatively narrow parameters.

Probably a much more significant question, both theoretically and practically, is this: "Why do the necessary (and sufficient) conditions for mobilization, incorporation and responsiveness to Hispanics and blacks occur (even within these narrow bounds) so seldom?" (Lindblom 1982, 15). But it is a question that much of the literature on minority politics has not addressed appropriately or adequately or very often (Wilson 1985). Future research needs to come to grips with these matters.

————THE LIMITS OF CONTEMPORARY, URBAN U.S. POLITICS

The study of minorities in urban politics needs to be more theoretically conscious in ways beyond those noted. Further evidence of this is a discussion of racial (black) transition in several American cities. Eisinger (1980) concluded a major study by delineating the "limits of American politics" that ultimately constrain the impact of what has been referred to here as incorporation and policy responsiveness. Eisinger refers to somewhat similar processes as ethnoracial transition or displacement. Eisinger's comments deserve attention, and emphases have been added to the quote that follows to indicate the points that seem most significant for our present contentions. Eisinger claims that

> in some larger sense . . . ethnoracial transitions [in cities] in the United States *do not challenge* the agreed upon *basic purposes* and *scope* of American politics. American politics is a process in which certain goods, services and honors are liable to *modest* redistribution or *extension* to the winners but in which certain *obligations and established privileges are also regarded as fixed*. This seems particularly true in cases concerning the use of political power by groups in office vis-à-vis other groups not in office but that compete in the *electoral arena*. Newly victorious ethnic groups, *even if they are relatively deprived* in American society, do *not* embark on radical transformations of the social, economic, or institutional structure. They operate *within limits* . . . which *preserve the broad established patterns and principles* of private ownership, taxation and income distribution. Change is aimed at the *extension* of goods to the new group . . . or *at most to incremental redistribution* (such as the opening of *government contracts* and *employment* to greater minority participation). These restraints raise some *serious*, though perhaps not unsurmountable, *problems* . . . for a politically victorious group seeking

to transform its political power into major social and economic advances. (Eisinger 1980, 192–193)

Indeed, evidence of these limitations of U.S. urban politics can be drawn from the Browning, Marshall, and Tabb study as well. Using various data presented in that study, a simple correlation (r) between minority incorporation (average for 1960 to 1979) and percentage of Hispanics and blacks in poverty in 1979 was undertaken. Notably, and consistent with Eisinger's "limitations" argument, the correlations were .667 and .442; that is, as minority political incorporation increased, so did poverty levels. When average Hispanic incorporation from 1960 to 1979 is taken alone (i.e., excluding blacks), the correlation with Hispanic poverty in 1979 is negligible, .067. But the correlation between average black incorporation from 1960 to 1979 and percentage of black poverty in 1979 is a rather strong .546. Thus incorporation may have significance for policy responsiveness as measured by Browning, Marshall, and Tabb, but it seems to have little or no impact on poverty.[6] If anything, the data just presented indicate that policy responsiveness, at most, is predicated on *needs*. Or, at worst, it increases the level of poverty.

_____SUMMARY AND CONCLUSION

The central purpose of this chapter has been to indicate the nature and extent of the biases and shortcomings that limit the ways in which Latino politics are studied. Latinos have received scant political science research attention, certainly less attention than they have gotten from several other social science disciplines. Some possible reasons for this were explored. When Latino politics are carefully and sensitively examined, the research may still be underlaid by questionable assumptions. Browning, Marshall, and Tabb's major study (1984) was considered the best mainstream research on Latino politics.

The Browning, Marshall, and Tabb study told a great deal about what has, and has not, occurred in politics in recent years with respect to Hispanics and blacks in a group of California cities. But, like much other research, the study was limited by the issues studied, how they were studied, and by inattention to the "limits" of U.S. urban politics. Research into Hispanic (and minority) politics must be more cognizant of these constraints and their impacts on research findings and interpretations. In short, the approach of most mainstream political research is capable when it deals with description and explanation; it is less compelling in its ability to provide *understanding* of the larger Hispanic public situation.

This critique also tentatively implies how the study of minority politics might be improved. Future inquiry into Hispanic politics might fruitfully address what American democracy means for–to Hispanic Americans (and their various subgroups), and vice versa. More specific to urban politics, these issues are important to "the city in the future of democracy" (Dahl 1967). And given developments in the nature and role of urban politics and governance (Stone, Whelan, and Murin 1986), an appropriate focus to link various issues in this literature together might be "democracy in the future of the city."

11

Latinos and the Political System: Two-Tiered Pluralism

_____The previous chapters have presented theories and evidence about research on Latinos and politics in the United States. What does it all mean? Can some overall interpretation of Latino politics be put forth? Although no definitive interpretation is possible at this juncture, an interpretation that moves toward a theory or that offers a perspective on Latinos in the U.S. political system is possible (Rocco 1977; Garcia and de la Garza 1977; Torres 1985, 186). Chapter 2 discussed several theoretical perspectives: pluralism, coalitional bias, and internal colonialism. These theories all have something to offer in that they provide insights into Latino politics, but they have limitations. Another view, one that partly draws on these perspectives but that modifies them and links them into a distinct interpretation, is offered here. This view also draws on other arguments and theoretical views presented in earlier chapters, such as second-generation discrimination in education and theories of urban politics. This perspective or interpretation is called two-tiered pluralism.

_____TWO-TIERED PLURALISM: DEFINITION

Two-tiered pluralism is easier to describe than define, for its manifestations are clearer than its essence. Basically, two-tiered pluralism describes a situation in which there is formal legal equality on the one hand, and simultaneously, actual practice that undercuts equality

189

for most members of minority groups, even if some individuals register significant achievements (Stone 1990; Hochschild 1984, 169). In other words, certain basic equalities and rights apply to all Americans, but because of the distinctive historical experiences and structural features of some groups, and because cultural or racial deficiencies are alleged to exist (Barrera 1979), equality is largely formal or procedural, not substantive. Significant political and social achievements are the exception, not the rule, for Latinos and other minorities.

Part of what two-tiered pluralism means is that there is a *marginal inclusion* of minorities in most or all facets of the political process. Indeed, formal but marginal inclusion is a pervasive phenomenon. But while this formal political inclusion exists, and in fact is touted, marginalization and stigmatization exist alongside it. The processes and outcomes of two-tiered pluralism emphasize, and perhaps reify, the subordinate status of minority groups. In the light of their meager resources, minority groups face a political dilemma: Should they continue to allow their problems to be ignored, hoping for change in the long run? Or should they support policies (e.g., affirmative action) and accept labels (e.g., minority or protected class) that indicate or give symbolic and perhaps policy recognition, or even "advantages," to them but also signify inferior status. That *both* recognition and connotations of inferiority occur simultaneously makes two-tiered pluralism powerful as both process and outcome. Two-tiered pluralism has many of the same double-edged qualities as a related concept, equal opportunity. And equal opportunity has been called "the keystone of U.S. liberal democracy" (Hochschild 1988, 168–169, 189).

Two-tiered pluralism suggests that pluralism, as generally understood by U.S. political scholars and practitioners, exists in form but not fully in fact for some groups—groups whose initial or "formative" relation to the United States was not entirely voluntary or consensual. Groups located in this second level, such as Latinos and African Americans, have the formal rights of citizens; indeed, they may have been given special protection, part of their belonging to the "protected classes." But from the standpoint of two-tiered pluralism, the very need for such protection is seen as indicating a flaw, as being as much a weakness as a strength of traditional pluralism as a description of, and prescription for, U.S. politics. Left to its own devices, without "reinforcement," pluralism does not really work as an ongoing group process. Programs for protected groups, while perhaps necessary, nonetheless suggest a "purchased" pluralism or a "symbolic" pluralism because they are needed to maintain the credibility of "real" pluralism. "Group competition . . . is not much of a theory if it requires constant . . . government support" (Lowi 1979).

Another name for two-tiered pluralism might be "limited" pluralism because of the implied link to the idea of "limited" government. Or two-tiered pluralism might be called "dual" pluralism or "complex" pluralism (as distinct from "simple" pluralism) or "bifurcated" pluralism.

Central to the argument of two-tiered pluralism is that pluralism, that is, conventional pluralism, exists and functions to some degree, but that there are essentially two tiers, or levels, of pluralism. Also, the relationship between the two tiers is interdependent, perhaps even symbiotic. In the discussion that follows, we consider how two-tiered pluralism functions and is maintained or continues, and the specific processes and outcomes that are central to these patterns.

_____HOW TWO-TIERED PLURALISM FUNCTIONS

The first tier of two-tiered pluralism is in some respects all-encompassing, for it actually encompasses the second tier. With regard to certain individual rights (but not privileges), including the right to vote and formal equality before the law, everyone in both tiers is included. Formal rights and formal equality are necessary, though not sufficient, conditions for significant political power. The power and decisions of the first tier, particularly its upper reaches, extensively and deeply affect everyone. Conventional pluralist analysis focuses on and is quite successful in explaining the first tier.

The second tier of two-tiered pluralism is much more limited than the first in its political and social influence, and it is the tier in which minority groups are heavily concentrated. Pluralism with respect to minority groups, as distinct from ethnic groups and other interest groups, has historically been limited in that the equality of such groups has been constrained, both formally and informally. For example, the legal status—a clearly inferior status—of blacks as slaves and of Native Americans was indicated in the U.S. Constitution. And after the abolition of slavery, such legal doctrines as "separate but equal" were controlling for many years. Even after the removal of formal constraints, the political, social, economic and, ideological legacy of those constraints, along with "informal" mechanisms and practices, effectively limited political and social change.

The political and social status of Latinos has also been formally shaped, if less visibly so than for blacks and Native Americans. This occurred through the original "conquest" of Latinos and through such subsequent actions as land-rights decisions and water-rights policies, "arranged" entrance programs—for example, the Bracero program and programs to encourage Puerto Rican migration when needed—and other practices (see Chapter 3; Barrera 1985). The manner in which immigration laws and policies have been enforced is another example (Moore and Pachon 1985). On the whole, the Latino situation has been shaped less formally and has been less explicitly articulated in law than has the black situation. The Latino experience has in many respects revolved around—and the group's inferior status has been attributed to or explained and legitimated by—cultural factors. In the context of political and socioeconomic inequality, what may be cultural "differences" became defined and treated as cultural "deficiencies" (see Chapter 3; cf. Barrera 1979; Meier and Stewart 1991).

Two-tiered pluralism implies differences in the *kinds* of situations faced by some groups; there are not only differences in degree, as is the case within the mainstream, or first tier, of pluralism (Stone 1986, 1980). Because of historical factors and other structural features, pluralism functions, or is in reality played out, as something akin to coalitional bias. That is, the *legacy* of conquest and related historical issues, along with the physical proximity of the Latino countries and the relationships of these countries to the United States, which have had at least some colonialist flavor, has led to a diminished form of pluralism for Latino groups, particularly Mexican Americans and Puerto Ricans.

Noting some parallels with historically similar processes may be useful. Two-tiered pluralism acknowledges that there is a formal or de jure pluralism. But two-tiered pluralism suggests that there is no de facto pluralism. Viewing these issues in terms of historical development, what has happened for minorities, including Latinos, is a shift from de jure segregation—exclusion, to de facto exclusion—segregation, to de jure pluralism. Evidence of the latter can be seen in such policies as desegregation (e.g., the *Brown* decisions), the Civil Rights Act of 1964, voting rights legislation, and affirmative action. But de facto two-tiered pluralism continues.

At another level, two-tiered pluralism is reminiscent of constitutional debates on the "separate but equal" concept. To a degree, the "separate but equal" status of minority groups in relation to other groups concerning programs such as affirmative action—and within the U.S. political system and U.S. pluralist thinking—has actually been less than equal despite the advantages presumably bestowed on minority groups. The political language has changed, however; how that language has changed and the messages implied in that language are important. These separate programs are now typically called "special," rather than considered "separate." And they are ostensibly *equalizing* or compensatory—at least in their stated intent—rather than *equal*. Indeed, critics view them as highly unequal, as reverse discrimination. The formal equality and the stated equalizing intent of these "special" policies have served as a kind of political and intellectual (or theoretical) safety net. That is, the policies are often seen as indicating the *achievement* of essential equality, and as vindicating pluralist theory, at least implicitly (see Chapter 10).

Another feature of two-tiered pluralism is the recognition that the concerns of disadvantaged groups are more likely to be dealt with through mediating institutions, such as welfare bureaucracies, most often by street-level bureaucrats and nonprofit organizations (Lipsky 1980; Lowi and Ginsberg 1990, 304–331; Stone, Whelan, and Murin 1986). Dominant groups deal more directly with governments, either through clientele agencies or, quite often, with "those at the top." Commonly, however, the political access of relatively influential groups is not visible, which makes those groups *more*, rather than less, powerful.

Furthermore, a public–private distinction is made when it comes to one set of circumstances, but the nature and extent of that distinction is different for the two tiers of pluralism. In the first tier, public–private cooperation is sometimes challenged on the basis of noninterference with the marketplace. But such cooperation is often justified and implemented by an ideology that, in recent language, has been embraced under concepts of public–private partnership, tax incentives, and the like. With respect to lower-class and minority groups, there is a clear-cut concern about not undermining incentives or a willingness to work through welfare or other redistributive programs. Indeed, these differences are central to distinctions between developmental or distributive policies, on the one hand, and redistributive policies, on the other.

These attitudes and biases result in a major burden for minority groups. Their efforts to wield political influence seem inevitably to require *explicit* political activity, often taking the form of redistribution, and to appear as *demands* (or complaints). Established mainstream groups, in contrast, are much more able to practice an *implicit* politics that builds on existing understandings and circumstances, to appear as system support, consistent with a "commercial republic" (Elkin 1987; Lowi and Ginsberg 1990, 71), as mere tastes, preferences, priorities, or issues. Thus the political goals and policies that minorities pursue are seen as nonincremental and redistributive; those of established groups appear as normal, incremental politics. There is a strong element of what has been called a "mobilization of bias" (Schattschneider 1975). Partly for these reasons, the political and social opportunity costs for minority groups are substantially higher than those for other groups (Stone 1986).

In some respects, two-tiered pluralism indicates yet another dimension of the tension in U.S. politics and political thinking about liberal democracy, that is, between liberalism and democracy (Hochschild 1984; Barber 1990). The predominantly low status of Latinos and other minority groups highlights new dimensions of that tension; two-tiered pluralism suggests an important political and theoretical dilemma (Myrdal 1944). U.S. liberal democracy, according to some, has numerous "internal weaknesses and contradictions, many of which grow more intractable as the American system ages and as its internal contradictions gradually emerge" (Barber 1990). The situation of minority groups and a description of two-tiered pluralism may be indicative of these contradictions.

———————AN OUTLINE OF TWO-TIERED PLURALISM

An outline of how two-tiered pluralism looks and works in the broader socioeconomic and political system can be suggested. Figure 2 illustrates two-tiered pluralism; it seeks to depict, summarize, and place in a broad perspective the political and economic situation of Latinos (and blacks) in the U.S. political system. By extension, it may provide a general understanding of politics in the United States, but with particular attention to minorities (Barrera 1979).

Several points depicted in the figure require explanation and elaboration. The large "diamond" represents the Anglo–white population (comprising 70 to 80 percent of the total U.S. population) and its socioeconomic distribution—a relatively large middle class and smaller upper and lower classes (Barker and McCrory 1980). The two smaller, pyramid-shaped figures represent the black population (about 12 percent of the total U.S. population) and the Latino population (about 6 to 8 percent of the U.S. total). The pyramid shapes for Latinos and blacks suggest the socioeconomic distribution of these two groups:

small upper classes and sizable lower classes (underclasses?). The pyramids underscore the fact that few Latinos and blacks are among the most politically or socioeconomically advantaged.

The theoretical frameworks delineated along the edges of the diagram (and discussed in earlier chapters) further underscore the notion of two-tiered pluralism. Stone's discussion (1980) of kinds and levels of urban political power are juxtaposed to the socioeconomic and political distributions indicated in the figure. The juxtaposition illustrates that minority political activity is largely confined to the decisional arena of local politics; the "higher" the form or level of power, the less likely it is that Latinos are involved (see Chapter 10).

Similarly, Peterson (1981) developed a theory of urban politics based on three kinds of public policy: developmental, allocational, and redistributive (see Chapters 8 and 10). Building on Peterson's work, Sharp (1990) puts forth the idea of bifurcated urban politics, claiming that there are two major domains of urban politics, the allocational and the developmental. Decision making regarding allocational politics

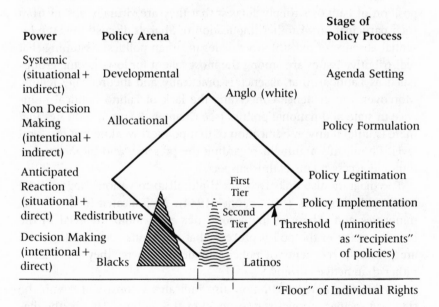

Sources: Data on Power are from Stone 1980; on Policy Arena, from Peterson 1981, Sharp 1990; on Stage of Policy Process, from C. Jones 1984.

FIGURE 2
Two-Tiered Pluralism—A Schematic Presentation

tends to have *high visibility* and *high levels of controversy,* and its overall pattern of power is pluralistic (i.e., conventional pluralism). Typical participants in allocational politics are elected officials, such as mayors and city council members, public-sector bureaucracies, and neighborhood organizations. As suggested earlier (see Chapters 8 and 10), Latino politics and most political science research have centered on the allocational policy domain (Sharp 1990, esp. chap. 11). But Latinos have been substantially underrepresented even among the institutions, bureaucracies and elected positions, and organizations that are most important in this domain (McClain and Karnig 1990). Moreover, some of Peterson's later work (1986) implies that allocational politics are relatively unimportant in the "big picture" of city politics (B. Jones 1990).

The developmental policy domain is characterized by low visibility of decision making and generally low levels of controversy; the overall pattern of power is elitist (but see Sharp 1990, 263–268). Typical participants in the developmental domain are banks, developers, downtown businesses, and corporate leaders. The socioeconomic status and position of Latinos strongly suggest that they are virtually absent from such participation. Another implication of Sharp's discussion is the essential absence of redistributive issues in urban politics. Assuming that redistributive issues are among the most salient for low-income groups (such as Latinos), that absence is practically and theoretically telling. Moreover, the evidence concerning the lack of Latino political influence in state and national politics (see Chapters 5 and 6) indicates that there is little, if any, modification of that political weakness at the local level. Pluralism's argument regarding the presence and importance of multiple access points is thus suspect.

The diagram also links two-tiered pluralism to various stages of the public policy process (see C. Jones 1984). As indicated in the figure, minorities and others in the second tier are seldom involved in the broadest stage of the policy process, that of agenda setting. Minorities are primarily recipients of policies made by others; they are clients, rather than active citizens.

The schematic representation also indicates a consistency with the standard socioeconomics status model of U.S. politics. That is, the diagram suggests that as one moves from the top of the "diamond" down, socioeconomic and political power and influence decrease. The distinct pyramids for the two minority groups, however, suggest additional and distinct conditions.

Also, the pyramids indicating the Latino and black populations are placed as they are from left to right to indicate patterns of political ideological leanings. Latinos are more ideologically moderate, and more ideologically split, than blacks, who are more liberal. (The figure cannot fully capture the complexity of the situation; for instance, there certainly are Latinos who should be placed more toward the conservative and liberal ends of the continuum.)

That the socioeconomic structure (and size) of the dominant (Anglo or white) group in society is somewhat different from that for blacks and Latinos (Barker and McCrory 1980, 53) has implications for the several groups, for both intergroup and intragroup relations. Not only is the white–Anglo population substantially larger numerically and proportionally, its middle class is larger than its lower or upper classes. The minority groups' pyramid-shaped socioeconomic structure suggests a small middle and upper class, in an already small population relative to the nation's overall population. If, as is often assumed, political leadership is most likely to come from the middle class, minority groups are hindered by the small size of their middle (and upper) classes, as well as the groups' overall size. As Stone and others (Vigil 1987; Wolfinger 1974) have argued, this can make a minority group particularly susceptible to the use of selective incentives (in return for political support), recognition politics, cooptation, and related processes. These processes underpin two-tiered pluralism and are major links between the two tiers.

Also, the upper class of the minority group is fairly similar in status to the Anglo middle class. This may enhance its ability to work with or interact with the dominant group's middle class. At the same time, the line (indicating the top of the minority pyramid) intersected or divided by the Anglo structure (see "threshold") may imply a distance or a division between the Latino middle and upper classes from the group's remaining, and substantially larger, segments. This is suggestive of the "dual validation" that affects Latino political officials and the constituencies to which they must appeal (Baird 1977).

The figure also implies that issues related to minorities and the U.S. political system are complex and potentially dynamic. The importance of racial–cultural factors, on the one hand, and socioeconomic factors–variables, on the other, are important; also, the interplay of racial–cultural and socioeconomic factors (taken together) with political activities and influence is suggested. The diagram indicates, and much data suggest, that while Anglos–whites as a group have lower *rates* or levels of poverty, they constitute the largest *numbers* of the socio-economically disadvantaged. Also, Latinos and blacks are dispropor-tionately concentrated among the nation's lower socioeconomic levels. (As noted earlier, however, specific patterns for the two minority groups may vary by the indicator used—for example, income vs. edu-cation.) The figure also implies that the two minority groups, although a substantial element of the lower classes, are also distinct population sectors within those levels.

Latinos are in some ways more in the U.S. social (and sociopolitical, attitudinal–ideological) mainstream than are blacks. The placement of the Latino population seeks to indicate that and related points. Latinos are not as racially distinct, or as residentially segregated, as blacks and in general are somewhat higher in terms of several measures of socio-economic status (education is the major exception). Also, there may be less "social distance" between Latinos and Anglos (Meier and Stewart 1991); that the Latino pyramid is not clearly "bounded" is intended to suggest this. (Yet there has been less *political* success for Latinos, as indicated by the most frequently used measures.)

Two other aspects of the Latino population are conveyed by the Latino pyramid. First, the "squiggly" lines in that pyramid suggest cer-tain differences between Latino and non-Latino populations. Most im-portant are language and cultural differences. Also, the two vertical lines extending from the bottom of the Latino pyramid represent the undocumented ("illegal") or noncitizen population. Also implied is that some, probably most, of the most disadvantaged Latinos are situ-ated here; because of their "illegal" status, they lack many basic indi-vidual rights.

The Latino situation is further complicated because of the internal diversity of the groups—regionally, historically, socioeconomically, and so on. Central to that diversity is, of course, that there are several identifiable Latino groups, which has had certain implications. Diver-sity affects internal group cohesion; it also makes the group rather eas-ily divided by "outside" influences. For instance, according to some observers, the Republican party has looked at Cubans as "their" His-panics. A substantial portion of the Latino population is conservative on a fairly wide array of issues, making it politically easy to appeal to whatever orientation or "tradition" one might wish to court. Issues include appeals to an immigrant, patriot–anticommunist, equal oppor-tunity, family ideology—all ostensibly used by the Republican party— or a minority group, social-welfare perspective, which is favored by the

Democratic party. As suggested in earlier chapters, both orientations are possible, and at least partly accurate, given the complex history of Latinos in the United States. Related appeals have focused on values or perspectives, such as European or non-European (e.g., the term Hispanic vs. Latino or Chicano), family or group (cultural) values, material or symbolic concerns. Overall, these factors make Latino politics somewhat diffuse.

_____TWO-TIERED PLURALISM: LATINOS AND BLACKS

With respect to the two largest minority groups, two-tiered pluralism may work differently for each group. For blacks, two-tiered pluralism has a greater flavor of what might be called "parallel" pluralism; that is, out of various historical reasons and necessities, blacks developed *parallel institutions*. The black state colleges and universities in the South, ostensibly created in order to maintain and in most respects reinforce racial segregation and inequality, along with the various private black institutions, were important in developing a black intellectual class. Also, and contrary to interest-group–pluralist analysis claiming that geographical dispersion is beneficial to group influence, residential segregation has *enhanced* black representation on governing bodies, particularly city councils, through district elections (but see Grofman and Handley 1989).

Latinos, and here let us speak most directly about Mexican Americans, were often disadvantaged culturally, especially regarding language, and in terms of the compatibility of customs and institutions in relation to those of the dominant (Anglo) group. Both early and recent events indicate this. That Mexican American citizens lost much land following the Mexican-American War has been attributed to the different assumptions and practices of the Anglo versus Spanish and Mexican legal systems. Less residential segregation of Latinos seems to have lowered their political representation at local levels (Taebel 1978; Zax 1990). And bilingual education programs, ostensibly developed to help Latinos and other language minorities, have instead served to "track" Mexican American and Puerto Rican children negatively and are generally related to lower levels of educational achievement (Meier and Stewart 1991).

Another distinction that might be drawn is that the relationship between the majority population and Latinos seem *bicultural*, while that of blacks to the dominant group might be called *subcultural*. To a considerable degree, the issues and problems of Latinos are related to cultural matters. This is evident in several ways. First, the notion of Anglo (rather than "white") in relation to Chicano, Hispanic, Latino, and the like implies a cultural more than a racial difference. Most Latinos consider themselves white, although the Chicano Movement often emphasized race by calling for "brown" or "bronze" power. Concerning public policy, among the distinct policy concerns of Latinos are such issues as bilingual education, Official English or English Only measures, and immigration policy. Also important is the low political participation among Latinos, which researchers have often attributed (to some degree) to language and (related) cultural attachment, or to "ethnic estrangement" (but see Meier and Stewart 1991, 159–160).

Latinos have had a tenuous relationship to U.S. society (Falcon 1984). For Mexican Americans, this has been manifest in terms of citizenship status and loyalty issues (de la Garza, 1985). For Puerto Ricans, their dual-citizenship status appears central. For Cuban Americans, their earlier intense focus on politics in Cuba probably influenced perceptions (including self-perceptions) of them as an "exile" group. In all instances, culture and attachment have been, or at least have been perceived as, important elements in this "tenuousness."

The cultural variables seem linked to the distinct structural features that Glazer argues affect Mexican Americans, and seem to affect other Latino groups. Relatedly, a strong belief among the general population that speaking English is an important part of "what it means to be an American" is integral to understanding support for Official English or English Only measures (Citrin et al., 1990). Because of their different language, Latinos may be perceived as "less" American. This would seem particularly so, given the perception that language is a *choice* that persons can make. The perception, then, is that Latinos *choose* not to use English, which may be seen as a justification for inequality. The element of choice may also make Latinos a "less deserving" minority group in the eyes of the non-Latino population.

The situation for blacks has been one defined in relationship and response to the dominant U.S. society and culture. Language and cultural issues have been important in different ways for blacks than for Latinos. Blacks have not had the same relationships to or with foreign societies and foreign nations qua nations, partly because there is not the same physical proximity of black nation–states that exists with Latino groups.

The diffuseness (again, implied by the "squiggly" lines of the Latino pyramid) and the somewhat more mainstream politics of Latinos may provide insight into Latinos' political status. To some degree—and to what degree is highly debatable—the lower levels of Latino political success (particularly compared to blacks) *may* be a result of some level of social integration and attachment to culture and community (Barrera 1985; Calvo and Rosenstone 1989.)

Another, more directly political phenomenon—indeed, one that many contemporary writings focus on—is also implied. Because there is probably a larger pool of minorities in the upper part of the minority groups than there once was, the election of such candidates, especially at the local level, becomes more possible and, indeed, has become more frequent. But it does not necessarily follow that the lower-status elements of the Latino population benefit socioeconomically (Eisinger 1980).

Yet another point is implied. Latinos and blacks, concentrated in the lower level (second tier of pluralism), will interact and perhaps compete—primarily with lower-class whites but not infrequently with each other—for socioeconomic and political benefits. Discussions about affirmative action as "reverse discrimination" (or, as some critics have called it, affirmative discrimination) have often been most intense at the practical political level between working- or lower-class whites and minorities. The diagram implies that whites may feel "threatened" by minorities and special programs (Meier and Stewart 1991).

TWO-TIERED PLURALISM IN INSTITUTIONAL PRACTICE

Two-tiered pluralism is evident in institutional structures and practices, practices that seem to have evolved in ways consistent with broader social and political processes. We can note examples of this. Studies of minority-group efforts to gain voting rights have claimed that strategies to limit those rights have changed from vote denial to vote dilution. Instead of outright denial of minority voting rights, more subtle mechanisms such as vote dilution have been used to lessen the impact of minority voters (Ball 1986).

Education provides another example. As we saw in Chapter 9, second-generation discrimination occurs in academic grouping, disciplinary policies, and educational outputs. Education policies have been justified in terms of administrative efficiency and necessity, and in some cases the need for "special" treatment. Notably, the turn-of-the-century reform movement also addressed alleged ethnic-group "parochialness" or "private regardingness" through administrative and governmental structural means. "Natural specialization" is now invoked in the name of "universal" educational goals. Second-generation discrimination is a clear instance of two-tiered pluralism. A specific example with reference to Latinos is bilingual education (see Chapter 9).

Another example is the *Richmond* v. *Croson* (1989) decision (see Chapter 5), in which the U.S. Supreme Court limited affirmative action *primarily* to policies where no "special qualifications" (i.e., no "high" qualifications) were necessary. That is, minorities could receive preference for lower-level jobs (second tier?) but not for business contracts (first tier?). Similarly, that Court decision indicated that the City of Richmond would have to *prove* that specific discrimination had occurred in the past in contracting policies and thus required rectification. Specific proof was demanded despite abundant evidence of various forms of discrimination historically in Richmond, and discrimination in many business practices throughout the United States. Whatever the legal wisdom of the decision, programs to provide incentives for general economic development are seldom subject to the same burden of proof. The need to provide incentives or to "induce" is assumed or institutionalized in the link between the economic and political structures (Williams 1990; Lindblom 1980).

Another institutional development that seems especially germane to minority political development is that power in urban bureaucracies appears increasingly to be shifting from more visible line agencies to less visible and allegedly more "universalist" staff agencies. This shift probably makes attention to minority policy concerns more difficult because of the leanings and imperatives of staff agencies (Stone, Whelan, and Murin 1986). (It might be hypothesized that minority presence in bureaucracies is lowest in staff agencies or in staff agencies within line agencies.) This development is especially powerful because it is underlaid with notions of bureaucratic professionalism, neutrality, and the like.

Also notable is the extent to which these patterns are apparent in research. According to several sources, study of the kinds of social and political issues addressed throughout this book have been relegated to a secondary status in social science research. Minority politics has been "shut out of the conversation or marginalized in it by the establishment of academic slums and backwaters with names like Afro-American studies, or women's studies" (Barber 1990; cf. Barrera, 1979). To this list some would add "ethnic studies," "Chicano studies," or related programs.

In view of Barber's arguments, it is not surprising that professional organizations, including the formal apparatus of academic disciplines, might also manifest this. Over the past decade or so, professional associations (such as the American Political Science Association) have established committees on the status of minority groups—for example, the Committee on the Status of Chicanos/Latinos in the Profession. The existence of a committee on status is a pretty certain indicator that the particular group has low status. Committees that have broader foci and thus do not have such "particular" designations are in effect—but not in name—essentially committees on the "status of status" in the particular profession. That they are never so named further legitimizes them because they do not seek—they feel no need for—justification. The existence of a particular set of institutions, structures, and organizations, with their attendant established norms, goals, and procedures, are powerful mechanisms for determining what is and should be "legitimate" academic and social concerns.

Academic disciplines, including political science, "continue to reflect the inequalities and disparities of power found in the society" that those disciplines seek "objectively" to study (Barber 1990: 40). Issues and groups excluded from the scholarly "clubs are disempowered in a subtle but consequential fashion; their intellectual powerlessness in the conversations of the club mirrors the social and economic powerlessness of the groups they represent." Academic professions and disciplines may not only reflect political and social inequalities, they may reinforce them. A major problem of professional political science, Barber adds, is its "inability to achieve genuine inclusiveness."

_____BROADER IMPLICATIONS OF TWO-TIERED PLURALISM

In recent years, there have been several interrelated debates in American politics regarding the distribution of power and authority. In one way or another, these debates have addressed the issue of how much equality exists in U.S. politics and society, and why. Some have viewed equal opportunity as the central issue in this debate and, in turn, the central tenet of pluralist theory. But, as suggested in an earlier chapter, equal opportunity is a double-edged sword (Hochschild 1988). Two-tiered pluralism implies that minorities have the *opportunity* to achieve equal opportunity but that equal opportunity is not necessarily a given. That is, equal opportunity assumes a certain level of equality; it also seems to assume a certain level of awareness and understanding of the social and political system and its accompanying opportunities that may not actually exist. Two-tiered pluralism, then, has some "mixed blessing" qualities in contemporary U.S. politics. The nature and extent of them must be understood.

While dominant groups use the political system to maintain and enhance their power and status, minorities pursue politics to try to achieve a modicum of equality, to realize equal opportunity in the first place. The purposes are quite different. That minorities have to struggle to achieve what is presumed to be a given casts them in an unfavorable light. Jones (1984, 7) has referred to the "preferential pluralism" enjoyed by powerful groups"; the political situation is more difficult for minority groups, partly *because* of the preferential or privileged position of some groups. Stone (1986) speaks of the much larger "opportunity costs" that minority groups must incur compared to mainstream groups.

Two-tiered pluralism does not deny that some minority individuals or groups have realized some accomplishments or success. These accomplishments, such as the election of a Latino as mayor of a large city, suggest that the disadvantaged status of minorities are not "anomalous," that not *all* members of minority groups suffer inequality. Therefore, the extent of the negatively exceptional or anomalous status of the minority group as a whole is diminished; that is, black and other minority-group "exceptionalism" is diminished as an explanation of U.S. politics, and the political system is viewed more positively, as more consistent with conventional pluralism. These successes also undermine the argument that minority subordination is a "necessity" in the U.S. social and political system (see Hochschild 1984). The idea that minority-group subordination is neither an anomaly nor a necessity is conventional pluralism's answer to the "dilemma" of minority groups in American politics and society. But the answer leaves much to be explained.

Understanding Latino and minority politics, then, is partly a matter of which aspects of the minority experience are stressed. Some have stressed the political accomplishments that have occurred above the social and political threshold; this is the domain that traditional or conventional pluralist writing and accompanying behavioral research has emphasized. Others have stressed the historical and continuing disadvantaged political and socioeconomic status of the mass of the Latino and black populations and their growing underclass, a group that did not decrease despite the economic expansion in the 1980s and the political successes in the "decade of the Hispanics." Two-tiered pluralism suggests that—and how—the two aggregates and situations can continue to coexist.

The concept of institutional discrimination encompasses much of this. Barrera has argued that institutional discrimination must be understood in terms of interests, that institutions are biased because particular economic, social, and political interests benefit from particular institutional arrangements and outcomes (Barrera 1979). That is difficult to dispute. It should be added, however, that social institutions and structures also manifest a tension or dialectic between interests and ideals. It seems that the ideals of U.S. politics—freedom, equality, democracy, and the rest—lead to the ability on the part of institutions to respond favorably to certain disadvantaged groups, but institutional interests limit the nature and extent of that response. Thus, pluralism as an ideal has been achieved; it is limited—it is two-tiered, or dual— because of the need to protect interests. The interplay of ideals and interests also shapes the nature of the ideology used to explain and justify the status quo. That is why pluralism and the sociological deficiency theories (see Chapter 2), particularly the internal social structural and cultural deficiency theories, are extensively and comfortably linked.

Theory and research about U.S. pluralism and liberal democracy need more directly, consciously, and self-critically to come to terms with the presence and persistence of ethnic–racial minority groups. Blacks and Native Americans are the leading examples, but they are not the only "dilemma" for analysis of U.S. politics. Because of their in-between status in the U.S. social and political system, the presence of Latinos in that system is important in itself and has broad implications for the development of U.S. politics.

The suggestion that culture, an important but often nebulous concept, plays a major role in understanding Latino political status in the United States is in no way an acceptance or endorsement of cultural deficiency theories; indeed, assertions that cultural deficiency explains important policy issues (e.g., education) are increasingly suspect (Meier and Stewart 1991). Instead, I suggest that cultural *differences may* have been defined as *deficiencies*. Unequal sociohistorical, economic, and political status—central to two-tiered pluralism—have both permitted and required that.

Notes

CHAPTER 3

1. What seems especially significant is that much of the social and economic decline of Mexican Americans was affected extensively by what were formally legal processes. While there was also, to be sure, much overt hostility and discrimination, formal and legal dispossessions—through tax policies, land-claims decisions, and the like—exemplify what is today referred to as "institutional discrimination." Overall, these and related processes "cemented" the underclass status of a majority of Mexican Americans.

CHAPTER 4

1. Several reasons may explain why the findings are inconsistent. First, the research took place at different points in time. Mexican and Mexican American—Chicano politics began receiving scholarly and public attention only in the late 1960s. Although attention has increased, studies are still limited and sporadic. And what attention there has been has not really matched the political and conceptual developments that have occurred. For instance, in the early 1970s, Chicanos were sometimes called an "awakening" minority. The 1980s were called the "decade of the Hispanics." Yet the term "Hispanics" was not even widely used ten years earlier. Thus, if one were doing research during the early 1970s on ethnic self-identification, for example, "Hispanic" would probably not have entered into the research. It is therefore difficult to compare patterns of self-identification directly, and so research findings on this issue, as well as on a number of related questions, are different. The research methods typically used are inadequate for grappling with dynamic social and political processes.

Second, researchers who have considered issues of Latino politics have asked different questions; there has been little or no consistency in the queries. For instance, some researchers interested in political ideology have asked respondents to self-identify as liberal, moderate, or conservative; others have asked respondents to signify whether they are left-wing, liberal, moderate, conservative, right-wing, or "other." And when close-ended questions have been used (which is usually the case) the choices given have shaped responses. Resultant findings and conclusions are, of course, similarly affected. Different choices or degrees of choice, or no "choices" at all (i.e., open-ended questions) might have led to different findings and conclusions.

Third, clearly there have been major differences in who or what is (or is not) included in the various research efforts. Survey research has sampled from several different populations, for example, all Spanish-surnamed people; Hispanics, but excluding noncitizens; or only Hispanics who are registered voters.

Fourth, much of the research has focused on particular locales. Research has, for instance, studied Latino behavior and attitudes in San Antonio (de la Garza and Weaver 1985), Houston (MacManus and Cassell 1988), and so on. Yet the variety of social and political experiences, historical and current, to say nothing of formal political structures and processes, has been extensive.

CHAPTER 8

1. Using Browning, Marshall, and Tabb's question (1984, 280), I sought to assess the extent of Hispanic demand–protest in Denver and Pueblo. Interview responses in Denver indicate that it was perceived as moderate to high (mean of 3.7) on a scale of 5 (high) to 1 (low); in Pueblo, the mean response was 3.0. For this question, and for other issues on which I refer to *interview or respondents' comments*, I interviewed a number of people in the two cities. These included six city council members in Denver and two in Pueblo; two administrators in each city; leaders of organizations promoting Hispanic interests, two in each city; and two local reporters (cf. Browning, Marshall, and Tabb 1984, 269).

2. The evidence, such as interviewee responses and little electoral support for Hispanic council candidates, would suggest greater resistance in Pueblo than Denver, however.

3. For how this is measured, see Hero 1990. I also examined "electoral mobilization" using Browning, Marshall, and Tabb's question (1984, 282) regarding the "extent to which [Hispanics] organize to control [Hispanic] candidacies." Respondents rated Hispanic electoral mobilization as moderate to low (2.8 on a 5–1 scale) in both Denver and Pueblo.

4. Following Browning, Marshall, and Tabb (1984, 272–273, 30), I first assigned one point for each Hispanic council member. But where Hispanic representatives were not part of the dominant coalition, a maximum of two points was assigned, even if there were more than two Hispanic council members. Two additional points were assigned if Hispanic representatives (regardless of number) were part of the dominant coalition on the council. Three additional points were given if a Hispanic held the mayor's office. The additional points for Hispanic occupancy were assigned only to independently elected mayors (also see Hero 1990).

5. In addition to the two noted, the other practices dealt with city set-asides that went beyond federal requirements; city ordinances requiring firms to meet affirmative action criteria; the city council pushing for greater minority contracting; the city setting specific goals for minority contracting (Browning, Marshall, and Tabb 1984, 284–285).

6. It is difficult to compare Denver and Pueblo with the California cities, for two reasons. The time periods are different, and, Browning, Marshall, and Tabb (1984, 157) did not distinguish Hispanics from blacks in their calculations.

7. It is difficult to draw comparisons with the California cities because of problems of data adequacy and comparability of time periods.

CHAPTER 10

1. Previous chapters, especially Chapters 7 and 8, carefully and uncritically followed the Browning, Marshall, and Tabb (1984) study. If imitation is the highest form of flattery, that study has been extremely flattered. I hope that the comments that follow help improve our understanding of a significant issue in U.S. urban politics and society. I feel certain that the authors of *Protest* share the hope that a better understanding of the Hispanic and black political situation can be achieved, for they have made a major contribution in that direction.

2. A plausible case might be made that affirmative action in employment is *not* a redistributive policy. The notion of redistribution implies that something is taken from one person or group and given to another. Affirmative action does not *take* jobs from person or group and give them to another. It basically seeks to allocate existing or future job opportunities differently (in the future). To call minority hiring redistributive would assume that nonminorities are somehow entitled to government jobs. Therefore, it seems that minority employment is better understood as "expanded" or "extended" distribution (see Eisinger's discussion below).

3. The agenda of this group lists education (elementary, secondary, and higher) as the first priority. And various social service concerns, such as employment, housing, and health and human services, are also discussed. But whether these concerns are addressed by the policy responsiveness measures is not self-evident. And many of the concerns raised in the "Agenda" are not addressed by the policy responsiveness measures. Also, data from a 1979 survey by Pueblo Action, a poverty agency in Pueblo, Colorado, would not suggest that the policy responsiveness measures deal with matters most salient to Pueblo's (poorest) Hispanics (see Pueblo Action, "A Profile of Pueblo's Poor" 1979). The need for jobs was mentioned most often, but, again, there was apparently no preference expressed for city government jobs.

4. Weinstein and Weinstein (n.d.) refer to such a definition as a "privation

of possibility." They suggest that "politics occur in that fragile domain between relations in which persons are regarded as mere materials of industrial art, factors of production, or variables within experimental designs, and relations of perfect solidarity characterized by mutual aid and compassionate appreciation" (p. 1).

5. One of the few cities in which incorporation and responsiveness is greatest, Berkeley, seems unique, and one wonders whether it should even "count" (but see Sonenshein 1990). Not only is its "university town" status unique among the ten cities in the study, which would seem especially important, given its rather small population, but vast amounts of money coming into the city must surely be tied to the state government, supporting the University of California at Berkeley.

6. In their analysis of federal social programs, Browning, Marshall, and Tabb explicitly say that they do not believe that those programs can or should be evaluated by "grandiose" claims of eliminating poverty. They contend that their own evaluation focuses on whether and to what extent such programs helped bring about policy responsiveness. An important contrast to their position can be noted. A prominent black politician in Denver (whom I interviewed as part of a research project) said that the "real test" of minority influence would be whether the election and incorporation of minorities in city government would affect the black and minority masses and would mitigate such problems as poverty.

References

Acuña, Rodolfo. 1988. *Occupied America: A History of Chicanos.* 3rd ed. New York: Harper & Row.

Almaguer, Tomás. 1987. "Ideological Distortions in Recent Chicano Historiography: The Internal Model and Chicano Historical Interpretation," *Aztlan* 18, no. 1: 7–28.

Amaker, Norman C. 1988. *Civil Rights and the Reagan Administration.* Washington, D.C.: Urban Institute Press.

Anderson, Martin. 1967. *The Federal Bulldozer.* New York: McGraw-Hill.

Avalos, Manuel. 1989. "A Report to the Executive Council of the Western Political Science Association." Unpublished. Salt Lake City, Utah.

Baird, Frank L. 1977. "The Search for a Constituency: Political Validation of Mexican-American Candidates in the Texas Great Plains." In *Mexican Americans: Political Power, Influence or Resource,* edited by Frank L. Baird. Lubbock: Texas Tech Press.

Ball, Howard. 1986. "Racial Vote Dilution: Impact of the Reagan DOJ and the Burger Court on the Voting Rights Act." *Publius: The Journal of Federalism* 16, no. 4 (Fall): 29–48.

Banfield, Edward, and James Q. Wilson. 1966. *City Politics.* New York: Vintage.

Barber, Benjamin. 1990. "The Nature of Contemporary Political Science: A Roundtable Discussion." *PS: Political Science and Politics* 23, no. 1 (March): 40.

Barker, Lucius J., and Jesse J. McCrory, Jr. 1980. *Black Americans and the Political System.* Cambridge, Mass.: Winthrop.

Barrera, Mario. 1979. *Race and Class in the Southwest: A Theory of Racial Inequality.* Notre Dame, Ind.: University of Notre Dame Press.

———. 1985. "The Historical Evolution of Chicano Ethnic Goals: A Bibliographic Essay." *Sage Race Relations Abstracts* 10, no. 1: 1–48.

Baver, Sherrie. 1984. "Puerto Rican Politics in New York City: The Post-World War II Period." In *Puerto Rican Politics in Urban America,* edited by James Jennings and Monte Rivera, 43–60. New York: Greenwood Press.

Bean, Frank D., Georges Vernez, and Charles B. Keely. 1989. *Opening and Closing the Doors: Evaluating Immigration Reform and Control.* Lanham, Md.: The Rand Corporation and the Urban Institute.

Blauner, Robert. 1969. "Internal Colonialism and Ghetto Revolt." *Social Problems* 16 (Spring): 393–408.

Browning, Rufus P., and Dale Rogers Marshall. 1986a. "Black and Hispanic Power in City Politics: A Forum." *PS: Political Science and Politics* 19, no. 3 (Summer): 573–575.

———. 1986b. "Is Anything Enough?" *PS: Political Science and Politics* 19, no. 3 (Summer): 635–640.

Browning, Rufus P., Dale Rogers Marshall, and David H. Tabb. 1984. *Protest Is Not Enough: The Struggle of Blacks and Hispanics for Equality in Urban Politics.* Berkeley: University of California Press.

———. 1990. *Racial Politics in American Cities.* White Plains, N.Y.: Longman.

Bullock, Charles S., III, and Bruce A. Campbell. 1984. "Racist or Racial Voting in the 1981 Atlanta Municipal Elections." *Urban Affairs Quarterly* 20 (December): 149–164.

Bullock, Charles S., III, and Susan A. MacManus. 1990. "Structural Features of Municipalities and the Incidence of Hispanic Councilmembers." *Social Science Quarterly* 71, no. 4 (December): 665–681.

Cain, Bruce E., and Roderick Kiewiet. 1984. "Ethnicity and Electoral Choice: Mexican American Voting Behavior in the California 30th Congressional District." *Social Science Quarterly* 65 (June): 315–327.

Calvo, Maria Antonia, and Steven J. Rosenstone. 1989. *Hispanic Political Participation.* San Antonio: Southwest Voter Research Institute.

Caplan, Barbara. 1987. "Linking Cultural Characteristics to Political Opinion." In *Ignored Voices: Public Opinion Polls and the Latino Community,* edited by Rodolfo O. de la Garza, 158–169. Austin: Center for Mexican American Studies, University of Texas.

Carmines, Edward. 1974. "The Mediating Influence of State Legislatures on the Linkage Between Interparty Competition and Welfare Policies." *American Political Science Review* 68, no. 3 (September): 1118–1124.

Cervantes, Fred A. 1976. "Chicanos within the Political Economy: Some Questions Concerning Pluralist Ideology, Representation and the Economy." *Aztlan* 7 (Fall): 337–346.

Citizens Conference on State Legislatures. 1973. *The Sometimes Governments.* Kansas City, Mo.: Citizens Conference on State Legislatures.

Citrin, Jack, Beth Reingold, Evelyn Walters, and Donald P. Green. 1990. "The 'Official English' Movement and the Symbolic Politics of Language in the United States." *Western Political Quarterly* 43, no. 3 (September): 535–560.

Connor, Walker. 1985. "Who Are The Mexican-Americans? A Note on Comparability." In *Mexican-Americans in Comparative Perspective,* edited by Walker Connor, 2–28. Washington, D.C.: Urban Institute Press.

Dahl, Robert A. 1961. *Who Governs? Democracy and Power in an American City.* New Haven: Yale University Press.

————. 1976. "The Other Ninety-thousand Governments." In *Basic Issues of American Democracy*, edited by Samuel Hendel, 305–315. Englewood Cliffs, N.J.: Prentice-Hall.

————. 1982. *Dilemmas of Pluralist Democracy*. New Haven: Yale University Press.

de la Garza, Rodolfo. 1974. "Voting Patterns in 'Bi-cultural' El Paso—A Contextual Analysis of Chicano Voting Behavior." *Aztlan* 5 (Spring/Fall): 235–260.

————. 1977. "Mexican Americans: A Responsible Electorate." In *Mexican Americans: Political Power, Influence or Resource*, edited by Frank Baird, 63–76. Lubbock: Texas Tech Press.

————. 1985. "As American as Tamale Pie: Mexican-American Political Mobilization and the Loyalty Question." In *Mexican-Americans in Comparative Perspective*, edited by Walker Connor, 225–242. Washington, D.C.: Urban Institute Press.

————, ed. 1987. *Ignored Voices: Public Opinion Polls and the Latino Community*. Austin: Center for Mexican American Studies, University of Texas.

de la Garza, Rodolfo, and Janet Weaver. 1985. "Chicano and Anglo Policy Perspectives in San Antonio: Does Ethnicity Make a Difference?" *Social Science Quarterly* 66, no. 3 (September): 576–586.

De Leon, Richard. 1988. "Race and Politics in San Francisco." Paper presented at the annual meeting of the Western Political Science Association, San Francisco.

Dometrius, Nelson C., and Lee Sigelman. 1984. "Assessing Progress toward Affirmative Action Goals in State and Local Government." *Public Administration Review* 44 (May/June): 241–246.

Dye, Thomas R. 1969. "Inequality and Civil Rights Policy in the States." *Journal of Politics* 31 (November): 1080–1097.

————. 1984. "Party and Policy in the States." *Journal of Politics* 46 (November): 1097–1116.

Dye, Thomas R., and James Resnick. 1981. "Political Power and City Jobs: Determinants of Minority Employment." *Social Science Quarterly* 62, no. 3 (September): 475–486.

Dyer, James, and Arnold Vedlitz. 1986. "The Potential for Minority Coalition Building." Paper presented at the annual meeting of the Southern Political Science Association, Atlanta, Georgia.

Eisinger, Peter. 1980. *The Politics of Displacement: Racial and Ethnic Transition in Three American Cities*. New York: Academic Press.

————. 1986. "Local Civil Service Employment and Black Socioeconomic Mobility." *Social Science Quarterly* 67, no. 1 (March): 169–175.

Elazar, Daniel J. 1984. *American Federalism: A View from the States*. 3rd ed. New York: Harper & Row.

Elkin, Stephen L. 1987. *City and Regime in the American Republic*. Chicago: University of Chicago Press.

Erie, Steven P. 1980. "Two Faces of Ethnic Power: Comparing the Irish and Black Experience." *Polity* 13, no. 2 (Winter): 261–284.

———. 1985. "Rainbow's End: From the Old to the New Urban Ethnic Politics." In *Urban Ethnicity in the United States,* edited by Joan Moore and Lionel Maldonado. Urban Affairs Annual Reviews. Beverly Hills, Calif.: Sage.

Erikson, Robert S., John P. McIver, and Gerald C. Wright, Jr. 1987. "State Political Culture and Public Opinion." *American Political Science Review* 81, no. 3 (September): 797–813.

Estrada, Leobardo F., F. Chris Garcia, Reynaldo Flores Macias, and Lionel Maldonado. 1988. "Chicanos in the United States: A History of Exploitation and Resistance." In *Latinos and the Political System,* edited by F. Chris Garcia, 28–64. Notre Dame, Ind.: University of Notre Dame Press.

Falcón, Angelo. 1984. "Puerto Rican Politics in New York City: 1860s to 1945." In *Puerto Rican Politics in Urban America,* edited by James Jennings and Monte Rivera, 15–42. New York: Greenwood Press.

———. 1988. "Black and Latino Politics: Race and Ethnicity in a Changing Urban Context." In *Latinos and the Political System,* edited by F. Chris Garcia, 171–194. Notre Dame, Ind.: University of Notre Dame Press.

Flores, Henry. 1989. "The Selectivity of the Capitalist State: Chicanos and Economic Development." *Western Political Quarterly* 42, no. 2 (June): 377–396.

Flores, Henry, and Robert Brischetto. 1989. "Texas Mexicans in the 1988 Election." Paper delivered at the "Latinos and the 1988 Election Conference," Austin, Texas.

Garcia, F. Chris, ed. 1988. *Latinos and the Political System.* Notre Dame, Ind.: University of Notre Dame Press.

Garcia, F. Chris, and Rodolfo de la Garza. 1977. *The Chicano Political Experience: Three Perspectives.* North Scituate, Mass.: Duxbury.

Garcia, John A. 1981. "Yo Soy Mexicano . . .: Self-Identity Among the Mexican-Origin Population." *Social Science Quarterly* 62, no. 1 (March): 88–98.

———. 1986. "The Voting Rights Act and Hispanic Political Representation in the Southwest." *Publius: The Journal of Federalism* 16, no. 4 (Fall): 49–66.

Garcia, John A., and Carlos H. Arce. 1988. "Political Orientations and Behaviors of Chicanos: Trying to Make Sense Out of Attitudes and Perceptions." In *Latinos and the Political System,* edited by F. Chris Garcia, 125–151. Notre Dame, Ind.: University of Notre Dame Press.

Garcia, Jose, with Clive Thomas. 1987. "New Mexico: Traditional Interests in a Traditional State." In *Interest Group Politics in the American West,* edited by Ronald J. Hrebenar and Clive S. Thomas, 93–104. Salt Lake City: University of Utah Press.

García, Mario T. 1989. *Mexican Americans: Leadership, Ideology, and Identity, 1930–1960.* New Haven: Yale University Press.

Gimenez, Martha E. 1989. "Latino/Hispanic—Who Needs a Name? The Case Against a Standardized Terminology." *International Journal of Health Services* 19, no. 3: 557–571.

Glazer, Nathan. 1985. "The Political Distinctiveness of Mexican Americans." In *Mexican-Americans in Comparative Perspective*, edited by Walker Connor, 205–224. Washington, D.C.: Urban Institute Press.

Goldman, Sheldon. 1987. "Reagan's Second Term Judicial Appointments." *Judicature* 70, no. 6 (April–May): 324–339.

Gómez-Quiñones, Juan. 1990. *Chicano Politics: Reality and Promise, 1940–1990*. Albuquerque: University of New Mexico Press.

Goodsell, Charles. 1985. *The Case for Bureaucracy*. Chatham, N.J.: Chatham House.

Grofman, Bernard, and Lisa Handley. 1989. "Minority Population Proportion and Black and Hispanic Congressional Success in the 1970s and 1980s." *American Politics Quarterly* 17, no. 4 (October): 436–445.

Guerra, Fernando J. 1989. "Latinos and the 1988 Election in California." Paper delivered at the Latinos and the 1988 Election Conference, Austin, Texas.

Hahn, Harlan, David Klingman, and Harry Pachon. 1976. "Cleavages, Coalitions, and the Black Candidate: The Los Angeles Mayoralty Elections of 1969 and 1973." *Western Political Quarterly* 55 (December): 521–530.

Harmel, Robert, Keith Hamm, and Robert Thompson. 1983. "Black Voting Cohesion and Distinctiveness in Southern Legislatures." *Social Science Quarterly* 64, no. 1 (March): 183–192.

Harrigan, John J. 1989. *Political Change in the Metropolis*. Glenview, Ill.: Scott, Foresman.

Heilig, Peggy, and Robert J. Mundt. 1984. *Your Voice at City Hall*. Albany: State University of New York Press.

Henderson, Lenneal J., Jr. 1987. "Black Politics and American Presidential Elections." In *The New Black Politics: The Search for Political Power*, 2d ed., edited by Michael B. Preston, Lenneal J. Henderson, Jr., and Paul L. Puryear, 3–28. New York: Longman.

Hero, Rodney E. 1986a. "Mexican-Americans and Urban Politics: A Consideration of Governmental Structure and Policy." *Aztlan* 17, no. 1 (Spring): 131–147.

———. 1986b. "Explaining Citizen–Initiated Contacting of Government Officials: Socioeconomic Status, Perceived Need or Something Else?" *Social Science Quarterly* 67, no. 3 (September): 626–635.

———. 1987. "The Election of Hispanics in City Government: An Examination of the Election of Federico Peña as Mayor of Denver." *Western Political Quarterly* 40, no. 1 (March): 93–105.

———. 1989. "Mexican American Referenda Voting on Urban Economic Development and Governmental Structure Issues: Theory and Evidence." *Hispanic Journal of Behavioral Sciences* 11, no. 4 (November): 318–388.

———. 1990. "Hispanics in Urban Government and Politics: Some Findings, Comparisons and Implications." *Western Political Quarterly* 43, no. 2 (June): 403–414.

Hero, Rodney E., and Kathleen M. Beatty. 1989. "The Elections of Federico Peña as Mayor of Denver: Analysis and Implications." *Social Science Quarterly* 70, no. 2 (June): 93–106.

Herzik, Eric. 1985. "The Legal-Formal Structuring of State Politics: A Cultural Explanation." *Western Political Quarterly* 38, no. 3 (September): 413–423.

Hietala, Thomas R. 1985. *Manifest Design: Anxious Aggrandizement in Late Jacksonian America.* Ithaca, N.Y.: Cornell University Press.

Hinckley, Barbara, and Sheldon Goldman. 1990. *American Politics and Government.* Glenview, Ill.: Scott, Foresman.

Hirsch, Herbert. 1972. "Political Scientists and Other Camaradas: Academic Myth-Making and Racial Stereotypes." In *Chicanos and Native Americans: The Territorial Minorities,* edited by R. de la Garza, Z. A. Krusewski, and T. Arciniega. Englewood Cliffs, N.J.: Prentice-Hall.

Hispanic Policy Development Project. 1990. *A More Perfect Union: Achieving Hispanic Parity by the Year 2000.* New York and Washington, D.C.: HPDP.

Hochschild, Jennifer. 1984. *The New American Dilemma: Liberal Democracy and School Desegregation.* New Haven: Yale University Press.

———. 1988. "The Double-Edged Sword of Equal Opportunity." In *Power, Inequality and Democratic Politics,* edited by Ian Shapiro and Grant Reeher, 168–200. Boulder, Colo.: Westview Press.

Holloway, Harry. 1968. "Negro Political Strategy: Coalition or Independent Power Politics." *Social Science Quarterly* 49, no. 4 (December): 534–537.

Holmes, Jack E. 1967. *Politics in New Mexico.* Albuquerque: University of New Mexico Press.

Horowitz, Donald L. 1985. "Conflict and Accommodation: Mexican Americans in the Cosmopolis." In *Mexican-Americans in Comparative Perspective,* edited by Walker Connor, 56–103. Washington, D.C.: Urban Institute Press.

Isaac, Jeffrey C. 1988. "Dilemmas of Democratic Theory," In *Power, Inequality and Democratic Politics,* edited by Ian Shapiro and Grant Reeher, 132–147. Boulder, Colo.: Westview Press.

Jackson, Byran O. 1988. "Ethnic Cleavages and Voting Patterns in U.S. Cities: An Analysis of the Asian, Black and Hispanic Communities of Los Angeles." Paper presented at the Conference on Comparative Ethnicity, University of California, Los Angeles.

James, Franklin J., et al., eds. 1984. *Minorities in the Sunbelt.* New Brunswick, N.J.: Center for Urban Policy Research.

Jennings, James. 1988. "The Puerto Rican Community: Its Political Background." In *Latinos and the Political System,* edited by F. Chris Garcia, 65–80. Notre Dame, Ind.: University of Notre Dame Press.

Jones, Bryan D. 1990. "Public Policies and Economic Growth in the American States." *Journal of Politics* 52, no. 1 (February): 219–233.

Jones, Charles O. 1984. *An Introduction to the Study of Public Policy.* 3d ed. Belmont, Calif.: Brooks/Cole.

Judd, Dennis R., and Randy L. Ready. 1986. "Entrepreneurial Cities and the

New Politics of Economic Development." In *Reagan and the Cities*, edited by George E. Peterson and Carol Lewis, 209–247. Washington, D.C.: Urban Institute Press.

Kahn, Ronald. 1985. Review of *Protest Is Not Enough: The Struggle of Blacks and Hispanics* by R. Browning, D. R. Marshall, and D. Tabb. *American Political Science Review* 79, no. 2 (June): 520–521.

LARASA (Latin American Research and Service Agency). 1989. *Hispanic Agenda Poll.* Denver, Colo.: LARASA.

Lindblom, Charles E. 1980. *The Policy-Making Process.* Englewood Cliffs, N.J.: Prentice-Hall.

———. 1982. "Another State of Mind." *American Political Science Review* 76, no. 1 (March): 9–21.

Lineberry, Robert L., and Edmund P. Fowler. 1967. "Reformism and Public Policy in American Cities." *American Political Science Review* 61, no. 3 (September): 701–716.

Lipsky, Michael. 1980. *Street-Level Bureaucracy.* New York: Russel Sage Foundation.

Lipsky, Michael, and David J. Olson. 1976. *Commission Politics: The Processing of Racial Crisis in America.* New Brunswick, N.J.: Transaction Books.

Lopez, Manuel M. 1981. "Patterns of Interethnic Residential Segregation in the Urban Southwest, 1960 and 1970." *Social Science Quarterly* 62, no. 1 (March): 50–63.

———. 1986. "Su casa no es mi casa: Hispanic Housing Conditions in Contemporary America." In *Race, Ethnicity, and Minority Housing in the U.S.,* edited by Jashid Momeni, 127–145. New York: Greenwood Press.

Lovrich, Nicholas. 1974. "Differing Priorities in an Urban Electorate: Service Priorities Among Anglo, Black and Mexican-American Voters." *Social Science Quarterly* 55, no. 2 (December): 704–717.

Lovrich, Nicholas, and Otwin Marenin. 1976. "A Comparison of Black and Mexican Voters in Denver: Assertive Versus Acquiescent Political Orientations and Voting Behavior in an Urban Electorate." *Western Political Quarterly* 29 (June): 284–294.

Lowi, Theodore. 1967. "Machine Politics: Old and New." *Public Interest* 9 (Fall): 83–92.

———. 1979. *The End of Liberalism,* 2d ed. New York: Norton.

Lowi, Theodore, and Benjamin Ginsberg. 1990. *American Government: Freedom and Power.* New York: Norton.

Lyons, William. 1978. "Reform and Response in American Cities: Structure and Policy Reconsidered." *Social Science Quarterly* 59, no. 1 (June): 118–132.

MacManus, Susan A. 1990. "Minority Business Contracting with Local Government." Paper presented at the annual meeting of the Southwestern Political Science Association, Little Rock, Arkansas.

MacManus, Susan A., and Carol A. Cassel. 1988. "Mexican Americans in City Politics: Participation, Representation, and Policy Preferences." In *Latinos and the Political System,* edited by F. Chris Garcia, 201–212. Notre Dame, Ind.: University of Notre Dame Press.

McClain, Paula, and Albert K. Karnig. 1990. "Black and Hispanic Socio-economic and Political Competition." *American Political Science Review* 84, no. 2 (June): 535–545.

Manley, John. 1983. "Neopluralism: A Class Analysis of Pluralism I and Pluralism II." *American Political Science Review* 77, no. 2 (June): 368–383.

Marquez, Benjamin. 1988. "The League of United Latin American Citizens and the Politics of Ethnicity." In *Latino Empowerment: Progress, Problems, and Prospects,* edited by Roberto E. Villareal, Norma G. Hernandez, and Howard D. Neighbor, 11–24. New York: Greenwood Press.

Martinez, Arthur. 1990. *Who's Who: Chicano Officeholders, 1990–1991.* Silver City, N. Mex.: n.p.

Meier, Kenneth, and Joseph Stewart, Jr. 1991. *The Politics of Hispanic Education.* Albany: State University of New York Press.

Melville, Margarita. 1988. "Hispanics: Race, Class, or Ethnicity?" *Journal of Ethnic Studies* 16, no. 1: 67–83.

Mindiola, Tatcho, Jr., and Armando Gutierrez. 1988. "Chicanos and the Legislative Process: Reality and Illusion in the Politics of Change." In *Latinos and the Political System,* edited by F. Chris Garcia, 349–362. Notre Dame, Ind.: University of Notre Dame Press.

Mladenka, Kenneth R. 1980. "The Urban Bureaucracy and the Chicago Political Machine: Who Gets What and the Limits to Political Control." *American Political Science Review* 74, no. 4 (December): 991–998.

———. 1989. "Barriers to Hispanic Employment Success in 1200 Cities." *Social Science Quarterly* 70, no. 2 (June): 391–407.

Mladenka, Kenneth R., and Kim Q. Hill. 1986. *Texas Government: Politics and Economics.* Monterey, Calif.: Brooks/Cole.

Mollenkopf, John. 1990. "New York: The Great Anomaly." In *Racial Politics in American Cities,* edited by Rufus P. Browning, Dale Rogers Marshall, and David H. Tabb, 75–87. New York: Longman.

Moore, Joan. 1970. "Colonialism: The Case of the Mexican American." In *Introduction to Chicano Studies: A Reader,* edited by Live Isauro Duran and H. Russell Bernard, 363–372. New York: Macmillan.

———. 1981. "Minorities in the American Class System." *Daedalus* 110: 275–298.

Moore, Joan, and Harry Pachon. 1985. *Hispanics in the United States.* Englewood Cliffs, N.J.: Prentice-Hall.

Moreno, Dario, and Christopher L. Warren. 1988. "The Conservative Enclave: Cubans in Florida." Manuscript.

Morgan, David R., and John P. Pelissero. 1980. "Urban Policy: Does Political Structure Matter?" *American Political Science Review,* no. 4 (December): 999–1006.

Mormino, Gary R., and George Pozzetta. 1987. *The Immigrant World of Ybor City: Italians and Their Latin Neighbors in Tampa, 1885–1985.* Urbana: University of Illinois Press.

Morris, Milton. 1975. *The Politics of Black America.* New York: Harper & Row.

Munger, Michael C. 1988. "Allocation of Desirable Committee Assignments: Extended Queues versus Committee Expansion." *American Journal of Political Science* 32, no. 2 (May): 317–344.

Muñoz, Carlos. 1970. "Toward a Chicano Perspective of Political Analysis." *Aztlan* 1 (Fall): 15–26.

———. 1989. *Youth, Identity, Power: The Chicano Movement.* New York: Verso.

Muñoz, Carlos, and Charles P. Henry. 1990. "Coalition Politics in San Antonio and Denver: The Cisneros and Peña Mayoral Campaigns." In *Racial Politics in American Cities,* edited by Rufus P. Browning, Dale Rogers Marshall, and David H. Tabb, 179–190. White Plains, N.Y.: Longman.

Myrdal, Gunnar. 1944. *An American Dilemma: The Negro Problem and Modern Democracy.* New York: Harper & Bros.

National Association of Latino Elected and Appointed Officials. 1990a. *National Report* 10, no. 4.

———. 1990b. *National Roster of Hispanic Elected Officials.* Washington, D.C.: The Association.

Neighbor, Howard. 1988. "New Rules in Voting Rights Cases Demand New Strategy for Chicano Employment." In *Latino Empowerment: Progress, Problems, and Prospects,* edited by Roberto E. Villareal, Norma G. Hernandez, and Howard D. Neighbor, 105–120. New York: Greenwood Press.

Nelson, Dale. 1979. "Ethnicity and Socioeconomic Status as Sources of Participation: The Case for Ethnic Political Culture." *American Political Science Review* 73, no. 4 (December): 1024–1038.

Nice, David C. 1983. "An Intergovernmental Perspective on Urban Fragmentation." *Social Science Quarterly* 64, no. 1 (March): 111–118.

Nivola, Pietro S. 1978. "Distributing a Municipal Service: A Case Study of Housing Inspection." *Journal of Politics* 40: 59–81.

O'Connor, Karen, and Lee Epstein. 1988. "A Legal Voice for the Chicano Community: The Activities of the Mexican-American Legal Defense and Educational Fund, 1969–1982." In *Latinos and the Political System,* edited by F. Chris Garcia, 255–268. Notre Dame, Ind.: University of Notre Dame Press.

Omi, Michael, and Howard Winant. 1986. *Racial Formation in the United States: From the 1960s to the 1980s.* New York: Routledge and Kegan Paul.

Pachon, Harry. 1985. "Political Mobilization in the Mexican American Community." In *Mexican-Americans in Comparative Perspective,* edited by Walker Connor, 243–258. Washington, D.C.: Urban Institute Press.

Padilla, Felix. 1985. *Latino Ethnic Consciousness.* Notre Dame, Ind.: University of Notre Dame Press.

Pedraza-Bailey, Silvia. 1985. *Political and Economic Migrants in America: Cubans and Mexican Americans*. Austin: University of Texas Press.

Perez, Louis A., Jr. 1990. Book Review in *American Political Science Review* 84, no. 1 (March): 364–366.

Perry, David C., and Alfred J. Watkins, eds. 1977. *The Rise of the Sunbelt Cities*. Vol. 14. New York: Sage Urban Affairs Annual Reviews.

Peters, B. Guy. 1986. *American Public Policy: Promise and Performance*, 2d ed. Chatham, N.J.: Chatham House.

Peterson, George E. 1986. "The Block Grants in Perspective." In *The Reagan Block Grants: What Have We Learned?* edited by George E. Peterson, et al., 1–31. Washington, D.C.: Urban Institute Press.

Peterson, Paul. 1981. *City Limits*. Chicago: University of Chicago Press.

Portes, Alejandro, and Rafael Mozo. 1988. "The Political Adaptation Process of Cubans and Other Ethnic Minorities in the United States: A Preliminary Analysis." In *Latinos and the Political System*, edited by F. Chris Garcia, 152–170. Notre Dame, Ind.: Notre Dame University Press.

Pursley, Robert D., and Neil Snortland. 1980. *Managing Government Organizations*. North Scituate, Mass.: Duxbury.

Raspberry, William. 1987. "Overcoming an Aversion to Capitalism." *Denver Post*, November 9, 6B.

Regalado, James. 1988. "Latino Representation in Los Angeles." In *Latino Empowerment: Progress, Problems, and Prospects*, edited by Roberto E. Villareal, Norma G. Hernandez, and Howard D. Neighbor, 91–104. New York: Greenwood Press.

Rocco, Raymond A. 1970. "The Chicano in the Social Sciences: Traditional Concepts, Myths, and Images." *Aztlan* 1 (Fall): 75–97.

———. 1977. "A Critical Perspective on the Study of Chicano Politics." *Western Political Quarterly* 30, no. 4 (December): 558–573.

Saiz, Martin. 1988. "Progressive Politics and Fiscal Authority: The Experience of the Peña Administration." Paper presented at the annual meeting of the Western Political Science Association, San Francisco.

Sanchez-Jankowski, Martin. 1986. *City Bound: Urban Life and Political Attitudes among Chicano Youth*. Albuquerque: University of New Mexico Press.

Sanders, Heywood T., and Clarence N. Stone. 1987. "Developmental Politics Reconsidered." *Urban Affairs Quarterly* 22 (June): 521–539.

Schattschneider, E. E. 1975. *The Semisovereign People*. Hinsdale, Ill.: Dryden Press.

Shapiro, Michael J. 1981. *Language and Political Understanding: The Politics of Discursive Practices*. New Haven: Yale University Press.

Sharp, Elaine B. 1990. *Urban Politics and Administration: From Service Delivery to Economic Development*. New York: Longman.

Sigelman, Lee, and N. Joseph Cayer. 1986. "Minorities, Women, and Public Sector Jobs: A Status Report." In *Affirmative Action: Theory, Analysis and*

Prospects, edited by Michael W. Combs and John Gruhl, 91–111. Jefferson, N.C.: McFarland.

Sonenshein, Raphael. 1990. "Biracial Coalition Politics in Los Angeles." In *Racial Politics in American Cities,* edited by Rufus P. Browning, Dale Rogers Marshall and David H. Tabb, 33–48. New York: Longman.

Southwest Voter Research Institute (SWVRI). 1988. *Southwest Voter Research Notes* 2, no. 6 (September–December).

———. 1989. "The 100th Congress: How They Voted on Issues of Concern to Latino Leaders." *Southwest Voter Research Notes* 3, no. 1 (September).

Stein, Robert M. 1989. "Market Maximization of Individual Preferences and Metropolitan Municipal Service Responsibility." *Urban Affairs Quarterly* 25, no. 1 (September): 86–116.

Stone, Clarence N. 1980. "Systemic Power in Community Decision Making: A Restatement of Stratification Theory." *American Political Science Review* 74, no. 4 (December): 978–990.

———. 1986. "Race, Power, and Political Change." In *The Egalitarian City,* edited by Janet K. Boles, 200–223. New York: Praeger.

———. 1990. Personal correspondence.

Stone, Clarence N., Robert K. Whelan, and William J. Murin. 1986. *Urban Policy and Politics in a Bureaucratic Age.* 2d ed. Englewood Cliffs., N.J.: Prentice-Hall.

Taebel, Delbert. 1978. "Minority Representation on City Councils." *Social Science Quarterly* 59, no. 2 (June): 142–152.

Tarrance, Lance, Jr. 1987. "Hispanic Vote Behavior: Selected Findings from Past Research Conducted by Tarrance & Associates." In *Ignored Voices: Public Opinion and the Latino Community,* edited by Rodolfo O. de la Garza, 63–75. Austin: Center for Mexican American Studies, University of Texas.

Thernstrom, Abigail M. 1987. *Whose Votes Count? Affirmative Action and Minority Voting Rights.* Cambridge, Mass.: Harvard University Press.

Thomas, Clive S., and Ronald J. Hrebenar. 1990. "Interest Groups in the States." In *Politics in the American States,* 5th ed., edited by V. Gray, H. Jacob, and R. Albritton, 123–158. Glenview, Ill.: Scott, Foresman.

Torres, Maria de los Angeles. 1988. "From Exiles to Minorities: The Politics of Cuban-Americans." In *Latinos and the Political System,* edited by F. Chris Garcia, 81–98. Notre Dame, Ind.: University of Notre Dame Press.

Vedlitz, Arnold, and Charles A. Johnson. 1982. "Community Racial Segregation, Electoral Structure, and Minority Representation." *Social Science Quarterly* 63, no. 4 (December): 729–736.

Verba, Sidney, and Norma Nie. 1972. *Participation in America: Political Democracy and Social Equality.* New York: Harper & Row.

Vigil, Maurilio. 1987. *Hispanics in American Politics: The Search for Political Power.* Lanham, Md.: University Press of America.

Villareal, Roberto. 1988. "The Politics of Mexican-American Empowerment." In *Latino Empowerment: Progress, Problems, and Prospects,* edited by Roberto

E. Villareal, Norma G. Hernandez, and Howard D. Neighbor, 1–10. New York: Greenwood Press.

Warren, Christopher L., John G. Corbett, and John F. Stack, Jr. 1990. "Hispanic Ascendancy and Tripartite Politics in Miami." In *Racial Politics in American Cities,* edited by Rufus P. Browning, Dale Rogers Marshall and David H. Tabb, 155–178. New York: Longman.

Weinstein, Michael, and Deena Weinstein. n.d. "Empirical Political Theory: The Privation of Possibility." Manuscript.

Weissberg, Robert, 1978. "Collective vs. Dyadic Representation in Congress." *American Political Science Review* 72, no. 2 (June): 535–547.

Welch, Susan. 1990. "The Impact of At-Large Elections on the Representation of Blacks and Hispanics." *Journal of Politics* 52, no. 4 (November): 1050–1076.

Welch, Susan, and John R. Hibbing. 1988. "Hispanic Representation in the U.S. Congress." In *Latinos and the Political System,* edited by F. Chris Garcia, 291–299. Notre Dame, Ind.: University of Notre Dame Press.

Welch, Susan, Albert K. Karnig, and Richard Eribes. 1983. "Changes in Hispanic Local Public Employment in the Southwest." *Social Science Quarterly* 36, no. 4 (December): 328–335.

Williams, Bruce A. 1990. "Regulation and Economic Development." In *Politics in the American States: A Comparative Analysis,* 5th ed., edited by V. Gray, H. Jacob, and R. Albritton, 479–526. Glenview, Ill.: Scott, Foresman.

Wilson, Ernest, III. 1985. "Why Political Scientists Don't Study Black Politics But Historians and Sociologists Do." *PS: Political Science and Politics* 18, no. 3 (Summer): 600–606.

Wilson, James Q., and Edward Banfield. 1964. "Public Regardingness as a Value Premise in Voting Behavior." *American Political Science Review* 58, no. 4 (December): 876–887.

———. 1971. "Political Ethos Revisited." *American Political Science Review* 65, no. 4 (December): 1048–1062.

Wolfinger, Raymond. 1974. *The Politics of Progress.* Englewood Cliffs, N.J.: Prentice-Hall.

Wolfinger, Raymond, and John O. Field. 1966. "Political Ethos and the Structure of City Government," *American Political Science Review* 60, no. 2 (June): 306–326.

Wright, Gerald C., Robert S. Erikson, and John P. McIver. 1985. "Measuring State Partisanship and Ideology with Survey Data." *Journal of Politics* 47: 469–489.

———. 1987. "Public Opinion and Policy Liberalism in the American States." *American Journal of Political Science* 31, no. 4 (November): 980–1001.

Yinger, J. Milton. 1985. "Assimilation in the United States: The Mexican-Americans." In *Mexican-Americans in Comparative Perspective,* edited by Walker Connor, 29–55. Washington, D.C.: Urban Institute Press.

Zax, Jeffrey S. 1990. "Election Methods and Black and Hispanic City Council Membership." *Social Science Quarterly* 71, no. 2 (June): 339–355.

Index

Ability grouping, as form of discrimination, 157
Academic grouping: and Cubans, 158–159; and Mexican Americans, 158–159; and Puerto Ricans, 158–159; and second-generation discrimination, 157–158
Accommodation, and Mexican Americans, 35–36
Affirmative action, and Latinos, 94–97, 201, 202
Age make-up, and assimilation, 51
Allocational policies: and study of Latino politics, 181–183; and urban politics, 135–136
Anglo: as term relative to Latinos, 200; as used in Southwest, 7
Anglo judges, and Mexican and Spanish land-owning laws, 34
Anglos: attitudes of, toward Latino groups, 32; and ideology of liberation, 32; and power thesis, 160–161
Anti–single shot rules, and impact on election of Latinos, 142
Arizona: inequality in, 101–102; Latino elected and appointed officials in, 113; and Latino presence in, 100; and Official English, 167–168; policy liberalism in, 112; and vote on Official English, 168
Assimilation: as consideration of Latino groups, 44–51; definition of, 44–45; group size and, 45–46; and political influence in urban government, 133–134; variables explaining, 44–51
Avalos, Manuel, 174–175

Bakke case, and equal protection/affirmative action, 97
Banfield, Edward, and ethos theory, 139
Barrera, Mario, 22–26; on Chicano history, 33; on Chicano Movement, 33; on communitarian concerns, 33; on egalitarian concerns, 33; on goals of Chicano groups, 33; on *mutualistas* (mutual aid societies), 33
Batista regime, in Cuba, 42
Bay of Pigs invasion, and Cuba, 42
Berkeley, Calif., 143, 210n.5
Bias theories, description of, 24
Bicultural education, 157
Bicultural politics, and Latinos, 200
Bilingual ballots, 94
Bilingual education, 157; classes and second-generation discrimination, 158, 202; and Official English, 156, 166, 200
Biological deficiency theories, 23–24
Blacks: compared to Hispanics, in northern California cities, 144; and electoral support for Federico Peña, 122–123; and Latinos, in workings of two-tiered pluralism, 199–202; and power thesis, 160–161; and second-generation discrimination regarding Hispanics, 159–160; and "subcultural" politics, 200
Bracero program: and immigration policy, 170; and Mexicans, 170
Browning, Rufus P., Dale Rogers Marshall, and David H. Tabb, 144; significance of research of, 176–178, 181–187, 209n.1; and study of Latinos in urban politics, 176–178
Brown v. Board of Education of Topeka, 93

Income (and poverty), in states with largest Latino populations, 101–102
Incorporation (political): in Denver, 148;
in Pueblo, Colo., 148; of Hispanics in
Miami, 154. *See also* Political incorporation
Independent power politics, and election
of minorities, 117
Individualistic political culture, description of, 104–105
Institutional discrimination: defined, 157,
207n.1; and two-tiered pluralism, 205
Integration, as subprocess of assimilation,
43
Interest groups: effects of, on political
system, 15; among Latinos, 35, 71–79;
Latinos as, in the states, 111
Interest in homeland, as factor in assimilation, 46, 50
Interests: and internal colonialism, 25–
26; and structural discrimination theories, 25
Intermediate scrutiny, and equal protection, 97
Internal colonialism: and ascriptive class
segments, 25–26; and coalitional bias,
47; debates over validity of, 47; description of, 17–18; evaluated, 27; and
Marxist theory, 25–26; as perspective
on politics, 17–18; and pluralism, 47;
and Puerto Ricans, 41; as structural
discrimination theory, 25; as theory of
American politics, 189

Johnson, Lyndon: administration of, and
programs affecting minority groups,
83–84; and Civil Rights Act of 1964,
83–84; and Great Society, 40–41; and
Voting Rights Act of 1965, 83–84; and
War on Poverty, 40–41, 83–84
Jones, Charles O.: and policy process,
195; and preferential pluralism, 204
Jones Act, and Puerto Ricans, 39

Kennedy, John F., election of, and Latinos, 82
Keyes v. *School District Number One (Denver, CO)*, 94
Key West, Fla., Cubans in, 41

Land grants, and dispossession of Mexican Americans, 34
Language: discrimination and Hispanic
education, 158; as factor in assimila-
tion of Latino groups, 46, 48
Language issues, and Latinos, compared
to blacks, 200
Language policy, significance of, 165
La Raza Unida party, 77–78; and Chicano Movement, 37–38; reasons for
decline of, 77–78
Las Gorras Blancas (White Caps), 34
Latino: education, 52–54; income, 52–
54; as label, term, 3; occupations, 52–
54; policy concerns, 67–69; socioeconomic status, 52–54
Latino elected and appointed officials: in
Arizona, 113; in California, 113; in
Colorado, 113; in Florida, 113; in
Texas, 113
Latino groups: age makeup and assimilation of, 51; coming from culturally
similar society, 46, 49; in contemporary situations, 31–32; and cultural attachment, 32; differences among, 33–
55; and discrimination, 46, 50; and diversity of class and occupation, 46, 49–
50; and education, 46, 50; and interest
in homeland, 46, 50; and language,
46, 48; length of residence of, 46–47;
and race, 46, 48; similarities in history
and culture, 32; summary of history,
44; and voluntary entrance to U.S., 46,
48–49
Latino politics: adequacy and appropriateness of research on, 178–180; biases in research regarding, 173–174;
normative and theoretical issues in
study of, 178; reasons for absence of
study of, 174–175; study of, 9, 173;
and theoretical frameworks, 5–6;
uniqueness of, 8–9
Latinos: and ability to affect presidential
selection, 81–82; and affirmative action, 202; and bicultural politics, 200;
and blacks in "second tier," 201; and
blacks and two-tiered pluralism, 199–
201; and colonial experience, 5–6;
communitarian goals of, 73–74; Congress and, 87–92; and courts, 92–94;
and cultural differences, 199–200; defined, 1; and Democratic party, 198–